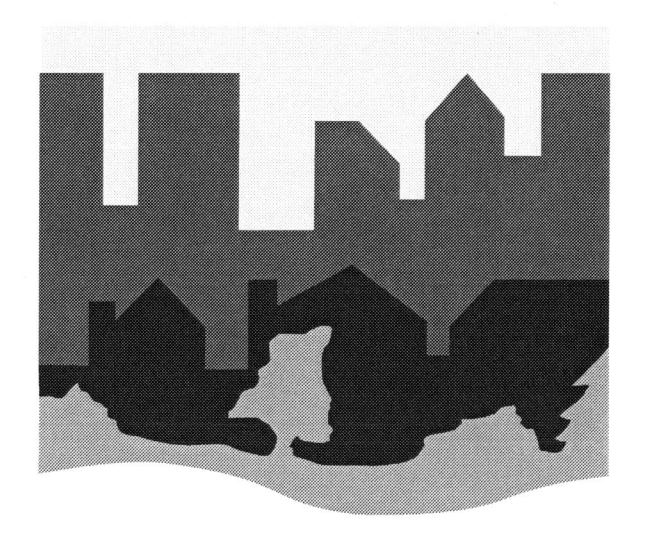

COMMUNITY FOUNDATION HANDBOOK:
What You Need to Know

Elaine Gast

COUNCIL *on* FOUNDATIONS

VISION

The Council's vision for the field is of

A vibrant, growing and responsible philanthropic sector that advances the common good.

We see ourselves as part of a broad philanthropic community that will contribute to this vision. We aim to be an important leader in reaching the vision.

MISSION

The Council on Foundations provides the opportunity, leadership and tools needed by philanthropic organizations to expand, enhance and sustain their ability to advance the common good.

To carry out this mission, we will be a membership organization with effective and diverse leadership that helps the field be larger, more effective, more responsible and more cooperative.

By "*common good*," we mean the sum total of conditions that enable community members to thrive. These achievements have a shared nature that goes beyond individual benefits.

By "*philanthropic organizations*," we mean any vehicle that brings people together to enhance the effectiveness, impact and leverage of their philanthropy. This includes private and community foundations, corporate foundations and giving programs, operating foundations and public foundations, as well as emerging giving and grantmaking mechanisms involving collective participation.

STATEMENT OF INCLUSIVENESS

The Council on Foundations was formed to promote responsible and effective philanthropy. The mission requires a commitment to inclusiveness as a fundamental operating principle and calls for an active and ongoing process that affirms human diversity in its many forms, encompassing but not limited to ethnicity, race, gender, sexual orientation, economic circumstance, disability and philosophy. We seek diversity in order to ensure that a range of perspectives, opinions and experiences are recognized and acted upon in achieving the Council's mission. The Council also asks members to make a similar commitment to inclusiveness in order to better enhance their abilities to contribute to the common good of our changing society.

All illustrations used in this book are copyright by and used by permission of The Cartoon Bank (www.cartoonbank.com). All rights reserved.

© 2006 Council on Foundations. All rights reserved.

This publication may not be reproduced without attribution to the The *Community Foundation Handbook* and the Council on Foundations. Revenue from publications sales supports the Council on Foundations and ensures its capacity to produce resources and provide services to promote responsible and effective philanthropy. Members of the Council on Foundations may obtain copies of this book and other Council publications at member rates by calling 888/239-5221.

Library of Congress Cataloging-in-Publication Data

Gast, Elaine.

Community foundation handbook: what you need to know/written by Elaine Gast.

      p. cm.

Includes index.
ISBN 1-932677-36-4 (alk. paper)
1. Community foundations-United States-Handbooks, manuals, etc.
2. Community organization-United States-Handbooks, manuals, etc.
3. Community leadership-United States-Handbooks, manuals, etc.
4. Charity organization-United States-Handbooks, manuals, etc. I. Title.
HN90.C6G37 2005
361.8068—dc22
      2005025984

COUNCIL *on* FOUNDATIONS
1828 L Street, NW, Suite 300
Washington, DC 20036-5168
202/466-6512 • Fax 202/785-3926
www.cof.org

TABLE OF CONTENTS

Acknowledgments v

Introduction vii

1) Community Foundations Overview 1
    Introduction 3
    Mission and History 4
    Trends 13
    Options and Opportunities 19
    Questions to Consider 23
    Resources for Community Foundations Overview 24

2) Governance and Accountability 25
    Introduction 27
    What Staff Needs to Know About Boards 29
    Building the Board 43
    Helping Good Boards Become Great 49
    Questions to Consider 55
    Sample Activity Chart for Board and Staff 56
    Resources for Governance and Accountability 57

3) Management, Finance and Administration 59
    Introduction 63
    General Management 64
    Human Resources 72
    Administration 85
    Legal and Fiduciary Responsibilities 99
    Questions to Consider 113
    Resources for Management, Finance and Administration 114

4) Grantmaking and Community Leadership ... 117
- Introduction ... 121
- Managing the Grantmaking Program ... 123
- Strategic Grantmaking ... 138
- Working with Grantees ... 150
- Working with Donors ... 153
- Community Leadership ... 155
- Questions to Consider ... 162
- Resources for Grantmaking and Community Leadership ... 164

5) Resource Development and Donor Relations ... 167
- Introduction ... 171
- Building a Climate of Giving ... 173
- Creating Funds ... 179
- Designing a Development Plan ... 192
- Legal Considerations for Resource Development ... 205
- Questions to Consider ... 208
- Resources for Resource Development and Donor Relations ... 209

6) Communications, Marketing and Public Relations ... 211
- Introduction ... 215
- Defining Communications ... 217
- Identifying Your Audiences ... 220
- Developing an Image ... 228
- Getting in the Public Eye ... 231
- Delivering Your Message ... 238
- Designing a Communications Plan ... 248
- Questions to Consider ... 251
- Sample Planning Tools ... 252
- Resources for Communications, Marketing and Public Relations ... 255

Sources ... 256

Community Foundation Resources ... 258

Glossary of Community Foundation Terms ... 261

Index ... 275

ACKNOWLEDGMENTS

To the Community Foundations Leadership Team of the Council on Foundations, for giving voice to the needs of the community foundation field.

To the Professional and Organizational Development Action Team, for developing a continuum of learning and training opportunities for community foundation staff and board.

To the Community Foundation Handbook Committee and editorial subcommittees, whose vision and foundation experience shaped this volume.

COMMITTEE MEMBERS

Peggy Ogden, President and CEO
Central New York Community Foundation
Committee Chair

Diana Haigwood, Administrative Director
League of California Community Foundations

Jennifer Leonard, President and Executive Director
Rochester Area Community Foundation

Donnell Mersereau, Director, Community Foundations
Council of Michigan Foundations

Suzanne Feurt, Managing Director, Community Foundation Services
Council on Foundations

EDITORIAL SUBCOMMITTEE MEMBERS

Community Foundations Overview

David Luckes, President/CEO, Greater Saint Louis Community Foundation
Bonnie Hindman Wallace, Vice President, Donor Services, Rochester Area Community Foundation
Linda Montgomery, President, Community Foundation of Greater Jackson
Chuck Slosser, President/CEO, Santa Barbara Foundation

Governance and Accountability

Ellen Bryson, Consultant, Bryson Consulting Group
Becky Cain, President/CEO, Greater Kanawha Valley Foundation
Eric Dewald, Executive Director, Central Susquehanna Community Foundation
Jack Stith, Porter Wright, Morris & Arthur LLP

Management, Finance and Administration

Dave Lindberg, CFO, Council of Michigan Foundations

Ann Lisi, Executive Director, Greater Worcester Community Foundation

J.T. Mullen, Senior Vice President/CFO, Cleveland Foundation

Lynn Sargi, Vice President for Human Resources and Administration, Cleveland Foundation

Grantmaking and Community Leadership

Mary Holmes, Executive Director, Cumberland Community Foundation

Jill McCormick, former Program Officer, Community Foundation Serving Richmond and Central Virginia

Natasha Gore, Program Officer, Winston-Salem Foundation

Donna G. Rader, Vice President, Grants & Programs, Winston-Salem Foundation

Marcia Rapp, Vice President, Programs, Grand Rapids Community Foundation

Resource Development and Donor Relations

Sheryl Aikman, Vice President, Development, Community Foundation of Western North Carolina

Catherine Gowen, Development Officer, Community Foundation Silicon Valley

Todd Lueders, President/CEO, Community Foundation for Monterey County

Karri Matau, former Donor Relations, Greater Everett Community Foundation

Alison Woods, Director of Development, Community Foundation of Southeastern Connecticut

Communications, Marketing and Public Relations

Jim Bower, President/CEO, Stark Community Foundation

Julie Hrabak, Communications & Marketing Associate, Cleveland Foundation

Cory Curtis, former Communications Officer, Community Foundation of Jackson Hole

Carl Little, Director, Marketing and Communications, Maine Community Foundation

Emily Jones Rushing, Communications Officer, Community Foundation of Greater Birmingham

Dianna Sutton, President/CEO, Community Foundation of the Florida Keys

INTRODUCTION

Welcome to the *Community Foundation Handbook*.

As a new or seasoned community foundation CEO or staff member, you are embarking on an exciting journey. You live in the community and hold insight to its strengths and needs. You have the skills, the knowledge and the desire to make a difference. Along with your colleagues and your community colleagues, you do make a difference, every day.

Your work is important and you know the value of improving it. The *Community Foundation Handbook* presented here will help. In the pages that follow, you will find six chapters focusing on different facets of community foundations:

1. Community Foundations Overview
2. Governance and Accountability
3. Management, Finance and Administration
4. Grantmaking and Community Leadership
5. Resource Development and Donor Relations
6. Communications, Marketing and Public Relations.

These six chapters feature information fresh from the field. Although there are nationally recognized standards and practices, the field remains amazingly diverse. The *Community Foundation Handbook* introduces you to the spectrum of choices available to community foundations in different aspects of their work. You will find ideas and tools for you to compare and evaluate, and perhaps even improve on your own foundation practices.

If you have questions about community foundations, the *Community Foundation Handbook* will help you find focused answers, fast.

WHO SHOULD READ THIS BOOK

The *Community Foundation Handbook* provides essential information for community foundation chief executive officers (CEOs) and their staff. Although written primarily for staff, the chapters are broad enough that board members and volunteers will find them just as valuable. For newcomers, this book can serve as a comprehensive orientation to the field. For seasoned staff, it can serve as a useful refresher on the continual path of professional development.

By reading each chapter, you will upgrade your understanding of community foundations and enhance your performance on the job. All six chapters, taken together, constitute a panoramic course on the governance, management and operations of a community foundation.

Because community foundations vary in size, location and operating style, these chapters speak to different levels of experience. Depending on your foundation's stage of development, you may find some of the tools here too basic. Others may be more sophisticated than you want or need at this time. Some of the practices may not be right for your foundation, but many of them will be. Use these guides as a starting place to work from, or as a point of comparison for what you do already.

HOW TO READ THIS BOOK

At the start of each chapter, you will find a list of topics for easy scanning. Within each chapter, sections begin with a sidebar called What You Will Learn, as an introduction to what follows. Through your reading, you will find interesting quotes and examples from your colleagues in the From the Field sidebars, as well as useful tips and tools. Each chapter concludes with a quick Questions to Consider sidebar, giving you a summary of questions to reflect on or take to your board for discussion. Some chapters also include sample tools for you to adapt and use as you need, and each ends with a list of publications and web resources for further research.

The *Community Foundation Handbook* will help you in many ways. What it won't do is replace your own hands-on experience and good, individualized legal and financial advice. This book presents a comprehensive overview of community foundations, but should not be your last word on any of these topics. Use it as an introduction and as a desk reference to dip into as needed, as well as a springboard to find other resources.

You will find that this book builds on old ideas and sparks new ones. It will help you continue and improve upon your good work. Enjoy.

CHAPTER 1
COMMUNITY FOUNDATIONS OVERVIEW

"Welcome aboard. You are now exempt from federal, state, and local taxes."

Community Foundations Overview

In This Chapter

Introduction 3

1) **Mission and History** 4
   What Is a Community Foundation? 4
   What Distinct Value Do Community Foundations Offer? 5
   What Sets Community Foundations Apart as Public Charities? 5
   How Did Community Foundations Start? 6
   How Did Community Foundations Grow? 6
   How Did U.S. Community Foundations Organize as a Field? 7
   How Did Community Foundations Spread Internationally? 8
   How Do Community Foundations Today Compare? 9
   What are the National Standards for U.S. Community Foundations? 9

2) **Trends** 13
   How Has History Affected Recent Trends? 13
       Shift from Trust to Corporate Structure 13
       Community Foundations Seek Permanent and Non-Permanent Funds 13
       Focus on Grants from Living Donors 14
       More Funds from Private Foundations 14
       Single Entity Requirements 14
       Variance Power 15

   What Trends Influence Community Foundations Today? 15
       Keeping Up With the Competition 15
       Donors Needs Have Changed 16
       Forming Regional Collaborations 17
       The Need to Know What Works 17
       Growing Professionalism in the Field 18

3) **Options and Opportunities** 19
   How Does Your Community Foundation Fit In? 19
   Why Was Your Foundation Formed? 20
   Who Are Your Local Constituents? 20
   What Are Your State and Local Laws? 21
   What Are Your Values, Vision and Mission? 22

Questions to Consider 23

Resources for Community Foundations Overview 24

COMMUNITY FOUNDATIONS OVERVIEW: AN INTRODUCTION

"In no other place can the intricacies and passions of our daily lives be better expressed than in the broad and far-reaching work of a community foundation."

—Karri Matau, Donor & Community Relations, Greater Everett Community Foundations

Over the past 90 years, community foundations have made positive change in neighborhoods, regions and locations across the entire American landscape. As a staff member at a community foundation, you work to change people's lives, improve conditions and better the area in which you live. You are in good company.

Today, community foundations make up one of the fastest growing sectors of philanthropy. Currently there are approximately 700 in the United States. These organizations range in size from a few thousand dollars to almost $2 billion in assets, and provide services and opportunities as varied as the communities they serve. About 70 percent of the community foundations in the United States have agreed to comply with the National Standards for U.S. Community Foundations. The idea has spread throughout the world, with an estimated 1,175 community foundations identified in 46 countries (as of 2004).

Years of valuable work have earned community foundations the confidence and trust they now enjoy. The field is incredibly diverse, and that's one of the reasons why it works so well. Each community foundation tailors itself to the resources and the needs of its particular area. Yet all have the same reason for existing—to engage donors, to serve communities and to improve the quality of life.

This chapter introduces you to the field of community foundations. In the following three sections, you will learn about:

1) **Mission and History**—Learn about community foundations, past and present. Read about the distinct value of community foundations, what sets them apart as public charities and how they have contributed to society. Learn how community foundations got their start, how they evolved and grew as a field and how the concept spread internationally. Compare community foundations today, and see how National Standards have raised the bar on effective practices.

2) **Trends**—Learn how history has brought the field to where it is today and where current trends are leading the field tomorrow.

3) **Options and Opportunities**—Discover your foundation's distinct local character and the many choices available to you.

1.
MISSION AND HISTORY

"As it's often said, community foundations connect people who care with causes that matter. It's time we became well known."

—Chuck Slosser, President/CEO, Santa Barbara Community Foundation

WHAT YOU WILL LEARN

In this section, learn about community foundations, past and present. Read about the distinct value of community foundations, what sets them apart as public charities and how they have contributed to society. Learn how community foundations got their start, how they evolved and grew as a field, and how the concept spread internationally. Compare community foundations today, and see how National Standards have raised the bar on effective practices.

What Is a Community Foundation?

Community foundations are independent, tax-exempt public charities created by and for the people in a local area. They enable people with philanthropic interests to support the issues they care about, easily and effectively. They create long-term assets for communities to sustain the people who live there.

Working within a specific geographic area, community foundations build permanent funds, through a gift of assets contributed by many donors. From those funds, community foundations make grants and engage in community leadership activities to address a wide variety of current and long-term needs.

Community foundations are different than any other kind of public charity. With a mix of roles, they act as grantmakers, community leaders, donor service providers and fund developers. At any given time, community foundations juggle these roles, making sure their work in each remains vital and always aligned with their mission.

Community foundations are also different from each other. In fact, no two community foundations are exactly alike. Because they are shaped by local traditions and local resources, even long-established community foundations vary in structure and focus. Community foundations enjoy a flexibility that adapts to their community needs, making it possible to create an organization fitted to individual strengths and circumstances.

Definition of a U.S. Community Foundation

A community foundation is a tax-exempt, nonprofit, autonomous, publicly supported, nonsectarian philanthropic institution with a long-term goal of building permanent, named component funds established by many separate donors for the broad-based charitable benefit of the residents of a defined geographic area, typically no larger than a state.

What Distinct Value Do Community Foundations Offer?

Why should people care about community foundations? There are many reasons. They build and strengthen the communities where people live and work. They bring to life a philanthropy that is visionary, diverse and inclusive. In doing so, they have become catalysts for improving communities worldwide.

Community foundations offer great value to donors, grant seekers and the community. They accept gifts of various sizes and types from individuals, local corporations, other foundations and government agencies, and they design giving plans for a range of donors. With this quality of customer service, community foundations give donors the best benefit from their gifts—and use those gifts to do the most good.

Community foundations offer:

- **Personalized, flexible giving opportunities for today:** Community foundations help individuals, families and businesses achieve their charitable goals by providing tools and resources that make giving easy, flexible and effective.

- **Flexible giving to make a difference in the future:** Donors can create lasting legacies, ensuring that the causes they care about will be supported after their lifetimes.

- **In-depth community expertise and leadership:** Community foundations understand the community's challenges and work closely with diverse groups and individuals to address the community needs, now and in the future.

For more on the value of community foundations, read the Community Foundation Message Points, National Marketing Action Team. Visit www.cfmarketplace.org.

What Sets Community Foundations Apart as Public Charities?

Most charitable nonprofit organizations serve the community in a direct way, such as by sheltering the homeless or counseling those in crisis. When donors give to these charities, they usually do so to help the organization perform its service.

Community Foundation Roles

- Builders and stewards of permanent community resources
- Grantmakers
- Service providers to donors
- Service providers to nonprofits and other grantmakers
- Community leaders
- Conveners, catalysts and collaborators
- Promoters of philanthropy

For more on the above roles, read the chapters "Resource Development and Donor Relations," "Grantmaking and Community Leadership" and "Communications, Marketing and Public Relations."

Community foundations also receive gifts from donors. From these gifts, they create funds from which they make grants in the community. Because community foundations receive funds from the public, they enjoy a different tax status than most other foundations. Community foundations are *public charities*, which gives them tax advantages over private foundations, and allows them to offer donors better tax deductions. As public charities, community foundations are accountable to the public, and to keep their public charity status, must meet a public support test. *See more on the public support test in the "Management, Finance and Administration" chapter.*

How Did Community Foundations Start?

Before there were community foundations, there was Frederick Harris Goff.

Goff, a banker and lawyer in Cleveland, had a simple but revolutionary idea. He fashioned a community-oriented foundation as a way to collect many charitable trusts under unified management and allow a group of citizens to ensure that the charitable goal of the funds fit changing local circumstances.

In 1914, Goff created the Cleveland Foundation. This was just one year after John D. Rockefeller gave $35 million to start the Rockefeller Foundation. A former attorney for Rockefeller himself, Goff had learned what it takes to turn vision into reality.

Through his study, Goff found that banks knew a great deal about investing money but little about giving money away. Therefore, he kept the foundation's investment and grantmaking arms separate—with banks managing the funds and a local board of citizens distributing the money earned from those funds.

Goff determined that the new organization would accumulate and manage permanent funds rather than raise annual operating funds. He also determined that while funds would always be guided by the donor's original intent, they wouldn't be limited by the "dead hand" of the donor if the original purpose became outdated.

Community foundations, he deemed, should consider the wishes of the donor but always retain the power to meet changing needs and priorities. Goff described his community foundation as "an agency for making philanthropy more effective, and for cutting off as much as is harmful of the dead past from the living present and the unborn future." This concept later became legally recognized as **variance power.**

Goff then took his "Cleveland Plan" around the country and in 1915 alone, eight new community foundations were created. This period gave birth to modern public institutions, such as health systems, social work, public libraries and high schools—some of which were started with philanthropic support.

How Did Community Foundations Grow?

Community foundations quickly spread from their Cleveland origins, especially throughout two particular regions: the Midwest, where community foundations fit into the civic culture, and the Northeast, where charitable organizations already played an important role.

During the Great Depression, the rate of new foundations slowed, with only 21 formed between 1930 and 1945. After World War II, however, as the economy grew again, communities formed more foundations. Local organizations other than banks began to sponsor community foundations, and by 1960, they formed at a rate of more than six per year.

The number of community foundations grew more dramatically after the **Tax Reform Act of 1969**, which gave community foundations the preferred tax status of public charities. Concerned about various abuses, the government tightened the law—and the tax breaks—for private foundations. The act divided all charitable organizations, including trusts, into either "private foundations" or "public charities." Private foundations were suddenly under increased scrutiny, as the government considered them less accountable to the public.

This division also created a problem for community foundations with multiple trusts. Initially, the Department of the Treasury wanted to classify each trust as a private foundation. However, following extensive negotiations, the community trust regulations, which took effect in 1976, allowed community trusts to meet the public support test as if they were one entity. That is, contributions to each of their trusts count as gifts to the community foundation as a whole, as long as the trusts meet specific requirements laid down in the regulations. These include control of the trust by the community trust's governing body, variance power and the absence of donor control. Trusts that meet these requirements are called "component funds" of a community foundation.

With the Tax Reform Act of 1969 and the 1976 regulations, community foundations attracted many donors, primarily because they could deduct a greater percentage of their gifts to community foundations than to private foundations. As income tax rates encouraged more growth, communities formed more than 300 community foundations in the next ten years.

In 1986, many community foundations received record amounts of new gifts as donors took advantage of as much as they could before the tax rates dropped.

In the 1990s, community foundations were one of the fastest growing forms of philanthropy. Community foundations boomed right along with the economy and continued to grow and expand. Donors had more assets to donate, and community foundations had greater returns on their investments. In 1991, with the advent of the Fidelity Charitable Gift Fund, the commercial financial services firms that had played a supporting role to nonprofit philanthropy showed they were ready to "sell direct to the customer." Other commercial enterprises quickly followed suit.

By the early 2000s, the commercial financial services sector had established itself as a major purveyor of philanthropic products, and community foundations found themselves focusing anew on organizational efficiencies and alternative streams of revenue. The field of philanthropy responded to the entrance of commercial firms by getting organized.

Excerpts of the above taken from On the Brink of a New Promise: The Future of U.S. Community Foundations, *by Bernholz, Fulton and Kasper, 2005.*

How Did U.S. Community Foundations Organize as a Field?

The first attempt at organizing the field came in 1920, when the American Bankers Association (ABA) established a Committee for Community Trusts. During the Depression, ABA dissolved the Committee for Community Trusts, and the field developed over the next 15 years without benefit of a service organization. In 1949, a group of concerned people formed the National Committee on Foundations and Trusts for Community Welfare to serve community foundations and generate publicity for the concept. For five years, the committee worked out of the offices of the Chicago Community Trust, receiving financial support from community foundations nationwide.

In 1957, a full-time national organization—the National Council on Community Foundations—was formed in New York. Seven years later, the council expanded its membership to include other kinds of foundations and changed its name to the Council on Foundations. For the first time, the foundation field had its own national center and voice.

How Did the Tax Act of 1969 Affect Community Foundations?

As a result of the 1969 act, public charity status and tax treatment of gifts to community foundations rest on three concepts: (1) whether the community foundation meets the test of public support, (2) whether it is one corporate entity or consists of a group of separate funds or trusts, and (3) whether a fund or trust is a component part of the community foundation entity or is a separate fund or trust.

The Council held its first annual conference solely for community foundations in 1985. Four years later, Council staff and members generated congressional support for a proclamation designating the first "Community Foundation Week."

The Council's Community Foundations Leadership Team (Leadership Team), composed of representatives selected by the field, addresses issues for U.S. community foundations. The leadership team scans the field to identify key issues on which to work. Some of these areas include, or have included, standards, legal and legislative advocacy; national marketing; technology; professional and organizational development; emerging issues; and financial services. The Leadership Team changes its priority areas to meet the changing needs of the field.

In 1999, a group of leaders from community foundations founded Community Foundations of America (CFA) to conduct research and develop products and services, especially in the areas of technology, relationships with financial institutions and accountability. In February 2004, the Leadership Team and CFA agreed to align their governance and operations.

In addition to forming national associations, community foundations joined together regionally to support the field. Regional associations of grantmakers (*see www.givingforum.org*) support the needs of their community foundation members across the country, and in some states, community foundations have also come together to form their own associations.

How Did Community Foundations Spread Internationally?

Although the first non-U.S. community foundation formed in Winnipeg, Canada, in 1921, it wasn't until the 1990s that there was a widespread growth of community foundations around the globe. Community foundations proliferated across Canada and the United Kingdom, followed by the rest of Europe and South Africa. Today there is similar community philanthropy in 46 countries (as of 2004), including those in Europe, Latin America, Africa, Asia, Australia and New Zealand.

In the 1990s, community foundations globally began to organize as a field. The Community Foundation Network (CFN) formed in the United Kingdom in 1991, followed by the Community Foundations of Canada in 1992. In October 1998, community foundations from around the world came together for the first time, joining with another association of support organizations, the International Meeting of Associations Serving Grantmakers (IMAG), to form Worldwide Initiatives for Grantmaker Support (WINGS). WINGS-CF now operates as a constituent group within WINGS, focusing solely on organizations supporting community foundation development.

In 2003, the World Bank Group, with foundation partners Ford and Mott, launched the Community Foundation Initiative to educate its staff on the concept and potential contribution of community foundations to development, and to identify and develop several pilot projects in various regions of the world, as a way to support and sustain non-government organizations (NGOs) worldwide.

Recently, community foundations have found more opportunities to band together across national borders. The Council on Foundations includes non-U.S. community foundations among its members and invites them to attend the annual Fall Conference for Community Foundations. Some organizations, such as the Trans-Atlantic Community Foundation Network and the German Marshall Fund, have established international exchange programs between North American and European CEOs to promote learning and sharing.

Of course, the Internet has made nearly instant communication and international networking easy. In just ten years, community foundations formed in isolation have joined in learning opportunities around the globe.

Excerpts of the above taken from the Community Foundation Global Status Report, *Worldwide Initiatives for Grantmaker Support (WINGS-CF) at www.wingsweb.org.*

How Do Community Foundations Today Compare?

Despite a slower growth in recent years, community foundations in the United States remain strong. To this day, community foundations exhibit some characteristics of the very first one. They must still qualify for status as a public charity. They can still vary the use of a fund where circumstances have changed. And they continue to serve the community needs and charitable goals in a defined geographical area.

Community foundations serve different geographic areas in different ways. While some serve purely metropolitan areas or counties, others serve entire states. All share the common goal of serving donors, nonprofit organizations and their communities. They make grants to a wide variety of nonprofit activities—human services, the arts, education, environmental projects, health, disaster relief and so forth.

Most community foundations today are professionally staffed, and new community foundations usually hire at least one professional staff member, typically the CEO, as part of their start-up process. In addition, many community foundations work extensively with volunteers.

With increased scrutiny from lawmakers and the media, community foundations created a push for more self-regulation. As a result, the field has raised the bar on accountability by developing the National Standards for U.S. Community Foundations, which were approved by and for the community foundation field in 2000. The Council on Foundations helps to support a National Standards Compliance process, collecting and disseminating effective practices and strengthening the quality of community foundation operations.

Community foundations now work to differentiate themselves from other charitable giving options. U.S. community foundations, as a field, now present a stronger, more consistent message on what they are and what their distinct value is to communities nationwide.

From the start, community foundations have had a versatility that allows them to change with the times and with their communities. Their flexible nature and diversity still exist as community foundations continue to evolve as individual organizations and as a field.

What Are the National Standards for U.S. Community Foundations?

Today, community foundations in the United States now are larger, more complex, more numerous and more active than at any time in the past. With this growth comes great need for information, best practices and shared principles.

In 2000, the field adopted the National Standards for U.S. Community Foundations, along with compliance indicators for these standards, providing a roadmap of legal, ethical and effective operational practices for all community foundations—new or long-established, large or small, urban or rural.

The standards provide the field with a set of tangible benchmarks for sound policies and accountable practices. They shape community foundations' capacity to carry out their missions and help distinguish them from others. As of April 2005, approximately 70 percent of U.S. community

---

Community Foundation Fast Facts

At the time of publication in 2006, community foundations:
- Numbered approximately 700 in the United States
- Numbered approximately 1,175 in 46 countries
- Held approximately $35 billion in the United States in combined assets in 2003
- Made grants of approximately $2.6 billion in 2003
- Received an estimated $3.8 billion in gifts in 2003
- Ranged in size from $1.7 billion in assets to some with assets of $100,000 or less.

COMMUNITY FOUNDATION TIMELINE

1914—The first community foundation is established in Cleveland. Within five years, community foundations formed in Chicago, Boston, Milwaukee, Minneapolis, Rhode Island and Buffalo.

1921— The Winnipeg Foundation, the first non-U.S. community foundation, forms in Canada.

1930—Twenty-one sizeable community foundations hold more than $100,000 in assets each.

1931—The first donor-advised fund is created in Winston-Salem, NC.

1949—The National Committee on Foundations and Trusts—an organization of community foundations and the predecessor to the Council on Foundations—is founded to "promote responsible and effective philanthropy."

1954—The National Committee on Foundations and Trusts is renamed the National Committee on Community Foundations.

1960—Following a strong period of growth, the number of community foundations nears 50.

1964–The National Council on Community Foundations, Inc., is renamed the Council on Foundations, Inc., and amends its bylaws to admit family and corporate foundations.

1969—The Tax Reform Act of 1969 gives community foundations the preferred tax status of public charities, providing the impetus for the field's penetration into most U.S. communities.

1976—Regulations establish rules for what kinds of gifts constitute a component fund. New tax advantages spur foundation growth.

1985—Council on Foundations holds its first annual conference for community foundations.

1986—Tax Reform Act of 1986 creates more incentives for living donors to contribute to community foundations.

1989—Council staff and members generate congressional support for a proclamation designating the first "Community Foundation Week."

1990s—The international community foundation field grows in Canada and the United Kingdom and eventually throughout Europe and South Africa.

1992—Fidelity Charitable Gift Fund offers donor-advised funds.

2004—Community foundations in the United States hold $39.4 billion in assets; $4.2 billion gifts received; and make $3 billion in grants.

2005—The Council on Foundations identifies approximately 700 U.S. community foundations—70 percent of which have agreed to comply with the National Standards for U.S. Community Foundations.

foundations had agreed to comply with the National Standards, and the field had designed a confirmation of compliance process. As a part of this system, trained practitioners review community foundation record books, checking 38 documents to see that they meet the key elements described by the National Standards.

What Do the Standards Include?

The 43 National Standards address six key areas of community foundation operations:

I. **Mission, Structure and Governance,** including standards defining board accountability, compensation, independence, fiduciary responsibility and representation of the community.

II. **Resource Development,** including parameters for administering funds, disclosures to donors and commitment to building long-term resources for varied community issues and causes.

III. **Stewardship and Accountability,** covering prudent investment and management of funds, transparent recordkeeping, use of funds for their intended purpose, annual audits and public availability of financial information.

IV. **Grantmaking and Community Leadership,** including standards related to due diligence and community responsiveness.

V. **Donor Relations,** including guidelines for informing, educating and involving donors in responding to community needs.

VI. **Communications,** including openness to public scrutiny and frequent communications about activities and finances.

To support community foundations' understanding of and ability to comply with National Standards, a Standards Best Practices Committee—composed of community foundation practitioners—developed an online database that contains descriptions of each standard, types of methodologies, examples of effective practices and more. *Visit the Standards & Effective Practices for Community Foundations database at http://bestpractices.cof.org.*

What Have Community Foundations Contributed to Society?

Since their inception, community foundations have changed the face of their communities and the lives of the people who live there. They have convened leaders around local needs and changed public policy. They have tackled issues on health and the environment, expanded arts programs and responded to tragedies and natural disasters. They have built the capacity of nonprofits and awarded scholarships allowing countless young people to fulfill their dreams.

Listed here are some of the many remarkable community foundation grants and leadership activities. For every one listed, thousands more exist.

- In 1954, television was still new, with only about half of American households even owning a set. The Boston Foundation contributed $10,000 to an experiment to see if the new medium might be used to educate as well as entertain the public. It helped create WGBH-TV, which launched the concept of public television.

- In 1983, the New York Community Trust made grants to a series of AIDS-related projects—the first private-sector funds to address the issue.

- After the Immigration Reform and Control Act of 1986, the California Community Foundation enlisted banks, private foundations, government agencies and an array of nonprofit organizations to help illegal immigrants apply for amnesty.

- Seeing the decay of public schools following the industrial decline and a bitter school desegregation struggle, the Dayton (Ohio) Foundation established the Public Education Fund, one of a national network of such funds, for Dayton and the surrounding suburbs.

- The San Francisco Foundation established a $7 million emergency fund to help put the Bay Area back together after devastating floods and mudslides.

- The Indianapolis Foundation gave $65,000 to the Central Indiana Council on Aging to develop the Home Emergency Area Response System (HEARS), an emergency response communication system to help senior citizens maintain independent living situations.

- The Community Foundation of South Wood County developed a Community Progress Initiative to help revive South Wood County and the town of Rome, Wisconsin, after the wood processing industry declined.

- In 2001, terrorists hijacked four commercial airliners and crashed them in New York City, Washington, DC, and Pennsylvania, killing thousands. Within hours, philanthropies nationwide responded by establishing funds, most notably The New York Community Trust's September 11th Fund and the Survivor's Fund of the Community Foundation for the National Capital Region.

2.
TRENDS

> **WHAT YOU WILL LEARN**
>
> Read this section to learn how history has brought the field to where it is today and where current trends are leading the field tomorrow.

How Has History Affected Recent Trends?

Shift from Trust to Corporate Structure

The first community foundation was organized to administer charitable trusts under unified management and to allow a group of citizens to ensure that the charitable goal of the funds fit changing local circumstances.

Most community foundations today organize as nonprofit corporations as opposed to trusts, and some converted from trust to corporate form or established a corporate form alongside its trust. State law generally allows corporations wider powers to conduct their affairs than trusts and provides greater flexibility for business operations. Unlike early community foundations in which the investments and grants were handled separately, the corporate form calls for one governing body, usually a board of directors, that manages both investment and distribution duties. The board may still delegate investment responsibility to banks or trust companies, as well as to other financial managers.

Community Foundations Seek Permanent and Non-permanent Funds

From the first community foundation, Frederick Goff determined that the organization would establish permanent funds that could be used to meet changing needs over time.

Community foundations today still seek permanent funds from many donors. The most common way to do this is to accept planned gifts from many separate donors and place those gifts into component funds. Component funds include the community foundation's unrestricted fund grants—which are made at the discretion of the foundation's board—and restricted funds—those for which donors specified a particular cause or charity beneficiary. From these funds, community foundations invest the principal and use the returns on those investments to make grants to benefit the community.

Community foundations build permanent funds to ensure a flow of money for grantmaking. As community foundations look to the future, many work to attract living donors, seeing them as a source for both permanent and non-permanent funds. Some community foundations now offer pass-through funds, which are temporary funds used to make immediate grants to the community.

For more information on component funds, see the "Resource Development and Donor Relations" chapter.

Focus on Gifts from Living Donors

The Tax Act of 1969 imposed a special challenge on community foundations. Typically, community foundations received most of their funds through bequests, leaving little predictability as to when the foundations would actually receive the gifts. This made it difficult for community foundations to plan the amount of support they would have in any given year and to know if they would receive sufficient gifts to meet the public support test.

How does this affect the way community foundations operate today? To maintain public charity status, community foundations have had to develop programs to attract and gain support from living donors. Community foundations now focus much of their activity on donor services, and some even devote entire departments to it. They attract donors who want to get involved in grantmaking and those who wish to see the positive affects of their gift, within their lifetime.

More Funds from Private Foundations

Individuals contribute most of the gifts community foundations receive. If there were a runner up, however, it would likely be private foundations. In the past, community foundations have received record high gifts from private foundations that terminated and continue to do so today.

The first recorded transfer of funds was in 1968, when a private foundation valued at more than $13 million delivered its assets to the Chicago Community Trust.

As community foundations grew in numbers and strength, private foundation trustees began to consider them possible partners as well as an alternative to sustaining a separate existence in perpetuity. By transferring assets to a community foundation, trustees could remain charitably active without the administrative burden of operating a private foundation.

Still today, private foundations can terminate by transferring assets to a community foundation, creating a fund in their foundation's name. Community foundations provide professional and cost-effective ways of administering private foundation assets. The community foundation provides the private foundation with professional management and investment practices, and ensures the foundation's purpose will be carried on in perpetuity.

Private foundations that wish to remain in business can also establish named funds at their local community foundation. This gives them an opportunity to give outside their private foundation's mission. It also builds strategic relationships with their local community foundations, allowing them to collaborate on important causes in their communities.

Many community foundations now offer a back-office operational service to private foundations, providing help with identifying and evaluating grantees, as well as ancillary and administrative services.

A ruling request currently pending at the International Revenue Service asks whether the provision of services to private foundations is related to a community foundation's exempt purposes. Although a final determination has not yet been made, the preliminary view of IRS staff, expressed during several conferences, is that such services are unrelated unless they are provided substantially below cost. Community foundations that offer services to private foundations should review this issue with their tax advisor.

Single Entity Requirements

Community foundations in the form of multiple trusts must comply with single-entity requirements for tax purposes. How did these additional requirements come into being? When Congress created a distinction between the tax treatment of private foundations and public charities, controversy arose over the tax treatment of community foundations in the form of multiple trusts.

After considerable negotiations, the Department of Treasury issued regulations that treated a community foundation as a single entity with many component funds. These regulations are significant in that a contribution to a separate trust or corporation is a contribution to a component part of a community foundation, which helps the community foundation satisfy the public support test.

Community foundations in the trust form must still meet these requirements today, which require them to meet several tests to qualify as a single entity. *For a full list of single entity requirements, see the "Management, Finance and Administration" chapter.*

Variance Power

When Goff formed the Cleveland Foundation, he realized that community foundations could not meet changing needs if they were always ruled by the "dead hand" of the donor. He advocated for a new legal device—the variance power, which would meet the donors' wishes but enable the community foundation to make changes if necessary.

Donors have the right to limit the use of their gifts to particular charitable causes or organizations. When a will or gift instrument contains such a restriction, the charity that accepts the gift must abide by it. Exceptions usually require court proceedings, and changes will be allowed only if the court determines that the terms or conditions have become illegal, impractical or impossible to carry out.

The variance provision requires community foundations to "modify any restriction or condition on the distribution of funds…if it becomes, in effect, unnecessary, incapable of fulfillment or inconsistent with the charitable needs of the community or area served."

The variance provision has become part of the National Standards, and most community foundations require it as a condition of accepting gifts of restricted income. *For more on variance power, see the "Management, Finance and Administration" chapter.*

> **NATIONAL STANDARDS II.E**
>
> A community foundation's governing body retains variance power by which it may modify any restriction or condition on the distribution and investment of assets, if circumstances warrant.

What Trends Influence Community Foundations Today?

Keeping Up With the Competition

In the past, community foundations were the primary vehicle for donor-advised funds. This has changed considerably in the last decade, as there has been tremendous growth in donor-advised funds—and in the organizations that offer them.

In 1992, Fidelity Investments created the Fidelity Charitable Gift Fund to enter the donor-advised fund market, and there are now similar funds established through financial institutions. Through these organizations, donors make a contribution and recommend grants from the fund. Today, other public charities offer donor-advised funds as well, including colleges, religious institutions, hospitals and special interest groups.

In addition, there are now more than 1,400 community-based United Ways in the United States. Once focused exclusively on workplace giving, American United Ways generated more than $4 billion in revenues in 2003–2004 and have expanded both their services and missions in recent years.

The competitive marketplace has changed the way some community foundations do business. For example, some now place considerable focus on donor-advised funds as the majority of their total assets and grantmaking. In another example, the community foundations work with commercial financial services firms. In April 2003, Merrill Lynch launched its Community Charitable Fund, supporting the efforts of community foundations by connecting them to the financial institutions field.

At the board level of almost all foundations, competition has caused members to chew on cross-cutting issues, such as:

- Who is the primary customer—donors or the community?
- Should the focus be on restricted or unrestricted funds? Permanent or pass-through?
- Are financial institutions competitors or partners?
- What distinct value can community foundations offer?

The new marketplace has also changed the way community foundations promote themselves and work together as a field. To differentiate themselves from others, the field works to unify its message through national marketing materials. It also now actively publicizes the value of community foundations by providing more donor education, peer networking, community knowledge and philanthropic expertise. The National Marketing Action Team (NMAT) has developed a website (www.cfmarketplace.org) with support from the Council on Foundations and Community Foundations of America, providing strategy and support for local foundations to spread this message nationwide.

For more on distinguishing the value of community foundations, read the Community Foundation Message Points, National Marketing Action Team at www.cfmarketplace.org.

Donors Needs Have Changed

Just as donors are given more choices for their philanthropy, their needs and interests have changed. In the past, most donors gave to community foundations to start a legacy. Today, many donors want to see the immediate impact of their dollars. Younger and more active living donors have specific interests and want to be involved in setting funding priorities and in undertaking the grants process.

To meet donor needs, community foundations have raised the level and scope of their development *and* donor services. Many have upgraded their services to donors, for example, offering online fund account access, more frequent fund statements and a quicker turnaround on grants. Others have created entire donor relations departments to support and serve donors. Community foundations also work more directly with intermediaries—particularly professional advisors—to reach new donors.

As community foundations increase their services to donors and donor advisors, they must grapple with a higher demand on staffing and costs. In the short term, this trend may result in limited growth of unrestricted grantmaking resources. As community foundations juggle their need to build unrestricted permanent funds while serving the charitable interests of donors, they work to find the balance between a donor-centered or community-centered model.

For more on types of donors, see the "Resource Development and Donor Relations" chapter.

Forming Regional Collaborations

With new types of donors, new ways of giving and increased competition for charitable dollars, community foundations face new challenges. Many community foundations now collaborate regionally with one another, banding together for marketing, public policy and more.

Through region-wide initiatives, community foundations have created shared messages and publicity campaigns, and conducted joint seminars and events. They have promoted the National Standards for their members and worked with other foundations in grantmaking. Collaborative efforts like these have shown great success. In two examples of formal regional collaboration:

- The League of California Community Foundations has supported the creation of new community foundations in the state. In addition, it has built a successful statewide visibility effort and promoted standards among its members.

- The Michigan Community Foundations' Ventures, associated with the Council of Michigan Foundations, formed in the 1990s with two objectives: to create a common regional/statewide community foundation message and brand, and to emphasize that its members are independent, local organizations. Through the collaboration, the group also promotes standards for its members.

In addition to these two sophisticated efforts, regional collaboration takes place in many informal ways such as meetings, events and information-sharing nationwide.

Some community foundations question whether regional collaboration will take away from their local identity and limit their independence. Yet, most see that working collaboratively has great benefits. As the saying goes, there is strength in numbers. Collaborating reduces costs, provides opportunities to learn and connect with peers, and increases community foundations' visibility and credibility in the public eye. As more and more community foundations join forces regionally, the field will continue to consolidate and strengthen.

Source: Community Foundations: A Case for Regional Marketing, by Karin E. Tice, Ph.D. *For more information on regional marketing, see the "Communications, Marketing and Public Relations" chapter. For more on collaborations, see the "Grantmaking and Community Leadership" chapter.*

The Need to Know What Works

As marketing becomes increasingly important to community foundations, so does the need to measure what is and isn't working. The field realizes and takes advantage of the connection between marketing and evaluation. The more community foundations can understand how they are making a difference in their communities, the more they can promote themselves to others.

So how *do* community foundations evaluate what works? It used to be that if community foundations evaluated their work at all, they evaluated grants—period. Now, with changing roles and increased

---

Considering a Regional Collaboration?

Consider these questions:
- How do you define the region?
- What are the past/current social and economic relationships among the communities in the proposed region?
- What is the nature of the relationships of the community foundations? How well do the CEOs and boards know one another? Does any tension or conflict exist, or are there existing collaborative relationships?
- How far are people willing to drive to attend meetings?

accountability, community foundations want to show how all of their activities make an impact—their programs, leadership, services and organizational effectiveness.

As community foundations grow smarter about *what* to evaluate, they also look at how to evaluate. Instead of evaluating the impact of one grant during one period of time, community foundations might now look at the aggregate changes of grantees throughout a region, for instance, over a five-or-more-year period.

Technology makes it much easier today for community foundations to evaluate, not only locally, but also on a regional, and even nationwide, basis. Community foundations can now use online surveys, data tabulation tools and more, making evaluation more accessible and immediate, and requiring less labor and cost than ever before. *For more on evaluation, see the "Grantmaking and Community Leadership" chapter.*

Growing Professionalism in the Field

With the growth and complexity of community foundations today, the field needs good information, training, best practices and benchmarks. To meet this need, the field has expanded significantly, both in individual organizations and at a national level.

Community foundations have changed the way they work internally. Individual community foundations now attract and require more experienced staff. Many aim to provide "full service" staff with an ability to work in cross-functional teams (for example, where staff might work in both the program and donor services departments). Even those fully staffed foundations are merging job functions internally, going beyond the "silo effect" of serving donors, grantees and the community separately.

Technology has also changed the way community foundations work. With tools such as web-based marketing, PC-based design services and the Internet, technology enables community foundations to be small but act big. Technology streamlines certain processes, such as how to cultivate new gifts. Donors can now contribute and recommend grants right over the web. Additionally, community foundations are now more in touch with one another through the Internet. Many participate in Council on Foundations-sponsored e-mail lists that promote ongoing dialogue, peer support and best practices. *For more on technology, see the "Management, Finance and Administration" chapter and the "Communications, Marketing and Public Relations" chapter.*

At a national level, the field now sees more function-specific professional associations and issue-specific action teams, providing more information and support to members. The Community Foundations Leadership Team of the Council on Foundations, for example, has formed action teams to monitor the field and provide tools and training on top priority issues. These teams include, or have included, the Legal and Legislative Action Team (LLAT), the Professional and Organizational Development Action Team (PODAT), the National Marketing Action Team (NMAT), the Standards Action Team (SAT) and the Technology Steering Committee (TSC), among others. The leadership team scans the field to identify key issues on which to work and changes its priorities to meet the changing needs of the field.

As the field continues to strengthen and grow, so too will its professionalism. More and more professional development opportunities are now offered through the Council on Foundations, Community Foundations of America, regional associations of grantmakers and other groups. Community foundations can now take advantage of offerings by the Council, including the annual Fall Conference for Community Foundations and courses through the Center for Community Foundation Excellence.

For more information on professional development opportunities visit www.cof.org.

3.
OPTIONS AND OPPORTUNITIES

"If a community foundation stands still, it will become obsolete. Each must be proactive about its choices."

—Suzanne Feurt, Managing Director of Community Foundation Services, Council on Foundations

WHAT YOU WILL LEARN

This section serves as a working guide for you to discover your foundation's distinct local character and the many choices available to you. Consider these mission-related questions and take them to your board for discussion.

How Does Your Community Foundation Fit In?

Community foundations are as different as the communities they serve. They operate differently, they make grants differently, and they approach their work differently. Each celebrates its own distinct history, personality, resources and leadership style. Although the field has come a long way in improving its practices, community foundations still run the gamut of philosophies, methods and operating styles.

Now that you know more about community foundations as a field, take a closer look at your own foundation. If you want to start a community foundation or already have, how you operate depends on from many factors, both external and internal. Influences include:

- Type of community you serve
- Size of your region
- Income base and average age of the population
- History and dominance of charitable giving in your area
- Personality and continued influence of founders or long-time board or staff
- Growth of the board and staff
- Presence and quality of your leaders
- Type and amount of your resources
- Deep-seated values of your founders and board.

With countless influences facing community foundations, there is no "one right way" to operate. At every stage, your foundation must make choices—and anticipate the effects of those choices.

For example, suppose your foundation were given a large, unrestricted pool of money. Suddenly you would be faced with vexing questions about how to spend that money. For instance, *what kind of grantmaker do you want to be? Should you use the money to take on a leadership role? Should you staff up? Invest in technology? Initiate a marketing campaign? How will your choices affect current and potential grantees, donors? How will it change your reputation, and your image in the community?*

By learning in advance about your choices—and being mindful in how you will respond—you can prepare for the time when these important decisions are no longer hypothetical. Read below to learn about some of the common mission-related choices community foundations face as they evolve. Again, every community foundation is different. Bear in mind that these options don't necessarily imply an "either/or" decision. Many foundations operate in a variety of ways at different times. Even in regions where they have been established for a long period of time, community foundations will adapt their structure or emphasis to local conditions.

It's up to your foundation to find the right answers. This section will help you ask the right questions.

Why Was Your Foundation Formed?

Every representative of the community foundation—board, staff and volunteers—will want to know its basic history. The best place to start is by reading the founding documents. Review the articles of incorporation, bylaws and any other agreements or governing instruments. Look for contemporary accounts such as newspaper clips or minutes of board meetings to learn how your foundation got its start.

Consider these questions:

- Who were the original board members or incorporators, and why did they form the foundation?
- What were the startup assets and where did they come from?

Who Are Your Local Constituencies?

Community

A community embodies a complex, ever-changing array of organizations, interests, needs and opportunities. As a responsible and successful community foundation, you are an integral part of that community, where you exercise some leadership and influence for the greater good.

Consider these questions:

- How do you define your community—where is it, who is part of it, how do you limit it geographically?
- What makes your community unique?
- What's important to the people who live there?
- How does the community perceive your foundation?
- How can you expand your community foundation to keep pace with changing community needs?

Donors

In the past, most of the gifts community foundations received were bequests. More and more, however, community foundations attract and cultivate living donors. Foundations now encourage active involvement from their donors.

Consider these questions:

- How have major contributions by living donors come to the foundation?
- How does your board cultivate donors?
- Which group of donors do you primarily focus on?
- How can you build unrestricted funds?
- If unrestricted funds are your priority, how do you continue to serve donors' specific charitable interests?

Nonprofit Organizations

Many community foundations have changed the way they relate to nonprofits, offering them grants as well as a higher level of technical support. Taking an interactive approach to grantmaking, some community foundations appoint advisory groups to locate potential grantees, hold workshops for grant seekers, train nonprofit staff on management and make grants to build capacity.

Consider these questions:

- How can you serve nonprofits better?
- How do you inform them about available grants?
- What is your grantmaking strategy?
- How hands-on should you be with grantees?
- How do local nonprofits perceive your foundation?
- Should you consider giving outside of your geographic region? Does your charter allow you to do so?
- Will you focus on responding to the community's current programs or initiating new ones?
- Will you work independently or collaborate on grantmaking with others?

Board Members, Staff, Volunteers

Board members, staff and volunteers bring perspectives, expertise and interests to the foundation. Collectively, they form the skills and opinions needed to make good grant decisions and run the foundation effectively. Many community foundations use volunteers from the community, asking them to serve on a variety of committees. *For more on board committees, see the "Governance and Accountability" chapter.*

Consider these questions:

- Who are your internal audiences?
- How do you view your work?
- How can your board, staff and volunteers use the same message and language when talking about the community foundation?
- Who should serve on the board and for how long?
- How should the board be structured?
- What policies do you need for the board and staff?
- How involved should community members be in grantmaking?
- How can you engage and manage community volunteers?

What Are Your State and Local Laws?

States have laws that may affect your community foundation. Ask your legal counsel about relevant laws—especially sales tax and real estate laws; charity registration; charitable solicitation laws; and those pertaining to liability, conflict of interest, discrimination and Workers' Compensation. These laws vary by state. You might also check with your state's attorney's office to be sure you remain in compliance.

> **NATIONAL STANDARDS**
> **II.A**
>
> A community foundation is founded and operated for public benefit and has a well-defined, articulate mission.

What Are Your Values, Vision and Mission?

Every organization needs to define its fundamental purpose, philosophy and values. All day-to-day activities flow from your foundation's values, vision and mission. If they haven't done so, your board should define and periodically review these founding statements. Creating these statements requires dedicated time, thoughtful deliberation and sometimes the help of an outside facilitator.

If you are a new foundation that has yet to craft these statements, the best way to help your board is to define what these statements mean and show how they shape all foundation activities. If your foundation already has set these statements into word and action, get to know and understand them—and help your board members do so as well.

Values Statement: Describes your community foundation's core principles and culture. A values statement informs your work—how you interact with others in the community and among your own board, staff and volunteers.

Vision Statement: Describes your community foundation's aspirations—what you hope to accomplish in the future. Through its vision statement, your foundation defines its ultimate motivation, its dreams and its image of an ideal world.

Mission Statement: Defines the purpose of your community foundation's philanthropy—what you hope to accomplish in the present to bring about your vision for the future. The mission statement clarifies the reason for your foundation's existence. It describes the needs it was created to fill and specifies what geographic area you serve. Without a mission statement, your foundation won't be able to establish priorities.

The mission statement also helps assess your community foundation's success, verifying that you're on the right track and making good decisions. A powerful mission statement can be used as a tool for resource development, to attract donors, solicit volunteers and get the community involved.

There are certain requirements for your mission to comply with National Standards. Your mission statement should (1) show its commitment to public benefit, (2) clearly define the geographical region it serves, typically no larger than one state and (3) explain its long-term goal of securing resources to meet changing community needs. Many community foundations craft short mission statements but include these elements in different documents such as a values statement.

Once you have these statements in place, use them to develop your foundation's message and bring awareness to your community. If you need help developing these statements look to your community foundation colleagues for samples. *Find community foundations online at www.cflocate.org. For more information, see the "Communications, Marketing and Public Relations" chapter.*

Every decision your community foundation makes should reflect your values, vision and mission statements. Again, your board should consider reviewing them periodically to make sure they continue to change with the community you serve.

VALUES: What ethics guide you? How do you interact internally and in the community?

VISION: What do you aspire to? What would be ideal?

MISSION: What actions will you take to reach your vision?

RESOURCES: How can you attract funds to achieve your mission?

GOALS: What will you do today to work toward your mission?

OBJECTIVES: How do you meet your goals for fundraising, grantmaking, donor services, community leadership, etc.?

STRATEGIES: What methods do you use to accomplish your objectives?

Overview of Community Foundations: Questions to Consider

Consider these questions:

- How is your mission relevant and effective?
- How can you be sure your mission changes with the needs of the community?
- How do your mission-related choices affect operations? Your constituencies? Your strategic plan?
- How can you plan for the future?
- How are you "making a difference?"

RESOURCES FOR COMMUNITY FOUNDATIONS OVERVIEW

Publications

Community Foundation Global Status Report. Worldwide Initiatives for Grantmaker Support (WINGS-CF), 2005. www.wingsweb.org

Community Foundations and the Coming Intergenerational Transfer of Wealth: An Overview of Approaches and Strategies. The Philanthropic Initiative, 2000. www.tpi.org

Grantmaker Forum on Community and National Service. *Profiles of Success: Community Foundations in Service to Communities.* Grantmaker Forum on Community and National Service, 1999.

Mofson, Phyllis. *Leading the Field: Profiles of Community Foundation Leadership in Smart Growth and Livable Communities.* Funders' Network for Smart Growth and Livable Communities, March 2001.

On the Brink of a New Promise: The Future of U.S. Community Foundations, by Bernholz, Fulton and Kasper. Blue Print Research & Design, Inc., and the Monitor Institute, 2005. www.communityphilanthropy.org

Chapter 2
Governance and Accountability

"I don't think of us so much as 'the Board' as of a Walt, a Phil, a Pete, a Flo, two Chucks, and a Moe."

Governance and Accountability

In This Chapter

Introduction 27

1) **What Staff Needs to Know About Boards** 29
   What Do Community Foundation Boards Do? 29
   What Do Individual Board Members Do? 30
       Legal Duties 30
       Board Member Job Descriptions 30
   What Are the Roles of Board, CEO and Staff? 31
   How Does the CEO Work with the Board? 32
       The CEO Evaluation 33
       Board and Staff Relations 34
   How Does the CEO Help the Board Stay Accountable? 34
       Accountability 34
       Bylaws and Policies 35
   How Do Boards Work? 40
       Committees 40
       Strategic Planning 41

2) **Building the Board** 43
   How Can the CEO Support the Board? 43
       Board Recruitment 43
       Governance Committees 44
       Board Size and Structure 45
       Board Diversity 46
       Board Member Removal 47
       Change in Board Leadership 47

3) **Helping Good Boards Become Great** 49
   How Can the CEO Help the Board Become Better? 49
       Know What the Board Needs 49
       Orientation 49
       Effective Meetings 51
       Board Evaluation 53
       Professional Development 54

Questions to Consider 55

Sample Activity Chart for Board and Staff 56

Resources for Governance and Accountability 57

Governance and Accountability: An Introduction

"Community foundations remain flexible and responsive to changing community needs, while meeting the requirements of accountability and standards. Our field has taken the lead in this arena and will prove to be the testing ground not only for community philanthropy, but also for the art of good governance."

—Becky Cain, President/CEO, Greater Kanawha Valley Foundation

As a community foundation CEO, you hold a position of great challenge and great reward. The board sets the foundation's direction, allocates resources, and creates policies and procedures. You work closely with the board to implement their directives.

For your important role as CEO, you need skills that go well beyond basic management. You need a sophisticated understanding of governance and a firm grasp on how you can help your board lead well. The more you help your board do its best job, the better you can do your own.

Your board will face countless choices as it evolves—for example, how it involves members, makes decisions and assesses its work. As the CEO, you can actively bring these choices before your board, sparking discussion and encouraging members to plan into the future. By taking on this role, you become much more than an employee of the board. You become an agent of change.

The first step is to educate your board and yourself on governance and accountability. In this chapter, you will find information on:

1) **What Staff Needs to Know about Boards**—This section describes what community foundation boards do, as well as the roles of individual board members, the CEO and staff. Help your board raise its accountability by adhering to laws and standards, and by creating strong bylaws and policies. Learn how boards get their work done and how you can help them with committees and strategic planning.

2) **Building the Board**—How can you help your board decide who's on board? This section provides tools that will help your board with recruiting new members, building board diversity, removing board members and planning for leadership transitions. Find out about governance committees and if they are right for your foundation.

3) **Helping Good Boards Become Great**—This section outlines what your board needs to succeed. Share tools with your board on orientation, job descriptions, meetings, self-evaluation, professional development and opportunities to connect with their peers.

> **NATIONAL STANDARDS II.G**
>
> **A community foundation's governing body:**
>
> 1. Is responsible for the mission, direction, and policies of the organization
> 2. Ensures adequate human and financial resources and actively monitors and evaluates the organization's Chief Executive Officer
> 3. Approves policies to prevent perceived, potential, or actual conflicts of interest
> 4. Serves without compensation (exclusive of the Chief Executive Officer)
> 5. Is not controlled by any other nonprofit organization or by any single family, business, or governmental entity, or any narrow group within the community
> 6. Reviews and adopts an annual operating budget
> 7. Ensures that the governing documents include policies for size of the board, required number of meetings annually, limits of members' terms, and structure and responsibilities of standing committees
> 8. Ensures that the community foundation reflects the diversity of the community it serves
> 9. Ensures that the community foundation meets all laws and legal requirements
> 10. Approves all grants

Because the CEO is the designated staff who works directly with the board, this chapter is written specifically to the CEO's perspective. However, all community foundation staff or board members can gain insight here about how boards work and how to best support that work. This chapter provides an overview of governance, but should not be your only resource on this topic—or more important, your board's only resource.

Be sure to give your board a copy of *The Guide for Community Foundation Board Members*, 2003, which is a must-read for all new and seasoned board members and serves as a companion piece to this chapter. *Find this book by contacting the Council on Foundations at www.cof.org or BoardSource www.boardsource.org.*

"Staff can be agents for change by bringing choices before the board."

1.
WHAT STAFF NEEDS TO KNOW ABOUT BOARDS

"Living the public trust, community foundations face an awesome task—to spend carefully but creatively, to honor donors while exercising independent judgment, to move inexorably forward with fairness and accountability to all."

—Mariam C. Noland, "Grants: Giving Life to the Public Trust"

WHAT YOU WILL LEARN

This section describes what community foundation boards do, as well as the roles of individual board members, the CEO and staff. Help your board raise its accountability by adhering to laws and standards and by creating strong bylaws and policies. Learn how boards get their work done and how you can help them with committees and strategic planning.

What Do Community Foundation Boards Do?

Your community foundation is only as effective as your board. For you to make good grants and serve donors well, your foundation must have a stable governing body and enjoy a high level of trust from the community.

Governance refers to how your board "steers" the foundation. Your board has ultimate authority over the organization, setting the course, allocating funds and overseeing its performance. Board members have important legal and fiduciary responsibilities that require committing their time, skill and resources.

The board plays a role in your foundation's essential operations—finance, grantmaking and community leadership; resource development; and communications.

In broad terms, a community foundation board:

- Articulates the foundation's values, vision and mission.
- Creates bylaws describing how the foundation will be governed.
- Sets policies on foundation operations and practices.
- Guarantees accountability and compliance with legal and ethical standards.
- Creates and oversees an organizational strategic plan.
- Determines grantmaking and donor development strategies.
- Hires, supports and evaluates the CEO.
- Ensures and monitors financial resources and performance.
- Oversees and assesses the foundation's programs and activities.
- Assesses its work as a board.
- Recruits and orients other board members.
- Defines board member roles and responsibilities.
- Creates a positive image of the foundation in the community.

- Communicates its work to constituencies and the public.
- Oversees compliance with National Standards for U.S. Community Foundations.
- Authorizes grants.
- Helps secure money for the organization.
- Based on the policy of the community foundation, builds permanent funds.
- Ensures that donor agreements are honored.

As staff, the most important thing you need to know about governance is this: The board is in charge. In saying that, the *entire* board is in charge. A board can exercise its governing power only as an entity—not as individual members. Although individual board members may act as special advisors or offer expertise on certain issues, board members can set policy and make important decisions only when acting as a full board.

What Do Individual Board Members Do?

Legal Duties

Serving on a community foundation board is both a tall responsibility and a terrific honor. First and foremost, board members must understand their legal responsibilities in governing the foundation. Under the law, board members must make sure the foundation serves the public. They do this by meeting specific standards of conduct called Duty of Care, Duty of Loyalty and Duty of Obedience.

These three duties require board members to stay well informed, use good judgment and show reasonable caution. They must put aside personal and professional interests for the good of the organization. Moreover, they must ensure that the foundation stays true to its mission and purpose.

Beyond these duties, board members have a basic fiduciary responsibility—to act as stewards for the foundation's financial resources. The board is legally responsible for investing money and acting wisely on behalf of the community foundation. As a part of its stewardship, board members will develop investment policies, hire investment managers, document their investment decisions and review the foundation's portfolio performance. *For more on investment, see the "Management, Finance and Administration" chapter.*

If board members aren't aware of their legal and fiduciary obligations, you, as the CEO, can help them understand what is expected. By arming members with clear information, you will help the foundation stay out of trouble and remain in good public standing.

Board Member Job Descriptions

Community foundation boards have found that increasing individual board member accountability enhances board performance. More and more community foundations are creating job descriptions for their board members. Job descriptions help board members know what the foundation expects of them and can help them evaluate their individual performance on the board.

As the CEO, consider working with your board chair or, if applicable, the governance committee, to develop job descriptions for members. Job descriptions should include:

- A clear list of duties regarding legal responsibilities and decisionmaking
- An explanation of what it means to be on the board
- Any personal financial obligation or expectation to fundraise.

Your board will customize its job description based on individual expectations. For example, your board might ask its members to:

- Attend board meetings.
- Serve as an active member of at least one committee of the board.
- Participate in and support events.
- Make an annual gift to the unrestricted fund.
- Make a major gift to the unrestricted fund, or another type of gift, at least once every five years.
- Execute at least one planned-giving instrument during service.
- Ask others in the community to support the community foundation.
- Provide the names of potential donors and professional advisor contacts to the CEO.
- Publicize the importance of the community foundation to friends, neighbors and the community at large.
- Study the community to learn about its resources, needs and opportunities.
- Conduct an annual self-evaluation of their performance as board members.
- Participate in continuing education/board development each year.

When drafting a job description, remember that the responsibilities of the overall board are different from the duties of individual members. Give board members two job descriptions—one describing the board's collective responsibilities and the other describing individual board roles. Take care to craft the language carefully. For example, asking donors to "assist in fundraising for the foundation" can have a totally different implication than expecting them to "introduce the foundation to acquaintances to set the stage for fundraising."

Job descriptions can take many formats. Most are one or two pages and include the function, duties and desired characteristics of a board member. Some foundations use a "statement of expectations" or even a signed agreement to make responsibilities explicit.

To help your board create job descriptions, see samples from other community foundations in the Standards & Effective Practices for Community Foundations database, http://bestpractices.org, or visit www.boardsource.org.

What Are the Roles of the Board, CEO and Staff?

"The work of the staff is essential to the board."

A community foundation is a symbiotic partnership between the board and its employed staff. To put it simply, the board makes the rules defining "what to do," while the staff defines "how to do it."

The board establishes policy and oversees the foundation's progress, while the CEO and staff carry out that policy and implement activities. Both staff and board should share a common vision for the foundation's work and a commitment to its mission and goals.

Below are the typical roles of board and staff members:

The Board Chair:
The chair (also called chairperson or board president) leads the board. As the chief volunteer officer, the board chair presides over meetings, rallies the board, supports the CEO and facilitates communication between the board and the staff. Board chairs facilitate the foundation's direction.

Board Officers:
Board officers usually include a vice chair, treasurer and/or secretary and in some cases, the chief executive. Together, this leadership team shoulders specific additional board responsibilities.

The CEO:
Typically, the chief executive oversees the daily and long-term operations of the foundation and its staff: hiring staff and defining job responsibilities, overseeing implementation of activities, establishing and monitoring financial infrastructure, communicating fully and frequently with the board and acting in a leadership capacity on behalf of the foundation.

The Staff:
With the guidance of the CEO, staff provides information, assistance and leadership. The executive staff works with the board to provide overall management and leadership. The CEO hires staff to fill certain roles depending on the foundation's stage of growth. These roles might include grantmaking, development, finance, donor relations, communications and administration.

When a board hires executive staff for the first time, board members must make the critical transition from a "working board" to a "policy board." As the board separates policy from staff functions, confusion in roles may arise. To assist in this time of transition, help your board understand its roles and responsibilities and the individual and joint roles of staff. Offer your board sample job descriptions and activities of board and staff. *For a sample list of staff and board activities, see the end of this chapter. For more on hiring staff, see the "Management, Finance and Administration" chapter.*

How Does the CEO Work with the Board?

"To have a successful community foundation, no matter the size of its assets, there must be, first and foremost, a positive and mutually respectful relationship between the CEO and the board of directors."

—Peggy Ogden, President and CEO, Central New York Community Foundation

Both the board and CEO advance the foundation's mission. They hold different responsibilities and work from different perspectives, but their roles support and balance each other.

Although often thought of as a partnership, the board/CEO relationship is also one of employer/employee. The board as a whole hires, supports, oversees and evaluates the CEO. The CEO, in turn, supervises all other staff. As the CEO, your board should provide you with a job description outlining what they expect of you. If you haven't received a job description, discuss the need for one with the board chair.

In working with the board, it is your job as CEO to:

- Understand the goals of the board
- Determine the costs of operations
- Plan and coordinate board meetings
- Initiate the board's strategic planning process
- Secure board approval for the overall administrative costs
- Serve as staff liaison to the board and its committees
- Oversee the foundation's day-to-day operations according to the board's directives.

As the CEO, you will work closely with the board chair. For the CEO/chair relationship to be successful, both parties must communicate regularly and openly. It's a good idea to establish this communication right from the start. For example, the CEO might meet with a new board chair immediately, creating open dialogue about communication styles and the best way to work together.

Keep in mind, challenges may arise if the communication falters between the CEO and board. You and your board chair can circumvent these obstacles by providing one another continuous support and feedback.

Here are some tips for how you and your board can best support each other's work:

- **Have confidence in your board.** Be assured that the board members have the best interest of the foundation at heart and are willing to work for its good.

- **Give the board reason to have confidence in you.** Show the board that you are running the foundation well. Communicate openly with them.

- **Be sure everyone knows his or her role.** Provide clear job descriptions. An imbalance of power can undermine the authority of both board and staff and diminish morale.

- **Help the board avoid bottlenecks of control and micromanagement.** Offer members tools and resources on board roles. Communicate your concerns to the board chair.

- **Learn how to manage conflict.** Provide conflict resolution skills when needed. Model a positive, constructive attitude. Create appropriate channels for staff and board to voice concerns.

- **Encourage regular self-assessment.** Self-assessment opens communication, improves relations and increases the effectiveness of both board and staff.

- **Bring in an outside consultant.** If challenges arise between board and staff, you might suggest bringing in an objective expert to mediate and/or conduct a facilitated retreat.

The CEO Evaluation

As the CEO, you might make your board aware of its responsibility to evaluate your performance. To comply with National Standards, your board must evaluate your performance at least once every two years. In doing so, they must show the nature and extent of the review and what benchmarks are used in setting your salary.

Evaluation is more than a tool for the board to monitor your performance; it is highly beneficial for your role as CEO as well. Consider these advantages:

- As part of an evaluation, the board and CEO establish mutually agreed-upon goals for the coming year.

- Evaluations can be a formal time for you to address major concerns, budding disagreements or pressing issues.

- If the board is satisfied with your performance, this is an opportunity to agree on a salary increase.

The best CEO evaluations are simple but thorough. Many boards will ask the CEO to perform a self-assessment first, on which they then base their evaluation. Others ask the staff for feedback. If your board includes staff in the CEO evaluation, suggest that they keep staff comments confidential. Ask them to brief you and the staff first on their process and explain how the information will be used.

For sample CEO evaluations, visit the Standards & Effective Practices for Community Foundations database at http://bestpractices.cof.org or visit the Leader to Leader Institute at www.pfdf.org.

> **NATIONAL STANDARDS**
> **II.G.2**
>
> A community foundation's governing body...actively monitors and evaluates the organization's chief executive officer.

Board and Staff Relations

Relations between the board and staff are incredibly important and set a tone throughout the entire organization. A strong leadership team between the board and staff can propel a foundation to success. If the roles between board and staff aren't clear, however, it can create tension and misunderstanding. As the CEO, you hold a vantage point unlike any other and can help everyone understand their role.

Although you may be the only staff member who officially works with the board, you might provide some opportunities for board and staff to interact. For example, at your discretion, staff might coordinate board committees, make presentations at meetings or attend site visits with board members.

As the CEO, you and your board chair should consider setting clear guidelines for how the staff interacts with the board. Every foundation will have its own philosophy on this delicate matter. Sample guidelines might include:

- The board goes through CEO to arrange meetings with staff.
- Board members can request information and reports from staff, but may not direct staff work or micromanage operations.
- Staff attend board or committee meetings at the discretion of the CEO.
- Personnel grievances go through appropriate channels specified in the personnel policies.
- The board instills a whistleblower policy for staff to report unethical or illegal workplace activities.

For more on whistleblower policies, see the "Management, Finance and Administration" chapter.

How Does the CEO Help the Board Stay Accountable?

Accountability

Accountability means adhering to laws and regulations and taking steps to preserve the public trust. Your foundation should establish and carry out policies and procedures that demonstrate its transparency, credibility and integrity to donors, grantees and the community.

As the CEO, educate your board about how to build accountability. Make sure board members know the basics. The board must:

- Know federal regulations and your state laws.
- Understand their roles and responsibilities.
- Craft, communicate and enforce strong policies, including a conflict of interest policy and a code of ethics for board, staff and board committees.

- Discuss if your board is representative of the community it serves.
- Hire an independent auditor to conduct an annual audit or financial review.
- Make 990s easily available.
- Invest and monitor the foundation's money wisely.
- Familiarize themselves with intermediate sanctions, which prohibit providing more than fair market value economic benefits to disqualified persons.
- Set policy on records management and make sure files are maintained appropriately.
- Document corporate meeting minutes.
- Publish an annual report with financial data.
- Apply due diligence in grantmaking.
- Conduct a self-evaluation on the overall effectiveness of the board and foundation.

As a CEO, you can also encourage your community foundation board to comply with the National Standards for U.S. Community Foundations. If your board follows good governance practices such as those listed here, it can create a solid accountable foundation that strengthens the community, responds to change and avoids crises.

"I see a movement to assure the general public that we will be transparent in all we do. As we all know, if we don't do it ourselves it will be done for us."

—Chuck Slosser, President/CEO, Santa Barbara Foundation

Bylaws and Policies

Bylaws and policies are principles determined by the board to which the foundation adheres. Although the two are related, they are created at different times and used for different purposes.

As part of its founding documents, your board created articles of incorporation, as well as bylaws describing the internal rules that guide your board's activities. Bylaws often include:

- Foundation name and location
- Required number of meetings annually
- Board member nomination, election and/or appointment process
- Board structure including size, committees and responsibilities
- Terms for board service (e.g. two years, three years) and rotation policies
- Meeting guidelines (quorum, attendance policy)
- Evidence of variance power (if not included in the articles of incorporation or declaration of trust)
- Bylaw amendment process.

Your jurisdiction may have specific requirements for what your bylaws should include. Be sure to check with your state's secretary of state or similar government office for applicable laws relating to bylaws. Remind your board to periodically review the bylaws and amend them as needed. *For sample bylaws, visit the*

> **NATIONAL STANDARDS**
>
> **II.G.7**
>
> A community foundation's governing body...ensures that the governing documents include policies for size of the board, required number of meetings annually, limits of members' terms, and structure and responsibilities of standing committees.

Standards & Effective Practices for Community Foundations database at http://bestpractices.cof.org or the Nonprofit Management Assistance Program at www.mapfornonprofits.org.

Policies, as distinct from bylaws, provide directives on the foundation's daily operations and practices. Policies are determined by the board and easier to change.

What policies does your foundation need? The board should consider policies on the following:

- Conflict of Interest
- Code of Ethics
- Confidentiality
- Investment and spending
- Diversity and inclusiveness
- Gift acceptance
- Grant procedures
- Risk management
- Indemnification of board members
- Document integrity, retention and destruction
- Personnel issues
- Expense reimbursement
- Whistleblower protection.

As your board establishes policies, you, as the CEO, will communicate and implement them under the board's guidance. What is the best way to communicate policy to the board and staff? Provide every new board member with a board handbook describing bylaws and policies. The board handbook may be similar, or in some cases identical, to your foundation's employee manual.

Conflict of Interest Policy

Conflicts of interest are a normal part of doing business. A conflict occurs when a board member's outside involvements—business interests, personal or family relationships, political or other charitable activities—may make it impossible to remain unbiased. In any dynamic board, it's natural that these conflicts occur. More important is how board members disclose their conflicts to the board and how those conflicts are managed.

Your board should have a clear conflict of interest policy and guidelines in place. To comply with National Standards, the policy must:

- Commit to preventing conflicts, whether they are perceived, potential or actual conflicts.

- Apply to board, staff and individuals serving on standing board committees.
- Include procedures for handling disclosures of conflicts.

Moreover, to meet compliance you must show evidence that your foundation follows its conflict of interest policies. Such evidence may include samples of redacted disclosure documents, corporate records or minutes noting board members' disclosure of conflicts and so forth.

Most conflicts of interest involve a circumstance where a staff or board member benefits from the foundation in a personal, direct, tangible or economic way. An example would be if the foundation hires one of its board or staff members to perform a second, paid role for the foundation—such as an accountant, investment manager or real estate agent—or if a board or staff member takes part in a decision that brings personal gain. Direct conflicts or the appearance of a conflict may arise if a board member has a personal relationship with one of the foundation's grantees or grant applicants.

A conflict of interest policy identifies actual and potential conflicts and describes how the foundation will handle them. A good policy requires both board and staff to disclose financial and other interests that may interfere (or be seen by others to interfere) with their duty to put the foundation's interests first. A good policy will also provide that the person with the conflict will not participate in discussions about it, except to answer factual questions about the arrangement, and will leave the room to permit the remaining members of the board to discuss and vote on the proposal. Similar policies should apply to volunteers, such as the members of scholarship selection committees or those who recommend investments or the distribution of assets.

Because community foundations are public charities, it is generally legal for them to enter into conflict of interest transactions with board, staff and volunteers as long as the foundation has followed an appropriate process and the deal does not confer an excessive benefit on the individual with the conflict. However, foundations should consider that these transactions can be grounds for public criticism because of the appearance of favoritism to insiders and should avoid them whenever possible. Foundations that go ahead with a deal that involves a board member, a substantial contributor, a top staff member or any other person with the ability to influence the foundation's decisions should follow the three-step, rebuttable presumption process prescribed by the federal "intermediate sanctions" regulations. This process includes obtaining competitive bids to ensure a fair price and maintaining careful documentation of the basis for decisions. *For more information, see "Intermediate Sanctions Checklist" by Lloyd A. Mayer, www.cof.org/files/Documents/Legal/checklist.pdf.*

If a board or staff member acts in spite of having a conflict, the foundation should take disciplinary steps. Some boards form a task force or committee to analyze and deal with conflicts as they arise, with the board chair, staff or some other committee member designated as the lead person.

> **NATIONAL STANDARDS**
> **II.G.3**
>
> A community foundation's governing body…approves policies to prevent perceived, potential or actual conflicts of interest.

A good conflict of interest policy will help your board stay out of potential legal trouble. It will also keep the foundation from any questionable behavior that might harm its public standing. *For sample conflict of interest policies, Council members can visit the Standards & Effective Practices for Community Foundations database at http://bestpractices.cof.org.*

Code of Ethics
A code of ethics helps your community foundation demonstrate its accountability, values and transparency.

The board creates and oversees the code of ethics. To do so, your board might convene an ad hoc committee to determine what the code should include. A code of ethics commonly includes statements on:

- Personal and professional integrity and conduct
- Mission
- Governance
- Conflict of interest
- Legal compliance
- Responsible stewardship of resources and financial oversight
- Openness and disclosure
- Program evaluation
- Inclusiveness and diversity
- Integrity in resource development and grantmaking.

Once the board develops a code of ethics, you as the CEO will need to communicate the policy to all personnel. You might distribute the code to the staff and use its criteria as part of staff evaluations. Work with your board and staff to make sure they adhere to the code. *To customize your own code of ethics, visit www.independentsector.org.*

Confidentiality Policy
According to the National Standards, all private information obtained with respect to donors and prospects must be kept confidential. Your foundation should have a clear confidentiality policy outlining this requirement. *For more on what a confidentiality policy should include, see the "Resource Development and Donor Relations" chapter.*

Investment and Spending Policies
As its fiduciary duty, your board must safeguard the foundation's assets with a solid investment strategy. This strategy involves written investment and spending policies.

An investment policy describes the overall investment philosophy, including what the foundation is trying to accomplish with its permanent funds. The policy lists individual objectives and asset allocation criteria and how these contribute to the overall goals of the foundation. The investment policy also describes the spending policy, which is the annual percentage of assets the foundation will spend from its permanent funds. *For more information on these policies, see the "Management, Finance and Administration" chapter.*

Diversity
As the CEO, you should help board members commit to diversity in the board's composition and actively announce their commitment. Suggest that your board write a policy on diversity, perhaps as a "statement of inclusiveness," describing the community's demographics and the desired characteristics for the board. To

comply with National Standards, your board must document how it seeks diverse membership and different perspectives, such as age, gender and minority composition.

Gift Acceptance Policies
Gift acceptance policies protect your community foundations from accepting gifts and assets that could put it at substantial risk or create excessive costs. These policies describe the types of funds offered, the types of gifts accepted, the minimum amount to set up a new fund and more. *For more information on gift acceptance policies, see the "Resource Development and Donor Relations" chapter.*

Grant Policies
Grant policies describe your foundation's grantmaking goals, priorities, criteria and procedures. They communicate to grant seekers what the foundation will and will not fund, and guide them through the process of applying. They also guide your foundation's internal process for reviewing, awarding and monitoring grants. *For more information on grant policies, see the "Grantmaking and Community Leadership" chapter.*

Risk Management
Like any organization that works with people and organizations, community foundations face risks. Risk is any future event that threatens your foundation's vital assets and compromises its mission. Your board can minimize threats by developing risk management policies and procedures. One way boards do this is through an ad hoc "risk management committee" that identifies potential risks and plans ahead for how to intervene. All community foundations should have a general liability insurance policy and should consider the need for insurance covering events, professional errors and omissions. *For more on risk management, see the "Management, Finance and Administration" chapter.*

Indemnification of Board Members/Director's and Officer's Liability Insurance
You can never guarantee that a board member won't be implicated in a legal suit while acting on behalf of the foundation. Indemnification clauses usually occur in a foundation's bylaws, and state and federal laws may provide some protection for some causes of action. Even so, community foundations should purchase director's and officer's (D&O) insurance. Director's and officer's insurance is a specific insurance policy to safeguard board members as well as the foundation for causes of action not covered by a general liability insurance policy. Among other benefits, D&O insurance provides broad coverage for employment-related claims. *For more on D&O insurance, see the "Management, Finance and Administration" chapter.*

Document Integrity, Retention and Destruction
Legally you must maintain good records of receipts, contributions, disbursements, assets and other financial data. This helps your foundation maintain accountability in the event of an audit or public questioning. According to recent legislation, every nonprofit corporation should adopt a written policy setting forth standards for document integrity, retention and destruction. There may be strict punishments for altering or destroying any document with the intent to obstruct a federal investigation. *For more information on records management, see the "Management, Finance and Administration" chapter.*

Personnel Policies
Even the smallest community foundation needs to establish personnel policies and communicate them to staff. Written policies are the best way to clarify expectations and prevent misunderstandings. They also keep operations solid despite any staff transitions that might occur.

There are a variety of federal laws and executive orders on how employers must select, compensate and treat individuals in the workplace. Personnel policies are the best way to meet legal responsibilities and clarify rights and responsibilities of staff. Such policies might include those relating to hiring practices, work schedule, leave, substance abuse, violence in the workplace and more. *For more information on personnel policies, see the "Management, Finance and Administration" chapter.*

Whistleblowers

In the wake of recent public scandals, it is a best practice for community foundations in the corporate form to comply with the "whistleblower" provisions set forth by legislation. Whistleblower policies permit and encourage employees to alert management and the board to ethical issues and potential violations of law without fear of retribution.

Discharging, demoting or harassing an employee who provides true information about a potential federal offense is a felony under federal law. *For more information on whistleblower policies, see the "Management, Finance and Administration" chapter.*

How Do Boards Work?

Committees

Much of the board's work is accomplished through committees. When it comes to committees, some boards feel that less is more. Smaller, more cohesive boards may choose to manage the workload without committees, or perhaps with just one or two. This kind of structure might create more unity and focus, but it requires effective leadership and equal commitment from every member.

More recently, some community foundations have gone to a "zero-based" committee structure, where they abolish all committees at the beginning of each year and add them one by one as needed. This can help the board ensure that every committee counts.

By making your board aware of the many options available, you can help members find a structure that works well for them. Keep in mind that boards with too many committees risk immobilizing the power of the board, creating a situation where all the work is done at the committee level, leaving little for the overall board to do. Too many committees can also be labor-intensive for staff, as they are usually responsible for coordinating meetings and communications among members.

A good rule? Before adding any committee, the board should define its purpose. Your board will find its committees more effective if they launch a strategic function, rather than fill an administrative task. As the CEO, you should help your board plan the purpose of each committee. Suggest that they define clear tasks for each committee and monitor whether the work remains meaningful and effective. Here are some questions you might bring before your board:

- What committees does the board need to perform its work?
- How big should committees be?
- Who should participate on committees (board, staff, outside volunteers)?
- How often should committees meet?
- How much decisionmaking power should committees have?
- How can the board limit the scope of committees so as not to undermine the board as a whole?
- What will be the reporting mechanisms to the overall board?
- How will the board monitor the success of each committee?

Traditionally, boards have relied on standing committees, most commonly:

- **Executive Committee**—Acts on behalf of the full board between board meetings; its decisions are communicated to and approved by the full board. Boards should carefully consider the role and scope of the executive committee responsibilities in relation to the board as a whole, so as not to replace the decisionmaking authority of the entire board.

- **Nominating/Governance Committee**—Evaluates board composition and needs; coordinates board recruitment and elections; oversees board orientation and development. Some community foundations have other names for these committees, including "Organizational Effectiveness Committee."

- **Finance/Investment Committee**—Develops and monitors investment policies; hires and monitors investment consultants and managers. Monitors the foundation's financial status.

- **Development Committee**—Establishes a development strategy and creates a fund development plan, which is then implemented by all board members.

- **Grants/Program/Distribution Committee**—Develops the foundation's grant program, including its philosophy and guidelines, and oversees the grantmaking process.

- **Audit Committee**—Monitors the foundation's accounting and reporting; hires and assists an independent auditing firm to conduct the annual audit and reviews the annual audit.

In addition to standing committees, boards may add more throughout the year as needed. Often called ad hoc, advisory or task force teams, these committees focus on a special interest area or a short-term project. Sometimes, community foundations will use outside volunteers to serve on these committees. This enables busy community leaders to get involved with the foundation without too much time commitment, gives your board a chance to identify future board members and offers a "testing ground" for their performance.

For more information on board committees, visit BoardSource at www.boardsource.org.

Strategic Planning

Good boards don't just focus on what the foundation should do; they focus on the process to get there. This process is called strategic planning.

Community foundations create a strategic plan that describes what their long-term goals and objectives are and how they will work to fulfill those goals. As with any management tool, strategic planning helps the foundation do a better job. It focuses energy, ensures that the board and staff are working toward the same goals and adjusts direction in response to a changing environment.

Committee Tips

Good board committees have:

- A strategic instead of an administrative function
- Clear job descriptions and goals
- Members who are willing to work together to accomplish tasks
- A sense of being a part of the full board and not working in isolation
- An understanding that committees make recommendations; the full board makes decisions
- An evaluation process to assess its own work
- An awareness of when they need to change direction or disband.

Good strategic plans:

- Define the purpose of the community foundation
- Build a consensus about where the foundation is going
- Establish realistic goals and objectives consistent with its mission in a defined timeframe
- Describe how the foundation will communicate these goals to its constituents
- Focus foundation resources on key priorities
- Provide a base from which progress can be measured
- Develop a sense of ownership of the plan.

The board decides when it will undergo a strategic planning process. As a CEO, you might initiate this discussion among board members. Strategic planning most often occurs when a foundation is just getting started or when preparing for a new major venture. In addition, many community foundations engage in a full planning process once every three to five years. Once the strategic plan is in place, the board should annually review and, if need be, modify it to prepare for the coming fiscal year.

For a strategic planning process to be successful, the board must fully commit to it. Some boards form an ad hoc strategic planning team to guide the process. This committee "plans ahead" for the planning by outlining tasks, roles and timelines.

Some boards ask the CEO to facilitate the planning process. If the CEO has expertise in facilitation and planning, this can be a prudent choice. However, it might be better to hire an outside facilitator who can bring an objective view. This is especially true when the board is undergoing its first planning process or if past planning wasn't deemed successful. It can also be helpful when there is a wide range of ideas among members. Outside experts can bring a neutral opinion and can guide participants without fear of ruffling feathers.

Whether your board chooses to facilitate the process in- or out-of-house, here are some general steps to follow in strategic planning:

- **Get organized**—Get a commitment from the board, hire outside help if needed, form a planning team and schedule meetings and/or a retreat.
- **Analyze what's current**—Review the mission and history; identify each major area for discussion (e.g. financial management; fund development; accomplishments; perceived strengths, weaknesses, opportunities, threats)—(also called SWOT).
- **Develop a strategy**—Select whether your planning approach will focus on goals, critical issues (program emphasis, style of grantmaking, etc.) or scenarios (possibilities for the future).
- **Draft and refine the plan**—Select a format, develop a first draft, refine the plan and adopt the plan.
- **Implement the plan**—Communicate the plan to stakeholders, monitor performance, periodically review and update.

As anyone who has participated in strategic planning would agree, it's a process that requires much time and patience. Even the most effective foundations don't change overnight. Strategic planning will help your foundation evolve over time and help the board do more of its good work—even better.

"Our strategic plan fits on one piece of paper. It contains the four key result areas that drive our work: engaging donors, building philanthropy, strengthening community and ensuring organizational effectiveness."

—Peggy Ogden, President and CEO, Central New York Community Foundation

2.
BUILDING THE BOARD

> **WHAT YOU WILL LEARN**
>
> How can you help your board decide who's on board? This section provides tools that will help your board recruit new members, build board diversity, remove board members and plan for leadership transitions. Find out about governance committees and if they're right for your foundation.

How Can the CEO Support the Board?

Board Recruitment

It is the board's responsibility to cultivate, recruit, nominate and train new members. As with many leadership activities, however, the CEO supports the board in this work.

As a CEO, you and your staff should be on the lookout for qualified prospective board members. Once you've identified prospects, introduce them to your board. You might also participate in board recruitment activities, such as interviewing candidates before the election. Some CEOs maintain a file of community leader resumés and attend cultivation meetings with other board members and senior staff.

Most boards use set membership qualifications for who can serve on the board. Most set a minimum age requirement for participation. Some list additional qualifications such as knowledge of funding areas, standing in the community, professional experience and so forth. Some boards' organizing documents permit outside bodies, such as a chamber of commerce or local bar association, to appoint some members to the board as well. You and your board may work with these appointing authorities to ensure the individuals who are appointed meet the needs of the community foundation. To comply with National Standards, your board must reflect a diverse composition with different perspectives.

Help your board create a simple matrix where members list exactly what they are looking for and the criteria for joining the board. You might suggest the following selection criteria. Board members should have:

- Commitment to the values, vision and mission of the community foundation
- Wisdom and experience
- Ability and willingness to serve on the board

■ FROM THE FIELD: BOARD SELECTION CRITERIA

When one board decided to expand, the board governance committee set its sights on formalizing an eligibility process. The board governance committee designed a chart to assess the current board, using objective data such as ethnicity, gender, geography, religious denomination, age at time of appointment and areas of expertise. Each board member was asked what they believed were their top three areas of expertise, and the committee used this data to identify gaps. Next, they developed criteria to narrow the lists of potential board members. Categories included professional/volunteer status; special competencies; leadership skills; experience in philanthropy; knowledge of the community and its needs; and ethnicity, gender and geography.

- Community visibility
- High personal ethics
- Willingness to raise money
- Willingness to give money relative to their personal circumstances
- Legal or accounting knowledge, or contacts with professional advisors
- Contacts with banking institutions
- Contacts with high net worth individuals
- Civic leadership experience
- Experience as entrepreneurs and business leaders
- Management knowledge regarding internal policies and procedures
- Marketing and communications skills
- Knowledge of the community.

For sample board eligibility requirements, visit the Standards & Effective Practices for Community Foundations database at http://bestpractices.cof.org or the Nonprofit Management Assistance Program at www.mapfornonprofits.org.

Governance Committees

Traditionally, the nominating committee of community foundation boards identified and recommended new board members. Today, many foundations are replacing their nominating committees with governance committees. In addition to the role of nominating new members, governance committees work to sustain the entire board. They review the board's roles and responsibilities and assess board composition. They design and oversee the orientation process, as well as facilitate ongoing board education and evaluation.

Typically, a governance committee:

- **Identifies the needs of the board**—Identifies and recommends candidates to fill the board's needs; updates board members' roles and responsibilities (e.g., board job descriptions).
- **Cultivates and recruits new members**—Seeks nominees for the board.
- **Administers board orientation**—Plans and oversees orientation of new members; develops a mentoring program.

> ■ **FROM THE FIELD: GOVERNANCE COMMITTEES**
>
> When one community foundation board reviewed its nominating process, it realized that it wasn't fulfilling the needs of the organization. The foundation disbanded its nominating committee and replaced it with a governance committee. The new body took on all the responsibilities of the nominating committee, such as finding candidates and recommending them to the board. It also expanded the committee's activities, charging the committee with board orientation and molding new board members through mentoring. It helped educate board members with training sessions and guest speakers. And it continually worked to identify the needs of the board and cultivate new members. As one staff member said, "The governance committee finishes the work of the nominating committee, looking not just to the next board election but well into the future."

- **Engages all board members in the work of the board**—Tracks interests and availability; involves members in committees or task forces.
- **Educates the board**—Provides members ongoing education, retreats, board development and bylaw review.
- **Oversees the health of the board**—Rotates members, establishes term limits, leads board assessments, improves the effectiveness of board meetings and plans for board members succession.

As the CEO, you can inform your board members about governance committees, letting them decide if they are right for the board. *For more information on governance committees, order* The Guide to Community Foundation Board Members, *www.cof.org.*

Board Size and Structure

Before recruiting new members, your board should determine the best size and structure to accomplish its work. Legally, your board must be representative of the community. In a narrow legal sense, "representative" means that the board must not be controlled by a small number of the foundation's principal donors.

Beyond the legal requirements, how big should boards be? On average, community foundation boards range between eight and 18 members, and numbers vary from foundation to foundation. Larger boards don't necessarily mean better boards. In some instances, large boards can diffuse responsibility among members and create more administrative burden on the staff. That said, a board that is too small may miss the people power needed to serve on committees and perform its work.

Help your board decide on the size right for them. Common advantages of large and small boards include:

Larger Boards:

- may have more people and more connections to raise money
- allow for more working committees
- often use an executive committee to make decisions
- allow for more continuity in times of member turnover
- may be more representative of the community.

Smaller Boards:

- may make it easier for everyone to have a voice and make decisions
- allow members to know and communicate more effectively
- require fewer staff to support its work
- may create a stronger sense of ownership and responsibility among the board members.

Some foundation boards use a two-tier structure, in which former board members or others are elected to serve as honorary members. This structure maintains organizational history by allowing the former members to participate, without increasing the size of the board. The CEO and/or board chair meets with the honorary board at least once a year, to tap its expertise when necessary. Members might have a single, collective voting seat on the main board, with which they get one vote.

In sum, no one size is right for every board. Boards should only be as big as it takes to get the job done.
For more information on board structure, refer your board to The Guide for Community Foundation Board Members, *www.cof.org.*

Board Diversity

To qualify as a charitable organization, your community foundation must serve and be supported by a broad section of the public. Thus, your board should represent the same diversity as the community it serves.

By understanding diversity and using it appropriately, a community foundation board creates a foundation that is more responsive and effective. Why is diversity so important? For many reasons:

- The public expects community foundations to represent the community.
- Diverse boards demonstrate accountability and form a connection to the community.
- Diversity can bring innovation and creative thinking.
- It encourages varied opinions, approaches, attitudes and solutions.
- It sets an example for others in the foundation and in the community.
- It helps tap new sources of expertise and money.

As the CEO, you might suggest that your board write a statement of inclusiveness, describing the community's demographics and the desired characteristics for the board.

When considering diversity, your board might consider discussing candidates from the following demographic categories:

- Age
- Gender
- Ethnicity
- Socioeconomic background
- Geography
- Sexual orientation
- Skill sets
- Profession/occupation.

Your board should aim for a diverse mixture, choosing members based on their experience, skills and community knowledge—not because they fill a demographic slot. Suggest that your board recruit several members from the same group, if possible, to avoid creating "token" positions.

To comply with National Standards, be sure your board documents its nomination process, describing how it seeks diverse membership and different perspectives. Remind the board that with more diversity, members will enjoy new energy, new ideas and a richness of opinion. Board diversity can lead to better discussions and even better decisions.

For more information on diversity, read Cultures of Caring: Philanthropy in Diverse American Communities, *Council on Foundations, 1999, www.cof.org. For sample statements of inclusiveness, check with the Standards & Effective Practices for Community Foundations database at http://bestpractices.cof.org, your colleague community foundations or the Council on Foundations at www.cof.org.*

Board Member Removal

What happens when a board member becomes unable to perform his or her duties or prevents the board from working well? This can be a difficult situation, one in which the board might have to take disciplinary action or remove the member from service.

As a CEO, how can you help your board deal with this delicate matter? Suggest that they:

- In advance, create a code of conduct for member behavior, with consequences for noncompliance.
- Create and enforce term limits and rotation policies.
- Conduct a face-to-face intervention, offering opportunities for open communication and improvement.
- Call in an outside consultant for mediation.
- Offer the member a leave of absence.
- Ask the board member to voluntarily resign.
- Remove the board member by vote.
- Hold an open and confidential discussion with the board, after the fact, to help air feelings and prepare for the future.

Change in Board Leadership

What's the best way to undergo a change in board members? Your board should put a succession plan in place before the change in leadership occurs. Community foundation boards and CEOs should consider planning for the succession of all of its board members—particularly that of the board chair.

As the CEO, you can help your board create these plans. Discuss and agree with board members what should be included. For example, a good plan might address the following topics:

- **Orientation**—Discuss who among board and/or staff will lead the new chair orientation. Decide what materials should be presented and what activities the orientation will entail.

- **Public relations**—Agree on how the board will announce its new chair to stakeholders and the community. Prepare a sample news release announcing the change and a sample mailing list of organizations, field publications and local newspapers.

- **Training**—Consider what training and resources the board will offer its new chair. Keep a sample list of conferences and workshops offered by the Council on Foundations, Community Foundations of America, your regional associations of grantmakers, BoardSource and others.

- **Ongoing information**—Discuss with the board the best mechanisms for ongoing information exchange with the new chair.

As part of the succession planning, the board nominating or governance committee (or staff, on their behalf) should update board member job descriptions. Job descriptions are one of the best tools for board effectiveness and for succession. They brief the new chair on the purpose, responsibilities, duties and rationale for each board position.

Boards should not only develop the leadership skills of the current chair, but also develop those of the chair-elect and/or vice chair. Your board might create a job description for these roles, explaining what will be expected during the transition and beyond. This will open communication right from the start, giving the incoming chair an opportunity to ask questions of the current chair and CEO. It will also give the chair-elect a chance to practice skills for the future role. Some foundations even invite the chair-elect and/or vice chair to run a meeting or two.

3.

HELPING GOOD BOARDS BECOME GREAT

> **WHAT YOU WILL LEARN**
>
> This section outlines what your board needs to succeed. Share tools with your board on orientation, job descriptions, meetings, self-evaluation, professional development and opportunities to connect with their peers.

How Can the CEO Help the Board Become Better?

Know What the Board Needs

For your board to do its best job, it needs understandable and timely information about governance. As discussed earlier, board members need to know about the laws that affect the foundation. They need strong policies on how to govern and how the foundation will operate. And they need an understanding of stewardship and accountability.

Beyond these requirements, board members need tools to do the best job they can. As CEO, you can provide great service to your board by asking them what they need and informing them about available tools and resources. Here are some ideas to get you started.

To succeed, all boards need:

- A good orientation
- Job descriptions
- Effective meetings
- Self-evaluation
- Professional development
- Team building
- Ways to connect to the larger field.

Orientation

Orienting new board members requires a great deal of time and effort. It introduces new members to the foundation—its mission, programs and people. It also acclimates them to the board itself—its structure, operations and legal obligations.

How can you, as the CEO, ensure that your board receives the best orientation? Most foundations give new members a board handbook—a "bible" of board history, structure, practices, operations and more. This book introduces them to the board, but also serves as a useful refresher throughout their tenure. Give new members the handbook before their orientation; that way, they will know what to expect and come prepared with questions.

You and your staff should compile materials for the handbook. Consider including the following items:

- **Board directory and calendar**—A roster of board member names, contact and biographical information, job descriptions of the chair and members, committee lists, calendar of meetings.
- **Foundation background**—Values, vision and mission statements, history, description of grantmaking programs and process, long-range plan, annual report, current grantee list.
- **Board structure**—Terms and term limits, job descriptions for individuals and committees, members' responsibilities and their self-assessment forms.
- **Bylaws and policies**—Articles of incorporation and bylaws, board policies on indemnification and director's and officer's liability insurance, conflict of interest policies, code of ethics, attendance policy, expense reimbursements guidelines, document retention and whistleblower policies.
- **Staff**—Names and job descriptions, personnel policies, organizational chart.
- **Finances**—Investment policy and reports, budget, audit statement, financial procedures, IRS Form 990 (or pertinent excerpts).
- **Minutes and issues**—Minutes of recent board meetings, description of current issues for discussion, sample meeting agenda.
- **FAQs**—Frequently asked questions and their answers.
- **Glossary**—A list of philanthropic terms and jargon newcomers will likely encounter.

Once the orientation handbook is ready, you can help your board create an agenda. An orientation should always be held as a separate event—a retreat or before a regular board meeting, for example. Consider including breaks and at least one social meal.

The orientation agenda will vary based on the specific information your board wants to include. The session may start with a tour of the foundation's main office (if held on-site) and an introduction of key board members and staff. From there, a typical agenda might include an introduction to the field of philanthropy; an overview of the foundation's history, mission and values, together with a look at its strategic plan and communications; an explanation of the board's structure and committees; a discussion on legal responsibilities and what's expected of board members (for example, commitments of time and money); a review of finances and grantmaking programs, guidelines and processes; a discussion of liability and insurance coverage; and perhaps a site visit to grantees.

When it comes to the actual orientation, veteran board members—not the staff—should conduct most of the orientation. Remind your board that good governance is learned over time. Orientation provides continued education for seasoned members as well as incoming members.

Some foundations send new board members to outside training or workshops as a part of their orientation. Consider the Council on Foundations' Community Foundation Fundamentals, the Institute for New Board Members or similar workshops sponsored by the Council, regional associations of grantmakers or affinity groups. You might also consider giving incoming members a subscription to field publications, such as *Foundation News & Commentary* (www.foundationnews.org) and the community foundation electronic newsletter *CFSource* (e-mail cfsource@cof.org).

What Is a Consent Agenda?

A consent agenda is a voting procedure that can save your board time. Before the board meeting, your board groups routine items and resolutions under one package. Unless a board member requests the removal of an item ahead of time, the board votes on the entire package at once, with no discussion necessary.

Effective Meetings

Individual board members must actively participate for the board to be effective. Board members should stay informed, uphold the foundation's ethics and values, and represent the foundation in the community. They should attend meetings and events, participate on committees and carry out assignments.

Meetings bring board members together to do the real "meat & potatoes" work. Some boards might meet quarterly, for example, while others meet monthly or bimonthly. Because all other tasks flow from board meetings, the board must plan the annual meeting calendar in advance. Many times, the staff will schedule meetings and prepare and distribute a board meeting book to members before the date.

The board chair and CEO usually develop the agenda for meetings, which is included in the meeting book. The book also often includes other materials, reports and contact information that members should review before the meeting. *See sidebar for more ideas on what to include.*

Meetings are where the work gets done, and for that reason, you should make every meeting count. As the CEO, you can help your board chair lead a good meeting. Below are some tips you can share:

Before the meeting:

- Choose a meeting date, place and time
- Contact attendees well in advance
- Establish clear goals
- Prepare and distribute a meeting agenda and advance reading
- Assign advance roles and tasks if they are not clear.

During the meeting:

- Describe the meeting agenda and goals
- Encourage participation of all members
- Stay on task
- Use individual skills of members
- Use consent agendas where appropriate
- Stay connected to mission

Sample Board Meeting Book

A board meeting book typically includes:

1. Agenda
2. Contact list of board members
3. Previous meeting minutes
4. Financial information
5. Resource development director's report
6. Program directors' report
7. Proposal summaries with full proposal attached (if applicable)
8. New business materials
9. Next meeting announcement

- Record the minutes
- Recap the meeting's achievements.

After the meeting:
- Remind members of interim responsibilities
- Encourage contact and communication among members.

According to National Standards, your board must keep a record of its meetings. Usually, the board secretary or a designated staff person takes the minutes, or board members take turns. Minutes of corporate meetings are legal documents. Over the course of one year, the minutes should demonstrate the following: the board's approval and exercise of authority over the mission, direction and policies; the board's approval of the annual budget; the board's approval of all grants or delegation of this authority; the board's approval of the conflicts of interest policy; the board's review and acceptance of the audit or financial review; and evidence that the foundation reflects the community's diversity.

If board members have started to show low energy during meetings, or worse, not show up, it may be a sign that the board isn't engaging members or that board meetings have become repetitive. This might be a good time to hold a special meeting or retreat, reviewing the foundation's mission and perhaps making a shift in focus. If board meetings still feel repetitive, or members seem complacent or uninterested, work with your board chair to infuse energy into the meetings. You might want to:

- **Invite outside speakers.** Invite community members, program experts, board development specialists or grantees to speak at board meetings.
- **Identify "sacred cows."** Are there tough subjects the board avoids discussing or that have become too accepted to question? This usually can spark a good board discussion.
- **Discuss articles and policy papers.** Share publications that prompt discussion and keep members abreast of new developments in the field.
- **Tell stories.** Ask members to tell their story. For example, members might pick one word from the mission statement and describe what it means to them. This technique reveals why people joined the board as well as their underlying values.
- **Evaluate.** Evaluations of the board as a whole and individual board member performance can also be a catalyst to change what isn't working well.
- **Retreat.** Retreats offer an opportunity for members to spend more time together than they usually do and can strengthen communication, development and effectiveness.

■ FROM THE FIELD: WHEN THE BOARD LOSES ITS OOMPH

Has your board lost the energy and enthusiasm it once had? It might also be a good time for members to connect with the community—and be reminded of why they are doing the work.

When one community foundation in the South noticed this trend, they sent board members out into the community to ask questions and connect with people. "For our strategic planning process, the board went out and conducted community surveys," explained the president. "That got them fired up. They asked people in the community what their greatest need was and what we do to meet that need." The board came back full of ideas about how to improve and had a renewed sense of energy for the work.

Board retreats are special meetings organized around issues too significant to be handled properly within a normal meeting agenda. Most boards can benefit from an annual retreat simply to strengthen relationships and focus on future challenges. Retreats usually focus on one of the following topics:

- Conducting a board self-assessment
- Orienting new board members
- Refreshing board members' understanding of their responsibilities
- Strengthening board relationships and team-building
- Undertaking strategic planning and/or refocusing the mission and vision
- Working on a critical issue.

For information on planning a board retreat, contact the Council on Foundation's Governing Board Programs at www.cof.org, COF CODE: **Gov Boards**.

Board Evaluation

As part of its charge, a board strengthens what works and abandons what doesn't. Good boards regularly assess themselves and their work. Encourage your board to evaluate its work at least once a year. Remind them that assessment is nothing to fear; it can be a tremendous growth and awareness opportunity.

Boards typically hire an outside facilitator for the assessment process or conduct a self-evaluation. Facilitators might interview individual board members and sometimes staff or hold an all-day board retreat for evaluation as a group. For boards who choose to manage the process in-house, the board chair or an assessment committee might administer surveys to members and then discuss the results.

In a self-assessment process, your board should begin by evaluating their work as a group. You might suggest that your board discuss the following sample questions. *See the sidebar on "Board Assessment."*

Next, board members should evaluate their own individual performance and/or that of their peers. Some boards use a simple and confidential survey format, asking members to rate themselves on items using a scale of one to five. On any survey, it helps to also include open-ended questions to get a range of responses.

Board Assessment: Sample Questions

- Is the foundation's mission relevant?
- How is the board structure effective? How could it be improved?
- Who is the primary customer? What does the customer value?
- How well do board members know their roles and organizational relationships?
- What can the board do to improve its work?
- How well does the board communicate with stakeholders? With each other?
- Are there subjects the board avoids discussing?
- How well does the board perform in leadership and planning activities?
- What board development and organizational capacity building does the board do?
- How well does the board report and document procedures?
- How prepared is the board? What is the level of member participation?

> **WHERE TO FIND MORE ON GOVERNANCE**
>
> How can you help your board stay focused on policy and other big picture issues? The Governing Board Programs of the Council on Foundations offers resources for boards, including the latest research, training and tools. Learn more at www.cof.org, COF CODE: **Gov Boards**.

A peer review can be similar, using a one-page list of board members with the same scale. As part of evaluation, board members should receive feedback on their performance. As behavioral science has shown, feedback has an uncanny effect on performance. Sometimes knowing that performance will be monitored can prompt a positive change in behavior. *See the sidebar on "Member Assessment."*

For more information on board self-assessment, visit BoardSource at www.boardsource.org, the Leader to Leader Institute at www.pfdf.org or the Nonprofit Management Assistance Program at www.mapfornonprofits.org.

Professional Development

In addition to giving your board tools and information to help them do a good job, you should encourage them to take advantage of professional development. Professional development helps members continue their learning and stay motivated.

Professional development can range from inviting an outside speaker to a board meeting or sending board members to training. Ask board members what kind of professional development activities interest them. Find ways for the board to connect with members of the community—through site visits, events, meetings and so forth.

Inform your board of conferences, workshops and public talks. Check with the Council on Foundations (www.cof.org, COF CODE: **Events**) for a schedule, including the annual Fall Conference for Community Foundations, and the Center for Community Foundation Excellence courses (www.cof.org, COF CODE: **CCFE**).

In addition to the Council on Foundations, check for training opportunities through regional associations of grantmakers (www.givingforum.org); local organizations including development offices, colleges and universities; and other nonprofits. You could also

---

Board Member Assessment: Sample Questions

- How well do I understand and support the mission?
- How do I understand my roles and responsibilities?
- How well do I serve on the board?
- How do I prepare in advance?
- Do I regularly attend and participate in meetings? Events? Site visits?
- Do I volunteer for committees and serve effectively on them?
- Do I recommend individuals for board service?
- Do I recommend and make contact with potential donors, professional advisors, others?
- How well do I publicize the foundation to friends/associates? The public? The media?
- Do I participate in professional development?
- How do I give personally to the foundation?
- How do I find board service valuable?
- What could I do to improve my effectiveness?

contact neighboring community foundations (www.cflocate.org) to inquire where they send their board for professional development.

When boards connect with other grantmakers, they communicate their work, as well as learn the work of others. In addition to attending conferences and training opportunities, board members can join e-mail lists, connecting with colleagues right from their desk. To join an e-mail list for community foundation board members, e-mail cflistadmin@cof.org. In the subject line, write "Join CFBoardList." Include your name, title and community foundation in the e-mail text.

For a list of other community foundation e-mail lists, visit www.cof.org COF CODE: **CFLists.**

Governance and Accountability: Questions to Consider
- How can you help your board keep the mission vital?
- Do board members know their roles and what is expected of them?
- Are the roles between board and staff clear? How much should board and staff interact?
- What tools can you provide your board for recruiting and orienting new members?
- Does the board create and follow strong policies?
- How committed is the board to diversity?
- How does the board manage change and growth?
- How often does the board assess its work?
- What succession plans are in place for board leaders?
- Are there tough subjects the board avoids discussing? Or that you, as CEO, avoid discussing with the board?
- How has the board contributed to the growth and effectiveness of the foundation?
- Do board members have a sense of ownership, connection and satisfaction in their service?
- How does the board get the foundation from here to the future?

SAMPLE ACTIVITY CHART FOR BOARD AND STAFF

PLANNING:

Provide input to long-range goals	Board and CEO
Approve long-range goals	Board
Formulate annual objectives and budget	CEO and Staff
Approve annual objectives and budget	Board
Prepare performance reports on achievement of goals and objectives	CEO and Staff
Monitor achievement of goals and objectives	Board and CEO
Make investment decisions and monitor results	Board
Create policy	Board

OPERATIONS:

Assess community needs and issues	Board and Staff
Train volunteer leaders	Staff
Evaluate board and CEO performance	Board
Maintain records; prepare reports	Staff
Prepare preliminary budget	Staff
Finalize and approve budget	Board
See that expenditures are within the budget	Staff
Solicit contributions and cultivate donors	Board and Staff
Organize resource development campaigns	Staff
Review grant proposals	Staff and/or Board Committee
Approve grant proposals (or delegate authority)	Board
Communicate with grantees and grant seekers	Staff
Monitor and evaluate grants	Staff
Monitor and evaluate overall foundation performance	Board
Monitor and evaluate staff performance	CEO
Approve expenditures outside authorized budget	Board
Hire independent auditor for annual audit	Board

PERSONNEL:

Hire CEO	Board
Direct work of the staff	CEO
Hire and discharge staff members	CEO
Decide to add staff positions	Board
Settle discord among staff	CEO
Establish whistleblower policy	Board

COMMUNITY RELATIONS:

Publicize foundation to community	Board and Staff
Write articles and news releases	Staff
Provide media interviews	Board Chair and/or CEO

BOARD COMMITTEES:

Appoint committee members	Board Chair
Promote attendance at board/committee meetings	Board Chair and CEO
Recruit new board members	Board
Orient new board members	Board and Staff
Plan agenda for board meetings	Board Chair and CEO
Take minutes at board meetings	Board Secretary or Staff
Prepare exhibits, material and proposals for board and committees	Staff
Sign legal documents	Board or CEO

Source: Adapted from the Nonprofit Management Assistance Program at http://mapnp.nonprofitoffice.com

Resources for Governance and Accountability

Publications

Bryson, Ellen and Sandra Hughes. *The Guide for Community Foundation Board Members.* BoardSource and Council on Foundations, 2003. www.cof.org

Bryson, Ellen. *What Community Foundation Boards Are Saying.* Council on Foundations, 2002. www.cof.org

Cultures of Caring: Philanthropy in Diverse American Communities. Council on Foundations, 1999.

Accountability: The Buck Stops Here. BoardSource, 2002. www.boardsource.org

Andringa, Robert and Ted Engstrom. *Nonprofit Board Answer Book Practical Guidelines for Board Members and Chief Executives,* BoardSource, 2001. www.boardsource.org

Fletcher, Kathleen. *The Policy Sampler: A Resource for Nonprofit Boards.* BoardSource, 2000. www.boardsource.org

The CEO Viewpoint: A Report on a Survey of CEO's of the Largest 250 Foundations in the U.S. Center for Effective Philanthropy, 2004. www.effectivephilanthropy.org

Hughes, Sandra. *To Go Forward, Retreat!* BoardSource,1999. www.boardsource.org

Ingram, Richard T. *Ten Basic Responsibilities of Nonprofit Boards.* BoardSource, 2003. www.boardsource.org

Kurtz, Daniel L. Managing Conflicts of Interest: Practical Guidelines for Nonprofit Boards. Includes diskette with sample forms. BoardSource, 2001. www.boardsource.org

Lakey, Berit M. Nonprofit Governance: Steering Your Organization with Authority and Accountability. BoardSource, 2000. www.boardsource.org

Pierson, Jane and Joshua Mintz. *Assessment of the Chief Executive.* BoardSource, 1999. www.boardsource.org

Waterman Wittstock, Laura and Theatrice Williams. *Changing Communities, Changing Foundations: The Story of the Diversity Efforts of Twenty Community Foundations.* Minneapolis, MN: Rainbow Research, 1998.

Web

BoardSource—www.boardsource.org

Governing Board Programs, Council on Foundations—www.cof.org, COF CODE: **Gov Boards**

Nonprofit Management Assistance Program—www.mapfornonprofits.org

Director's and Officer's Liability Insurance and Indemnification, Council on Foundations—http://cof.npo-ins.com

Leader to Leader Institute—www.pfdf.org

Chapter 3
Management, Finance and Administration

"If Anderson is C.E.O., and Wyatt is C.F.O., and you're C.O.O., then who am I, and what am I doing here?"

Management, Finance and Administration

In This Chapter

Introduction 63

1) General Management 64
    What Makes a Successful CEO? 64
    How Does the Work Get Done? 66
        Planning 66
        Managing Teams 67
        Decisionmaking and Problem Solving 69
    How Can You Prepare for Staff Transitions? 69

2) Human Resources 72
    How Many Staff Does the Foundation Need? 72
    How Do You Hire Staff? 73
        Fair Recruitment and Employment Practices 74
        Using Search Firms 74
        Interviewing 75
        Making the Offer 76
    How Should Staff Be Compensated? 76
        Types of Benefits 77
        Payroll 78
        Salary Adjustments 78
    How Do You Work with Volunteers and Consultants? 78
    What Personnel Policies Does Your Foundation Need? 80
    What Is an Employee Manual? 81
    How Do You Evaluate Staff Performance? 82
    How Can Professional Development Help Staff Retention? 83

3) Administration 85
    What Technology Will Your Foundation Need? 85
        Technology Planning 85
        The Web 86
    How Can You Manage Risk? 90
        Safety and Security 91
        Insurance 92
        Maintenance and Service Contracts 93

What Is the Best Way to Manage Files and Records? 94
    Records Retention 94
    Filing Systems 95
    Paperless Office 95
    Archiving 96
How Do You Set Up a New Office? 97
    Location 97
    Space 97
    Office Furniture and Equipment 97

4) Legal and Fiduciary Responsibilities 99
What Legal Rules and Requirements Do You Need to Know? 99
Legal Structure: Trust or Corporate? 99
What Are Governing Documents? 100
What Is the Public Support Test? 102
What Are the Federal Requirements? 103
    Tax Filing 103
    Unrelated Business Income Tax 103
    Excess Benefit and Intermediate Sanctions 103
    Gift Substantiation and Disclosure 104
What Are State Requirements? 104
    State Filings 104
    State Charitable Solicitation Law 104
    Other Laws to Know 104
What Policies Does Your Foundation Need? 105
What Are the Material Restriction Rules? 105
How Do You Manage Foundation Assets? 105
How Do You Track Finances? 106
What Are the Basics of Budgeting? 107
What Are the Investment Basics? 108
    Developing an Investment Strategy 109
    Investment Committees 110
    Investment Consultants 110
What Are Uniform Laws? 111
What Should You Know About Audits? 112

Questions to Consider 113
Resources for Management, Finance and Administration 114

Management, Finance and Administration: An Introduction

A community foundation is an institution of almost limitless flexibility. With such flexibility comes the need for sound management. As a community foundation CEO or senior staff, your management function helps the foundation make the best use of its assets. Good management affects the entire organization and leads to good grantmaking, community leadership, donor services and resource development.

Every community foundation manages its operations differently. Community foundations operate with a mix of full- or part-time staff, volunteers, advisors, consultants and committees. This requires a high level of planning, coordinating and delegating on the part of community foundation senior staff.

This chapter will take you—the community foundation CEO or senior staff—through what it means to operate a community foundation. In the next four chapters, you will learn about:

1) **General Management**—Read about the role of the CEO in management and what it takes to get the work done. Find out about operating plans, managing teams, making decisions and solving problems. Plan ahead for staff transitions and learn how to prepare a succession plan for the CEO and other key staff before changes occur.

2) **Human Resources**—Learn the best way to recruit, retain and manage employees and consultants. This section walks you through hiring new staff and helps you make the best use of the staff already in place. Learn what personnel policies your staff needs and what goes in an employee manual. Find out how to evaluate staff performance and how to use professional development as a staff incentive.

3) **Administration**—This section is for those just establishing a community foundation office, as well as those who want to take their technology to the next level. Consider what technology platform your foundation needs, for example, a core operating system, web options and other applications. Learn how to manage risks through safety and security measures, insurance and good maintenance and contracts. Get to know the legal requirements and organizational tools for managing files, archiving material and setting up a new office.

4) **Legal and Fiduciary Responsibilities**—Legal issues surrounding community foundations are complex. Read here to learn the basics on legal structure, governing documents, the public support test, tax requirements, material restrictions and state laws. Learn what potential liabilities to watch for and what policies your foundation needs. Find out how to manage foundation assets and track finances, as well as the basics of budgeting and investment. Finally, learn what audits require and how you can prepare for them.

This chapter will give you tools and information to run your community foundation. With good management, your community foundation can be a powerful force for change.

1.
GENERAL MANAGEMENT

"A leader takes people where they want to go. A great leader takes people where they don't necessarily want to go, but ought to be."

—Rosalynn Carter, former First Lady

> **WHAT YOU WILL LEARN**
>
> Read about the role of the CEO in management and what it takes to get the work done. Find out about operating plans, managing teams, making decisions and solving problems. Plan ahead for staff transitions and learn how to prepare a succession plan for the CEO or other key staff before changes occur.

What Makes a Successful CEO?

Behind every successful community foundation there is an effective CEO. Community foundation CEOs are some of the most talented people around and for good reason. As a CEO, you must be able to juggle many skills at once—managing the foundation's resources, time, money and staff. This requires a diverse skill set and the ability to meet multiple demands daily.

As the CEO, you also have the edge on information. You are the key spokesperson for the foundation, as you have the broadest perspective on your foundation's capabilities and activities. You are responsible to the board as they rely on you to relay information and help determine the foundation's focus. You contribute to the board's planning process and implement their multiyear plan.

Your board, in turn, should clearly define your duties, responsibilities and their expectations for your role as CEO. To comply with National Standards, community foundations must have a CEO job description. Although each community foundation will have its own description, most include the following:

A CEO:

1) **Supports and administers board operations.** Advises and informs board members, interfaces between board and staff, and supports the board's strategic planning and evaluation processes.

Governance and Management: What's the Difference?

Governance creates the mission, purpose and direction; develops policies on operations, grantmaking, fund development and investment; and oversees the performance of the entire organization.

Management implements the mission, ensures that operations conform to policy, oversees staff and directs the business of the community foundation.

2) **Provides program, product and service delivery.** Oversees the design, marketing, promotion, delivery and quality of programs, products and services.

3) **Manages financial, tax, risk and facilities management.** Recommends a yearly budget for board approval and prudently manages the foundation's resources within those budget guidelines according to current laws and regulations.

4) **Manages human resources.** Manages the human resources of the organization according to personnel policies and procedures and conforms to current laws and regulations.

5) **Directs community and public relations.** Makes sure the staff, board and volunteers communicate about the foundation and its mission, programs and services with a strong, consistent message and positive image.

6) **Develops new resources.** Oversees resource development. Cultivates new donors and maintains relationships and credibility with current donors.

With these many CEO responsibilities, you confront a vast constellation of choices. As the foundation grows in money, reputation and capability, the community will expect endless things from you. *How will you choose what's important? How will you keep others informed and involved? How will you measure your impact?*

Every CEO has his or her own answer to these questions, as well as leadership style. Some community foundations hire CEOs for a specific set of skills—development skills, for example, or financial expertise and contacts in the field. Although these qualities no doubt add value, CEOs need to demonstrate good leadership.

Leaders have been described as falling into four basic types. An *entrepreneur* is a visionary with good ideas and great charisma. A *producer* is goal-oriented and gets the job done. An *administrator* is precise and systematic and sees that procedures are followed correctly, and an *integrator* values teamwork, harmony and consensus.

As the CEO of a community foundation, you shouldn't fall into just one of the above categories. Good leaders cultivate all of these skills and are able to call on them at different times. Some situations, for example, might call for a more authoritative style, where you must mobilize people toward a common vision. Other times, you may be served better by a democratic approach that motivates people to participate.

Successful CEOs must have the leadership to inspire and manage people of all skill levels. They must have passion for the work and be able to communicate and instill that passion in others.

So what's the key to being a good CEO? Know thyself.

As the CEO, the tone you set carries throughout the foundation. You must know and constantly reflect on your own style to understand its ripple effect. Consider these questions:

- What is my style of communication? How does that play out in how others communicate within, and outside, the foundation office?

- How well do I accept new ideas or approaches?

- How does the foundation handle controversy or difference?

- How do I incorporate different backgrounds and perspectives into my work?

Once you have an understanding of your own style, you can then cultivate your leadership skills and be prepared to demonstrate them at any stage or circumstance that occurs.

Know, too, that you are not alone; there are resources to help you. Management training and leadership workshops can benefit you as well as your executive staff. The Council on Foundations offers a variety of opportunities in this area, as do many state and regional grantmaking associations. *Visit www.cof.org to learn about the Council on Foundation's offerings, such as community foundation CEO Retreats. For more on the role of the CEO and board relations, see the "Governance and Accountability" chapter.*

"A good CEO has a passion for the work—and can communicate and instill that passion in others."

How Does the Work Get Done?

Planning

Who does the work of managing a community foundation? Although the board holds responsibility for developing policy, the reality is that both the board and CEO develop management policies and procedures. As the CEO, you are responsible for implementing them.

All work starts with planning. Planning is not one event. It is the continuous process of strengthening what works, making decisions, setting goals and adjusting as situations change.

For your community foundation to accomplish its mission, the board and CEO must engage in a planning process. Planning provides a framework for day-to-day operations and at the same time serves as a viewfinder into the future.

There are two types of plans: the **strategic plan** and an **annual operating plan**. The strategic plan articulates what the community foundation intends to be at some point in the future, usually over the next three to five years. The board is responsible for the strategic plan, although the CEO initiates and supports the process. *For more information on strategic planning, see the "Governance and Accountability" chapter.*

An operating plan focuses on specific steps to implement the strategic plan and move the foundation forward. While the strategic plan focuses on goals, the operating plan contains the objectives—or means—of meeting those goals.

Operating plans are most useful when they are simple and straightforward. In small foundations, the operating plan may be as simple as stating that each quarter the CEO will meet with the board to report on the progress of the strategic plan. For larger foundations, the plan will be more extensive.

Most operating plans are budget-driven and developed annually. Although the operating plan establishes objectives for the current year, it must also take the long term into account.

Good Leaders…

- Have passion for their work at the community foundation and can instill that passion in others
- Respond to the needs of donors, grantees and the community at large
- Make proactive decisions based on mission and resources
- Make staffing decisions based on responsibilities, training and capabilities
- Value board and staff members for their expertise and feedback
- Maintain strong credibility among constituents and the public.

Key Elements of an Operating Plan

Most operating plans include the following:

- A list of major tasks
- Timelines for accomplishing those tasks
- Staff responsible for each task
- Measures of success.

Often, senior staff (if applicable) will work with their staff to write measurable objectives for each department. The managers then tie these objectives to job descriptions and performance reviews for the coming year.

Most CEOs monitor progress on operating plans and report quarterly to the board. Larger foundations may require staff managers to write reports on their progress, which are then submitted to the board. At these quarterly reviews, the board might consider changes to the operating plan to respond to any unforeseen or changing circumstance.

Need help developing an operating plan? Visit the Standards & Effective Practices for Community Foundations database at http://bestpractices.cof.org or look to your colleague community foundations for samples.

"Planning helps a community foundation shape its vision for the community it serves."

Managing Teams

In any business, teams are an effective way to share the workload and accomplish a specific task. Teams bring people together and often create a better result. Much of the community foundation work is accomplished through teams—board members, volunteers, staff, consultants or a mix of all four. As the CEO, you will frequently direct teams and committees or delegate your staff to do so.

When managing teams, strive to be upfront and specific about what you expect of members, both individually and as a group. This can prevent misunderstandings and create a more efficient team environment. Write job descriptions for teams, especially for tasks that are ongoing or repeated year after year. Job descriptions will instruct current team members as to their duties, as well as bring continuity to tasks over time.

Make sure that members clearly understand the goals and tasks before them and that tasks are realistic and achievable. Structure tasks in a series of small but significant steps. Along the way, team members can gauge their progress and see tangible results of their efforts.

Tips for Team Management

When managing a team, provide members with the following:

- **Purpose**—Members should share a sense of why the team exists.
- **Priorities**—Members should know what needs to be done, by whom and by when.
- **Roles**—Members should know their roles in getting tasks done and when to allow a more skillful member to do a certain task.
- **Training**—Members should be given all the information and education they need to do their jobs efficiently.
- **Effectiveness**—Members should feel that their time is being well used.
- **Success**—Members should know when the team has met its goals and share equally in that success.

Dealing with Different Points of View
Teams include people of many personalities and points of view. As you will find when managing teams, disagreement—and sometimes even outright conflict—will occasionally occur. Although differences may on the surface appear disruptive, they can actually be useful in raising questions and issues that otherwise may not be addressed. These differences, and the discussions that ensue, may shed light on what is and what is not working within your organization. For that reason, any conflicts that arise should be dealt with quickly and openly and considered important to decisionmaking and growth.

Of course, there are conflicts and there are conflicts. Personality differences are just one type of conflict that a CEO must face. Because you have multiple demands placed on you in managing the foundation's resources, time and staff, much of what you do as a CEO is deal with conflicts—everyday, large and small. Good leaders manage conflicts according to individual circumstances as they arise, as well as with their own judgment and leadership style.

If a person becomes disruptive to the team or the foundation's work, however, you should take specific steps to reconcile the situation. Here are several suggestions that may help bring harmony to a troublesome situation.

You as the CEO or team manager should:

- Conduct a face-to-face intervention with the person or parties, offering opportunities for open communication and improvement.

- State your position, opinion or concern, even if it is in opposition to the person's point of view.

- Reflect your understanding of the other's position or opinion.

- Let the other person know that you value him or her as a person although you may share a different opinion.

- Agree to disagree, if necessary, to negotiate a compromise or solution.

- If necessary, offer a leave of absence or resignation from the team or assignment.

- Plan for ways to circumvent similar situations in the future.

By using these communication methods, you will likely alleviate any situation before it becomes harmful. Remember that it may take time to resolve certain conflicts. Like most community foundation responsibilities, managing teams requires a lot of practice and a lot of patience—but the rewards are many.

Cross-functional Teams
In any community foundation, it's important that "the right hand know what the left hand is doing." In other words, there needs to be good communication among staff and among individual departments.

Some community foundations have begun to merge job functions, even when fully staffed. They create cross-functional teams on certain initiatives to limit the "silo effect" of staff working isolated in their own departments. In doing so, they find that these teams bring new insights, ideas and creative thinking from different perspectives, adding value to the foundation's work on the whole.

If you are considering creating a cross-functional team:

- Choose a leader for the issue or initiative.

- Create clear and ongoing communication between all departments.

- Identify the role each department will play—what staff and other resources each will provide.

- Create opportunities for regular check-ins to monitor progress and keep activities on target.

- Develop internal communication procedures to provide ongoing information to all staff members, such as regular electronic updates, oral presentations at staff meetings and brown bag lunches with interested staff.

Source: Community Leadership for Community Foundations, www.cof.org, COF CODE: **CCFE**

Decisionmaking and Problem Solving

As the CEO or senior staff, everything you do involves making decisions and solving problems. When making decisions, it helps to have a rational approach as opposed to a reactionary one. There is no right answer to every decision or problem; nevertheless, all good decisionmaking and problem-solving methods follow a similar process. These tips can help:

- **Define, as specifically as possible, the decision that needs to be made.** Why is this decision important? When does the decision need to be made? Who will be affected by this decision? What values does this decision call into question?

- **Brainstorm alternatives.** Write ideas down as they come to you. If you only think of a few alternatives, you may want to get more information. Additional information generally leads to more alternatives.

- **Visualize the outcomes of each alternative.** For each alternative on your list, picture what the outcome of that alternative would likely be. Be sure to consider which alternatives are most likely to happen.

- **Choose the best fit.** Review your remaining alternatives and decide which one feels the most comfortable to you. If you feel you can live with both the alternative as well as the possible outcome, this may be your best choice.

- **Review your decision.** Are the outcomes what you expected? Do you want to let the decision stand or would you like to make some adjustments? If the decision did not evolve the way you planned, repeat the complete decisionmaking process again.

How Can You Prepare for Staff Transitions?

As a CEO, you should always have a clear succession plan in place, both for your position as well as the positions of other key staff. Even if you anticipate no change in the near future, a good plan can save a lot of time and confusion in the event of one.

You and your staff can prepare a solid transition plan in just a few simple tasks. Consider the following steps:

- **Update the administrative calendar for the organization.** Make a schedule of all major recurring activities during the year (e.g., performance reviews, special events, staff meetings, one-on-one meetings, lease/contract expiration dates, pay schedule)

- **Prepare a list of key stakeholders.** Make a list of key stakeholders the new CEO or other key staff should know about, e.g., donors, nonprofits, advisors (legal, accounting, real estate) and peer organizations.

- **Ask all staff members to document their activities.** Staff might share a "to do" list of their current major activities over the past month, planned activities over the coming two months and any major issues. These lists can help the new CEO or staff members get up to speed.

- **Create authorization lists.** In conjunction with the board chair, decide who will issue paychecks and sign them during a CEO or key staff transition. Often, the board treasurer and/or secretary will assume this role.

Tips for Outgoing CEOs

If you are a CEO leaving the community foundation, you and the other staff can help your board implement a succession plan. In addition to the tips listed above, you may want to:

- **Help the board appoint an acting CEO to serve during the transition.**

- **Complete performance reviews on all personnel before you leave.** This ensures that staff receives your feedback before you leave, giving personnel a fair opportunity to reflect on their past performance and giving the new CEO needed input about each employee.

- **Document your office facilities,** ensuring that there are labels on all documents and drawers. Meet with appropriate staff and board members to review where you keep files and important documents. Staff should retain a key to the office and appropriate board members should retain keys to the desk drawers and file cabinets.

- **Distribute emergency contacts to staff.** Give staff the names and phone numbers of at least two board members who they can contact if needed.

- **Hold weekly staff meetings.** Depending on the size of the organization, have weekly meetings of full staff (if small) or all managers (if large) during the transition, until a new CEO is hired. Have a board member attend the meetings. Have a designated staff member attend portions of the board meetings.

- **Meet with a board member once a week before you leave.** Review the status of work activities, any current issues, etc.

- **Help the board and staff prepare for new CEO orientation.** Discuss who among board and staff members will lead the orientation and what materials will be presented.

- **Discuss with the board how to handle public relations.** The community will soon hear that the CEO is leaving. Agree on how this message will be conveyed to the community.

Tips for Executive Staff

In times of CEO transition, the executive staff will often work closely with the board to ensure a smooth change. Once the new CEO is hired, staff will want to help the board orient the new hire, as well as assist the new CEO to integrate into the office. The following are tips for how executive staff members can assist the new CEO:

- **Ask the board chair to send a letter to stakeholders,** if the community foundation has not done so already, announcing the new CEO's arrival, start date, background and so forth. Be aware that transitions might affect donors or others in the field.

- **Send a news release announcing the change** to key organizations, community associations, field publications and local newspapers.

- **Familiarize the new CEO with the office.** Be sure to include keys; a tour of the office, and facilities and storage areas; an orientation to kitchen use and copy and fax systems; computer configuration and procedures; telephone use; and any special billing procedures for office systems.

- **Schedule any needed training,** e.g., computer training, including use of passwords, overview of software and documentation, location and use of peripherals and where to go to ask questions.

- **Support the new CEO with ongoing information exchange.** During the first six weeks, the executive staff may want to meet regularly with the new CEO to discuss the transition, hear any pending issues or needs and establish good working relationships.

Keep in mind that CEO transitions can be challenging on many levels. Community foundation staff—and CEOs, in particular—form important relationships with foundation constituents. It may take time for a new CEO to build credibility and trust among staff and board members and within the community at large. Change at the top, however, can be a positive experience for the foundation and one that can generate good publicity and a fresh vision.

For more on CEO transitions, visit www.transitionguides.com, which offers tools, ideas and services to strengthen organizations during leadership change.

2.

HUMAN RESOURCES

WHAT YOU WILL LEARN

Learn the best way to recruit, retain and manage employees and consultants. This section walks you through hiring new staff and helps you make the best use of the staff already in place. Learn what personnel policies your staff needs and what goes in an employee manual. Find out how to evaluate staff performance and how to use professional development as a staff incentive.

How Many Staff Members Does the Foundation Need?

A staff improves the efficiency and quality of operations. There are many factors that contribute to staff size and structure, and staff composition will vary according to strategic direction. In some cases, there may be separate staff to fill each organizational role. Smaller foundations often combine staff functions out of necessity—for example, senior staff may be responsible for donor relations and communications. Even in fully staffed foundations, community foundations have begun to merge job functions, creating cross-functional teams instead of isolated departments.

Staff usually works in one or more of seven traditional areas:

- **Executive**—Works in partnership with the board to provide overall management and leadership.
- **Finance and Administration**—Directs financial and accounting activities, human resources and technology.
- **Program**—Responsible for grantmaking activities.
- **Development**—Raises money or increases foundation assets.
- **Donor relations**—Works to meet needs of current or potential donors.
- **Communications**—Makes foundation visible in the community.
- **Administrative**—Provides daily organization and support.

As part of its strategic plan, your board will decide on the number and type of staff the foundation needs. Staffing requirements often correlate with the type of assets your foundation manages. Other factors may include the size of the board and committees and the frequency of meetings, the foundation's use of technology, the programs you support and the extent to which you decide to bring services in-house (for example, communications, event planning, training and scholarship administration).

Post Job Openings Online

Many websites offer job postings, including:
Council on Foundations—www.cof.org
Foundation Center—www.fdncenter.org/pnd/jobs
Chronicle of Philanthropy—www.philanthropy.com/jobs
Action Without Borders—www.idealist.org
Monster—www.monster.com

How Do You Hire Staff?

Before you begin to recruit for a new position, you will first draft a job description. The board develops job descriptions for the CEO, and the CEO or department manager develops those for all other staff.

A good job description includes:

- Position title.
- A brief description of the history of the foundation.
- Position's general and specific duties.
- Supervisory information.
- Supervisory responsibilities, if applicable.
- Particular skills required, such as accounting, project management, budgeting and investments, as applicable.
- Professional experience required, e.g. education, background, years in the field.
- The desired personal qualities, e.g. strong work ethic, sense of humor.
- Salary range.
- Application requirements, e.g. cover letter, resume, writing sample, references.
- Contact information.
- Closing date.

With job description in hand, you will next announce the job opening. Write a memo or news release with the job description attached. Send the announcement to national organizations, community foundation professional groups, philanthropy affinity groups, regional associations of grantmakers, local nonprofits and other community foundations. Ask them to post the opening on their office bulletin boards and in their newsletters and websites, if available. You may also want to advertise the job in field-related periodicals and in your local newspaper.

Important Federal Employment Laws and Regulations

- Employment Discrimination and Protected Classes
- Title VII of Civil Rights Act (1964)
- Age Discrimination in Employment Act (1967)
- Americans with Disabilities Act (1990)
- Equal Pay Act
- Immigration Reform and Contract Act (1986) and Illegal Immigration Reform and Immigrant Responsibility Act (1996)
- Employee Retirement Income Security Act (ERISA) (1974)
- Family and Medical Leave Act (1993) (FMLA)
- Health Insurance Portability and Accountability Act (HIPAA)
- Economic Growth and Tax Relief Reconciliation Act of 2001
- Fair Labors Standards Act (FLSA).

For more information on these laws, visit www.dol.gov/elaws.

Word of mouth can be an excellent way to find candidates. Talk to community foundation colleagues and local nonprofits. Spread the word at conferences and other workshops.

Fair Recruitment and Employment Practices

Community foundations should be approachable and responsive to the community at the staff and board level. The board and CEO should commit the foundation to fair employment practices and develop a formal policy that demonstrates that commitment.

Your community foundation should hire staff members who reflect the diversity of your community. Here are some tips for attracting diverse candidates:

- Publicize staff openings to all sectors of the community.

- Send job announcements to minority newspapers and other organizations that work with under-represented members of the community. Follow up with phone calls to be sure they received the announcement.

- Include in all job announcements that the foundation is an equal opportunity employer and welcomes applications from those of diverse ethnicities, heritages and backgrounds.

Using Search Firms

If your community foundation wants to search broadly for an executive position, you might consider hiring an executive search firm. A search firm can be useful if you don't have the time or ability to conduct a thorough search on your own. Firms usually begin by assessing where the organization is heading and what executive qualities the organization needs. In most instances, the search firm interviews board members and staff for their views. Although search firms can be costly, most guarantee their choice for up to one year.

Hiring a search firm may be the right decision when:

- You want to cast a wider net for candidates, such as a national search.

- Board or executive staff members do not have the capacity or the time to get involved personally.

- An outsider may help structure the process by contributing to drafting a job description, clarifying the expectations and defining a profile for the needed position.

If you decide to use a search firm, ask them the following questions:

- Who will staff the firm's search? Who will be the main contact?

- How many other engagements will the firm handle simultaneously?

- How does the firm conduct its search?

- What are the fees, expenses and payment schedules?

- What is the policy if the new hire doesn't work out?

To find a search firm, ask your community foundation colleagues or contact the Association of Executive Search Consultants (AESC) at www.aesc.org.

Interviewing

Interview as many candidates as possible in the first round to compare their experience and personal styles. Initial interviews can be relatively short—from 10 to 30 minutes. If you are interviewing many candidates or those that live far away, you might conduct first interviews by phone or in a central city. However, you will want to hold all final interviews at the foundation office, allowing candidates to see the work environment and meet the board and staff, as appropriate.

What do you ask in an interview? Everyone will have their own style of interviewing and questions they want to ask. Generally, you will want to design open-ended questions that show how well candidates think "on their feet."

Questions might include:

- What interests you about this job? How do you perceive the role of this job?
- Why are you in this field, or why do you want to enter this field?
- How do you organize and plan major projects?
- Describe your management/work style.
- What's your opinion/attitude about this community?
- What educational or personal development programs have best prepared you for this position?
- Describe your most notable accomplishments.
- Describe your most difficult management problem and how you resolved it.
- How would you define and communicate the mission of the community foundation?
- What can you bring to the community foundation that someone else couldn't?

In the final interview, discuss availability for possible start dates, as well as compensation and benefits requirements. Depending on the nature of the job, some foundations may conduct a skills test in the final interview.

Once you have narrowed your choices to two or three candidates, check references. Ask references about the candidate's former level of responsibilities and to describe any outstanding competency questions or concerns.

Interview Questions to Avoid

Be careful when interviewing potential employees. The Equal Employment Opportunity Commission (EEOC) and other government agencies may prohibit certain interview questions, such as those about:

- Family/marital status/children
- Age
- Ethnicity
- Religion
- Sexual Orientation
- Disabilities.

Making the Offer

Your community foundation should routinely use a written offer of employment when hiring staff. The offer should clearly state what is expected of the new employee in measurable terms and be specific about salary and benefits. In addition, the offer will describe the:

- Start date.
- Time period of employment, if applicable.
- Job responsibilities.
- Salary and benefits.
- Performance standards and review schedule.
- Length of review period.
- Nature and timing of performance reviews.
- Termination policies, including policies on substance abuse, professional conduct, sexual harassment, dispute resolution and conflicts of interest.
- Terms of the agreement.

Keep in mind that laws may vary by state on what must be included in a job offer. Contact your state's attorney's office for more information.

How Should Staff Be Compensated?

Staff compensation affects the type of employees you attract and retain. Competitive salaries and benefits packages attract and hold capable people, foster good morale and keep up with the competition.

When determining salary levels for employees, consider the following questions:

- How should the foundation's pay and benefit levels relate to the market?
- Should the foundation place more emphasis on the going market rate, the internal worth of the job's content or a blend of the two?
- What level of experience is the foundation willing to pay for?
- What kind of benefits is the foundation willing to offer?
- What steps should the foundation take to ensure that pay is administered in a bias-free manner?

Often, an employee's salary level and benefits package will be based on his or her work status and function within the community foundation. Employees are usually classified and compensated as follows:

- **Full-time**—Staff is responsible for planning and administration—in short, for making the organization run. The key full-time position is the CEO or executive director. Full-time staff is usually offered a full benefits package.
- **Part-time**—Part-time staff allow the foundation to stay flexible, meet its administrative needs and control operating costs. Many community foundations use part-time staff for tasks that are distinct and definable, require regular hours and demand a high level of accountability. Small community foundations especially rely on part-time staff. Part-time employees are usually offered a pro-rated benefits program based on the number of hours per week they work.

- **Temporary**—Community foundations will sometimes hire temporary employees to supplement a specific project or office task. Temporary employees are usually paid on a contract basis.

Generally, you will compensate staff based on their experience level and job responsibilities. The general rule for compensation is that it must be "reasonable." Reasonable is defined as the amount similar positions are paid for similar work at similar organizations in the same geographic area. In other words, compare the proposed rate with that of other community foundations in your region and relative to your asset size. Check the Council on Foundations' *Grantmakers Salary and Benefits Survey* each year, which reports on salary administration and compensation levels for typical positions. For the latest findings, visit www.cof.org.

The Council on Foundations strongly recommends that when reviewing and approving staff compensation—especially the CEO salary—foundations should adopt and follow the four-step procedure set forth in the intermediate sanction rules for public charities: (1) identify an organization's disqualified persons, (2) identify transactions with disqualified persons, (3) review and approve transactions with disqualified persons in such a manner as to ensure that they do not provide more than a fair market value benefit to the disqualified persons and (4) prepare and retain adequate contemporaneous documentation of each step.

For more information on this, read the "Intermediate Sanctions Checklist" by Lloyd A. Mayer, www.cof.org/files/Documents/Legal/check list.pdf or Recommended Best Practices in Determining Reasonable Executive Compensation at www.cof.org, COF CODE: **Gov Boards**.

> **NATIONAL STANDARDS**
> **IV.F**
> A community foundation ensures that the foundation's financial resources are used solely to further its mission. Salaries and benefits are within a range considered reasonable and customary for community foundations of similar size and taking into account the background and experience of staff.

Types of Benefits

By federal law, your foundation must offer its employees certain benefits, including Social Security, Unemployment Insurance and Workers' Compensation. Most community foundations offer other benefits as well, which may be optional or mandated according to state law:

- Medical
- Dental
- Disability
- Life insurance
- Retirement plan
- Flexible compensation (cafeteria plans)
- Leave—vacation, illness, holiday, other types of leave.

For these optional benefits, employers may choose to cover all the costs (employer-paid), some of the costs (cost-shared) or none of the costs (employee-paid).

A comprehensive package might also include other items to attract and keep good employees, such as service awards, education reimbursement and other perquisites appropriate to employee responsibility. When developing a benefits package, be sure to check your state law.

Payroll

The payroll function takes considerable knowledge and effort. Employees expect their paychecks to be completed correctly and delivered on time. If not, the foundation can have serious morale and legal problems. Good payroll recordkeeping is also critical for issuing W2 forms at the end of the year.

Many community foundations outsource payroll. Payroll services can provide assistance in complying with the law, and in most cases, fulfilling legal requirements such as issuing W2s and filing periodic reports.

Your community foundation should use a system for tracking personnel matters including vacation time, sick leave, performance review and cost-of-living increases. Ask your accountant or payroll company for sample timekeeping tools.

Salary Adjustments

A good compensation package is more than setting salaries and benefits; it also provides opportunities for advancement and promotion.

Your community foundation should consider rewarding employees for their service. As in any business, the best reward is a raise in salary. There are different factors upon which to base salary increases including:

- Cost-of-living
- Merit or performance
- Incentive.

Some foundations may give a cash bonus to those employees who have met or exceeded expectations. This program rewards employees and offers positive reinforcement for continued good work. Others use salary adjustments to reward good performance.

How Do You Work With Volunteers and Consultants?

Volunteers

Volunteers are an integral part of most community foundations, working on a variety of projects and tasks. Using volunteers brings large numbers of people into contact with the organization, thereby extending its reach into the community. Volunteer positions can help you identify and cultivate future board and committee members.

Federal Tax Withholding Warning

Like all employers, community foundations must follow federal law in withholding federal taxes from employee wages and paying the employer's share of federal employment taxes (e.g., Social Security and Medicare). Board members—including board members who are not compensated—can be held personally responsible for these payments, even if they did not know that the organization neglected its obligations. Fortunately, this happens only rarely, but it can be tempting for an organization under financial stress to postpone federal tax deposits to meet payroll or pay the rent. Board members of such organizations should make certain that federal tax deposits continue to be paid as they come due.

Although volunteers are unpaid, most community foundations reimburse their expenses. In some cases, using volunteers can reduce overhead costs; however, volunteers usually require a great deal of tact, time and supervision from staff.

If you are considering using volunteers, first ask why your foundation wants or needs volunteer support. Because your board determines the level of community involvement the foundation invites, be sure they support the plan for using volunteers. First, develop your plan for the program, explaining what you hope to achieve by involving volunteers. Describe the types of volunteers you will recruit and the way you'll manage them once you do. Next, bring your plan before the board.

Once you have a clear plan and board support, you can recruit volunteers. Target volunteers who have the necessary skill level as well as a genuine interest in the work of the community foundation. Understand the characteristics of your existing team and recruit volunteers who will mirror or enhance the team. Keep in mind that volunteer assignments offer a good "testing ground" for future staff or board membership and for cultivating new donors.

After you screen, interview and select volunteers, offer them a training program to orient them to the foundation and to the task. Provide them with the foundation's mission, organizational framework and codes of conduct that are enforced. Offer any project-specific training necessary to develop needed skills and be honest about the workload and time commitment involved. Be sure to give them a tour of the office or work area and ask them what they need to get started on the job.

At the end of a volunteer assignment, you should recognize those volunteers who participated, both formally (in an event, for example) and/or informally (such as a personal note or gift of thanks). You might also give public credit to volunteers, during media interviews or in your annual report for example. This shows volunteers that you value their support and may likely motivate them to stay involved with the foundation.

Consultants/Paid Advisors

Most foundations use consultants at one time or another, such as an accounting or audit firm, to perform a specific task for the foundation. Depending on the task at hand, consultants can bring expertise and an objective point of view that the foundation may not otherwise have available.

Consultants are usually paid on either a fee-basis or on retainer. The IRS maintains specific rules on what constitutes an employee versus a consultant. Always consult your attorney or accountant to make sure you are in compliance with these rules. *See the sidebar "Contractor or Employee?"*

Always consider your needs before hiring a consultant. Ask:

- What do you want to accomplish?
- Do you have the expertise, time and resources in-house to accomplish it?
- Do you have the objectivity in-house?
- Is hiring a consultant the best use of your resources at this time?
- If so, what do you expect of the consultant? Of each other? Are these expectations realistic?
- What product or result do you want at the end of the experience?
- What is your timeline?
- Who on the staff will oversee the consultant's work?

If you decide a consultant would be right for the job, look first for candidates by word of mouth. Ask community foundation colleagues for recommendations. Check with your national and regional associations or nonprofit periodicals. If your foundation needs a qualified lawyer or accountant, you can also contact local professional associations (e.g. the local bar association or your state society of public accountants).

Once you identify a list of potential candidates, consider drafting a Request for Proposal (RFP) that outlines your needs. Even if you don't use an RFP, ask potential consultants to prepare a proposal and work plan for your review. What they prepare for you will give a good sense of their skills and style.

When you are ready to hire, it is essential that you draft a letter of agreement or contract specifying the scope of the work and expectations. Most agreements also include:

- Length of work period
- Work setting
- Deadlines
- Fees and payment schedule
- Ownership of the work product
- Expectations for interim reports, evaluation and performance standards
- Termination clause.

As always, ask your attorney to review this written agreement.

What Personnel Policies Does Your Foundation Need?

Even the smallest community foundation needs to establish personnel policies and communicate them to staff. Written policies are the best way to clarify expectations and prevent misunderstandings. They also keep operations solid despite any staff transitions that might occur.

There are a variety of federal laws and executive orders on how employers must select, compensate and treat individuals in the workplace. Most notable are federal laws established by the Civil Rights Act, the Age Discrimination in Employment Act, the Americans with Disabilities Act, the Fair Labor Standards Act and the Equal Pay Act. As the CEO or senior staff, you should compile written policies into a personnel policy manual. These manuals clearly communicate legal compliance and serve as a policy and procedures reference guide throughout an employee's tenure. Every foundation should have its policy manual reviewed by legal counsel and consider policies in the following areas:

- Hiring practices.
- Employment laws and rights.
- Employer expectations.
- Work schedule.
- Hiring, orientation and professional development.
- Diversity, including equal employment opportunity, discrimination and so forth.

Contractor or Employee?

A person hired and paid to perform tasks for your community foundation may be an employee or an independent contractor. Proper classification is important because the foundation must withhold and pay employment taxes on behalf of employees. Just calling someone a "consultant" does not make them an independent contractor. If the IRS believes that the independent contractor classification is inappropriate, it will apply a 20-part test that examines the type of work being performed, how much supervision is given, whether the relationship is ongoing and whether work must be performed during set hours or at the foundation's office. Council on Foundations members can call the general counsel's office at 202/467-0466 for a free copy of the article *Worker Classification: Do It Before the IRS Does*.

- Performance standards and evaluation.
- Progressive discipline.
- Dispute resolution.
- Conflicts of interest.
- Ethics.
- Substance abuse.
- HIV/AIDS in the workplace.
- Safety and security including violence in the workplace.
- Harassment.
- Confidentiality.
- Compensation and benefits programs (including legally required, health and welfare, paid time-off, etc.).
- Payroll procedures.
- Whistleblower protection.

What Is an Employee Manual?

An employee manual provides staff with information on every aspect of the foundation. Many foundations treat their personnel policy manual (a description of all employee policies) and their employee manual (which may include other information about the organization and its procedures) as one and the same. Many also give the same manual to their board members, as both an orientation and an ongoing reference (although a board manual would also include other board-related materials).

An employee manual introduces new staff to the foundation and documents what staff members do. It describes the way the foundation works, outlines office procedures, includes a list of important records and more.

An employee manual might include the following:

- **Governing documents**—Articles of incorporation, bylaws, trust instruments and other legal documents that bind the foundation, and where these documents are kept.
- **Foundation Facts**—Annual report, fund information, grant guidelines, grant application procedures, strategic and operating plans.

What Is a Whistleblower Policy?

In the wake of recent public scandals, it is a best practice for community foundations in the corporate form to comply with laws that punish those who retaliate against "whistleblowers" in connection with federal investigations. The best way to avoid problems is to establish a whistleblower policy. These policies permit and encourage employees to alert management and the board to ethical issues and potential violations of law without fear of retribution. One foundation has taken measures to implement this policy by contracting with an organization called The Network, which operates 24 hours a day, 7 days a week, to receive confidential telephone calls to report unethical or illegal workplace activities. The Network confidentially reports this information to a member of the foundation's board, where it can be appropriately addressed. Other options include providing for reporting to the board chair or to the foundation's outside counsel.

- **Board of Directors**—Board/committee roster.
- **Staff**—Staff list, position descriptions.
- **Donors**—List of funds, types of gifts, privacy policies, gift acceptance policies.
- **Grant Process**—Proposal cover sheet, sample acknowledgement letter, sample award and declination letters, sample committee agendas, sample proposal worksheets.
- **Financial Information**—Investment and spending policies, budgets, chart of accounts, list of vendors.
- **Administrative**—Policies, procedures, organizational chart, operations schedule.
- **Resources**—National Standards for U.S. Community Foundations, list of key organizations, useful web links.

How Do You Evaluate Staff Performance?

Your foundation should develop clear job responsibilities and regularly evaluate staff performance. It is the board's responsibility to assess the CEO, and it is the CEO's responsibility to assess, or assign assessment of, the rest of staff. Typically, performance reviews are administered annually.

Why are regular performance reviews important? They:

- Develop staff
- Set measures
- Define and clarify expectations and responsibilities
- Improve communication

Tips for Performance Reviews

Most performance reviews rate employees according to:

- Job knowledge
- Professionalism
- Productivity and/or quality of work
- Communication
- Teamwork
- Initiative and ingenuity
- Planning and programming
- Leadership and management
- Judgment and responsibility
- Dependability and flexibility
- Punctuality and attendance
- Specific skills.

- In some cases, increase salary and provide incentives
- Document performance records in the event of termination.

Senior staff must set expectations with employees and communicate the consequences of success or failure in meeting those expectations. To positively influence staff behavior, managers should use rewards, reinforcement and, when needed, disciplinary action.

Performance reviews can be performed any number of ways. They can be formal or informal, simple or complex. In some cases, staff members evaluate their own performance first. The supervisor reviews the staff's self-assessment and then provides feedback. Another method is called a peer assessment, where managers ask staff to evaluate and comment on the work of their colleagues.

When planning a performance review, consider the following questions:

- Should the review focus more on past performance or on plans to improve in the future?
- How will the review focus on employees' training and development needs?
- How will the process support employees' career planning?
- How will performance reviews relate to the foundation's pay system?
- How will performance reviews relate to a disciplinary system?

Many community foundations use performance reviews as a time to evaluate the review process itself to see how well it works. In addition, it can be a good time to plan for an employee's annual professional development. Some questions you might ask the employee during the review include:

- What is the best way to measure performance?
- What are the critical areas or challenges for the employee in the coming year?
- What are the objectives for the coming year?
- What training, development or additional help is needed to accomplish these objectives?

How Can Professional Development Help Staff Retention?

When community foundations offer professional development opportunities, they show a commitment to their staff—one that both motivates and rewards. Staff will be much happier and more productive as they continually learn and grow professionally. With training and education, staff can stay abreast of developments in the field, make connections with peers and learn new skills.

Good senior staff use professional development to keep the work fresh and exciting. To start, ask employees: *What motivates you? What do you like most/least about what you do? What would make working here more rewarding for you?*

■ FROM THE FIELD: PROFESSIONAL DEVELOPMENT

One community foundation initiated a professional development program in its own office, creating an opportunity for distinguished foundation professionals to share their reflections with current foundation staff. The foundation invited long-time current and former philanthropy professionals from outside the foundation to share their experiences with, and their vision for, philanthropy in their region. The agenda allowed for some general visit time, about 20-30 minutes of remarks from the guest and 30 minutes of question/answer and dialogue. Holding four brown bag lunches over a 12-month period, this program provided "in-house" professional development and an opportunity to interact with colleagues from other foundations.

Recognizing the importance of professional development, most community foundations include it as a line item in their administrative budget. Some allocate a set dollar amount for each staff member, while others designate one lump sum. If a particularly attractive opportunity arises and there is no money for it, consider approaching one of your donors to cover the cost or asking the sponsoring organization to consider a scholarship.

Most community foundations try to send staff members to at least one national or regional conference each year. The Council on Foundations offers training opportunities for boards and staff of community foundations. (Visit www.cof.org.) Among them:

- Fall Conference for Community Foundations.

- Center for Community Foundation Excellence—including courses on community foundation fundamentals, resource development, financial administration, community leadership and more.

Check for training opportunities through your regional association of grantmakers (visit www.givingforum.org to find a regional association near you); local organizations including development offices, colleges and universities; and other nonprofits. You could also contact neighboring community foundations (visit www.cflocate.org) to inquire where they send their staff for professional development.

3. ADMINISTRATION

> **WHAT YOU WILL LEARN**
>
> This section is for those just establishing a community foundation office, as well as those who want to take their technology to the next level. Consider what technology platform your foundation needs, for example, a core operating system, web options and other applications. Learn how to manage risks through safety and security measures, insurance and good maintenance and contracts. Get to know the legal requirements and organizational tools for managing files, archiving material and setting up a new office.

What Technology Will Your Foundation Need?

Technology Planning

Technology is critical in supporting your foundation's operations. The sooner you can put your long-term platform in place, the better. To start, your foundation should develop an information technology (IT) strategic plan. Like any strategic plan, an IT plan identifies goals to support your mission and lists steps to achieve those goals. For information on developing an IT plan, visit www.cftech.org, the technology website for community foundations launched by the Technology Steering Committee (TSC).

Start planning for technology by assessing what operations you need to support. Review the components of the Technology Roadmap, developed by Community Foundations of America www.cfamerica.org and consider the following areas:

- Accounting and financial/tax reporting
- Investment management
- Gifts management
- Donor records
- Budgeting
- Grants management
- Word processing
- Office management
- Research (online access)
- E-mail and websites
- Timekeeping for staff
- Scheduling (for example, tracking board and other meetings)
- CD-ROMS and CD-RW disks.

■ **FROM THE FIELD:** *PURCHASE AGREEMENTS*

When purchasing a computer system, try to negotiate a performance-based purchase agreement. For example, one community foundation negotiated an agreement to pay 50 percent of the price up front and the balance when the equipment was installed and operating at capacity. Another foundation negotiated a maintenance contract giving the contractor five hours from the time it was called to get the system up and operating.

When determining your foundation's operational needs, it helps to include members from all staff areas in the discussion. Ask department managers and staff to develop project maps, describing specific tasks and how technology might assist them in those tasks.

Once you are more aware of the foundation's overall needs, you can then begin your search. It may help to get advice from other community foundations or nonprofit organizations of a similar size and region. Ask them, for example:

- What technology systems do you use?
- Where did you purchase your systems?
- What have you found most helpful about your service agreement?
- How have you used computer consultants or contractors? Do you know of anyone who could assist us?
- What software do you use that is helpful?

Once you have an idea of what you need, you can shop for a system. Computers are sold in many places—retail stores, direct vendors, online mail order firms and value-added resellers. If you know what you are looking for and don't need advice, your best bet is a retail store or a mail order firm. If you are looking for more advice, try direct vendors (such as Dell or Gateway) or a value-added reseller, who can customize a system based on your needs. Start your search on the Internet or in the phone book.

As you're considering a new technology platform, consider the costs in dollars, staff time, training, licensing and more. Depending on your strategy, size and budget, you should be able to come up with a technology solution that will work for your foundation.

Keep in mind: Technology isn't a one-time job. As time goes on, your operations will change and your operating systems will need updating. Your foundation must constantly assess and upgrade its systems to ensure they continue to meet your needs. It helps to keep lists of the equipment and software you use for when you do need to update your system.

For the latest information, ask a computer professional and visit websites such as www.pcmag.com, www.cnet.com or www.buyerzone.com for reviews and recommendations.

The Web

The World Wide Web has become the preferred venue for community foundations to share information with colleagues, grant seekers and the public. E-mail is the quickest way for staff to stay in touch, schedule meetings and discuss issues. With so many philanthropic and nonprofit resources on the web, Internet access is necessary to keep up in the field.

Community foundations use the web for other reasons as well, including to:

- Improve transparency.
- Communicate with board members or staff.
- Share fund information with donors.

How Do Foundations Use the Internet?

Grantmakers want to know what their peer organizations are doing online. Now you can find out with *Foundations for Success: Emerging Trends in Grantmakers' Use of the Internet*. This 56-page book is available for free in hard copy or downloadable PDF at www.iapps.com/success.

- Share program information and guidelines with grant seekers and the public.
- Market events, meetings and campaigns.
- Take donations online.
- Research other foundations, nonprofits and philanthropies.
- Participate in e-mail lists with colleagues.
- Keep abreast of news and upcoming events in the field.
- Collaborate with others or develop new programs.
- Streamline the grants cycle through online applications, eligibility screening, proposal review and grantee reporting.

More than ever, community foundations should have a web presence. Websites express a community foundation's mission and communicate its value to donors, nonprofits and the community. They also save valuable staff time, as staff can direct inquiries to the website to answer basic questions, download grant guidelines, retrieve a copy of the annual report and so forth.

Although the web has been around for more than a decade, it has been used as a broad communications tool for only a short time. For this reason, web strategies are new and continually evolving.

Unlike your other printed materials, a website is a continual work-in-progress. It allows you to start with something simple, which over time, you can steadily improve. It also puts new demands on staff and offers community foundations a new challenge.

If your foundation is considering a website, consider the following steps:

Step One: Planning

Consider these questions:

- Do you have the time, technology and expertise on staff to build and maintain a site?
- Who are the audiences you are trying to reach? Who will the primary users be?
- What are the three primary tasks you want the website to perform?
- What is the most important information the website should feature?

It helps to visit the websites of other community foundations, including those that have been recognized by the Council on Foundations' Wilmer Shields Rich Award, which showcases creative and strategic communications. *See www.cof.org, COF CODE:* **Council Awards,** *for the latest award winners.*

Step Two: Domain Name

A domain name is the address to your site (also called URL). Give your website a short, yet specific, domain name that users will be able to easily identify. You must register your domain name (for a fee) to ensure no one else uses it. *For more information, visit www.register.com or other domain registry sites through any search engine.*

Step Three: Web Hosting

A web hosting company (also called a web host or web server company) will store your website and make it available to the public. A number of companies offer website hosting services for a monthly fee.

When looking for a web host, know that there are options available specifically for foundations. For example, Community Foundations of America offers a web platform called VisionMgr that lets community foundations across the nation easily implement and maintain their own web presence.

Foundations can subscribe to VisionMgr to receive site set-up (including graphic design and customization), administrative tools to create and edit individual content, functions such as online giving and scholarship matching, access to frequently updated philanthropic information, articles and more. *Visit the VisionMgr website at www.visionmgr.org to learn more.*

The Foundation Center also offers foundations an opportunity to post information online—for free. This service provides you with an immediate web presence and makes basic information about your foundation available online. *For more information on setting up a foundation folder, visit www.fdncenter.org.*

These are just two examples, among many, of web hosts. For the latest in emerging services for foundations, visit www.cftech.org.

Step Four: Designing the Site

Should you use a web designer or design the site in-house? If one of your staff members has web expertise, it can save the foundation from paying for design services. It will, however, require a lot of staff time to design and maintain the site—something to consider over cost savings.

When creating a website either in- or out-of-house, you can expect to incur the following costs:

- Fees for the web hosting company
- Fees for the designer or firm (if applicable)
- Fee for the domain name (a website's specific address)
- Costs for maintaining the site (staff, consultant or volunteer time).

If you choose a firm, be sure to check referrals and review the designer's work before contracting. If you do decide to design the site in-house, your staff can learn HTML or purchase HTML conversion programs, which can be as simple as a fill-in-the-blank template with instructions. Popular software packages include DreamWeaver (www.dreamweaver.com), Homesite (www.macromedia.com/software/homesite), Microsoft FrontPage (www.microsoft.com/frontpage) and Adobe GoLive (www.adobe.com/products/golive/main.html).

Step Five: Site Content

Websites can be valuable tools for communicating the foundation's mission, fund options and grant guidelines to the community. Typical community foundation sites can include the following sections:

- About the Foundation—mission, history, board and staff names
- For Donors—why to give, how to give, types of funds
- For Grantseekers—grant guidelines, application, recent grants, annual report
- For Advisors—giving options, resources
- News, events, press information, calendar
- Job postings
- Contact information.

Step Six: Publicize the Site

There are several ways to promote your site. You can announce the launch of your site and any major changes in your newsletter. You might also announce your new site by sending postcards to everyone on your mailing list. Place your web address on all printed materials including newsletters, brochures, press releases, letterhead, fax cover sheets, business cards and the signature line on staff e-mails. Request links on association sites such as the Council on Foundations (Council members can e-mail webmaster@cof.org), the Foundation Center (www.fdncenter.org) and your local regional association of grantmakers (www.givingforum.org). You will also want to submit your page to the top ten web directories and search engines. There are many professional search engine submission sites that offer this service for free.

For more information on creating a website, see the "Communications, Marketing and Public Relations" chapter.

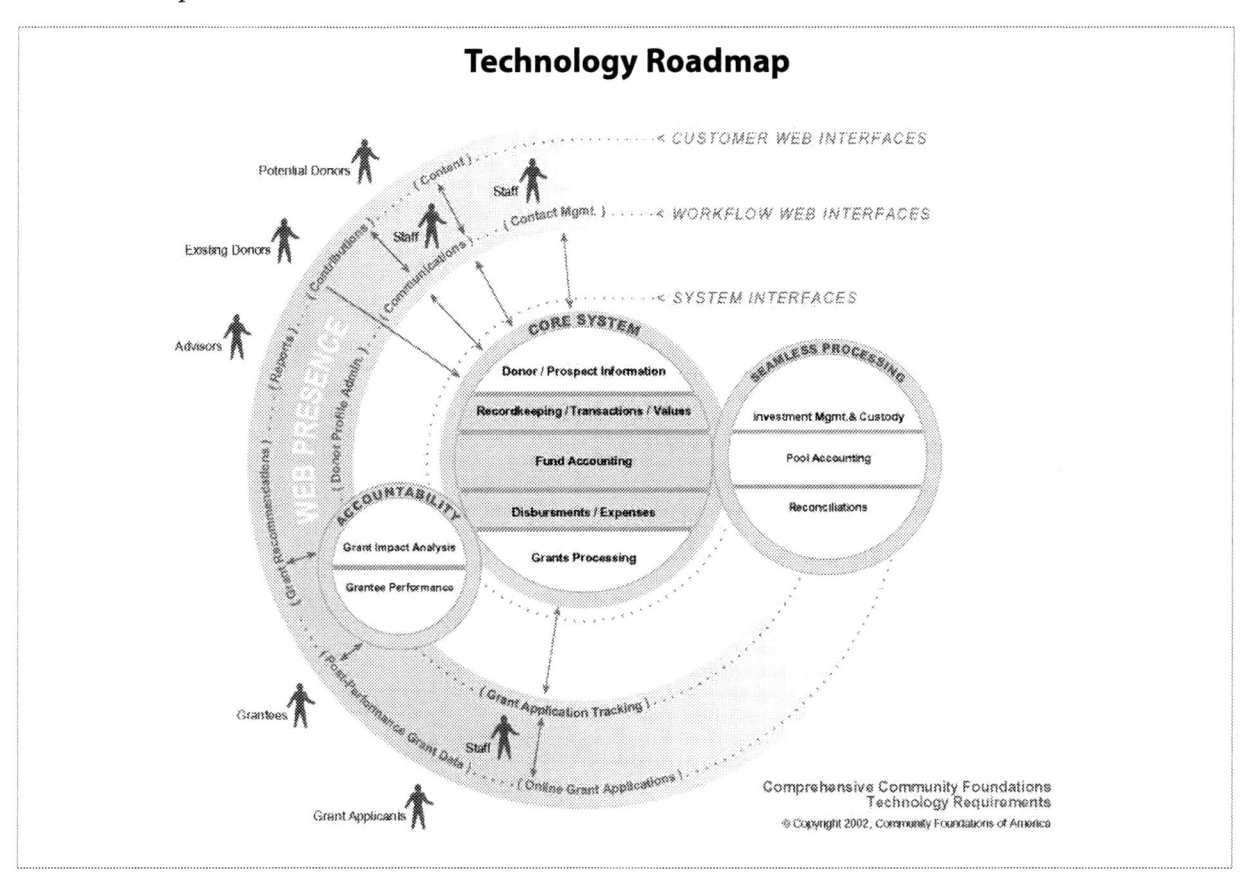

Technology Roadmap

Printed with permission of Community Foundations of America, www.cfamerica.org.

What Is the Technology Roadmap?

The Technology Roadmap defines the functional requirements needed for a competitive community foundation infrastructure and management information system. The five essential technology components include:

- A core system of integrated donor information, accounting and grant processing functionality, including robust customer relationship management (CRM) functionality.
- Internet interfaces of the core system to donors, advisors, non-profits and other important constituents.
- A web presence that delivers the interfaces, branding, dynamic content and interactivity to key constituents.
- Seamless processing capability linking the core system to investment managers and custodians, and automated pool accounting and reconciliations.
- Grant performance measurement and donor information tools that provide accountability information about the effectiveness of community foundation grants and grantees.

Your website is an integral part of the community foundation field as a whole. To learn more about the Technology Roadmap, visit **www.cftech.org**.

How Can You Manage Risk?

Nobody likes to think about potential disasters, yet risk and disaster can be an inevitable part of life. Community foundations must be prepared if they are to protect themselves and continue to forward their mission.

Generally, risks can affect four key areas of community foundations:

- People (board members, volunteers, employees, donors, the public)
- Property (buildings, equipment, materials, intellectual property)
- Finances (sales, grants and contributions)
- Goodwill (reputation, stature in community).

Risks include natural disasters such as fire, hurricane or earthquake; imposed disasters such as terrorism, theft or vandalism; and legal liabilities such as failing to meet fiduciary responsibilities or fair employment practices. The good news is that if you plan ahead for potential crises, your foundation can limit potential risks. Establish an ad hoc team to identify risks and develop appropriate prevention strategies. Because you will integrate the plan at all levels of the foundation, the team might comprise operations staff as well as board members.

How Can You Plan Ahead for Disaster?

To begin, your risk management team might ask themselves the following questions:

- What disasters could affect the organization?
- Of the foundation's assets, what are priorities to protect?
- What activities are necessary to prevent and/or mitigate the effects of potential disaster?
- Who will be responsible for these activities—before and during the disaster?
- How can the foundation restore order as quickly as possible after a disaster strikes?

How to Back Up Your Data

The single most important thing about your operating system is backing up your data. It's easy to do, but you have to make sure to do it regularly. To back up, you will need hardware (the drive) and accompanying software. Most data storage systems come prepackaged with software. If you have a small office, you can use a CD-RW or a tape drive (which stores more data than a disk back-up).

If you do purchase a back-up program, ask the following questions:

- Is it fast and easy to use?
- Do I have to be there during the backup?
- Will the system hold the amount of information I'll be backing up?

It helps to use at least two sets of backup media, alternating them in case one is destroyed. Always keep backup files away from your computer and store one outside the office. Always keep your computer backups and photocopies of your important documents off-site—away from the "threat zone."

Disaster Recovery Checklist

A good disaster recovery plan outlines different levels of risk management, including prevention, response, recovery and restoration. It covers issues of safety and security, insurance use and maintenance contracts. In your plan, consider how you will protect:

- People
- Property
- Financial data
- Copies of signed contracts
- Equipment
- Databases
- Custom software
- Human resources files
- Insurance files
- Proof of ownership/proof of loss.

For more information on risk management, visit the Nonprofit Risk Management Center at www.nonprofitrisk.org.

Safety and Security

Your community foundation needs procedures on office safety, emergencies and other security incidents. The CEO or delegated senior staff should establish these procedures and discuss them with employees, making sure everyone knows what to do and to whom they report.

Protecting Computers from Disaster

There are basic requirements to maintain any computer network and protect it from a host of external and internal threats. Talk to an IT professional, if you do not have one on staff, to find out how your network may be vulnerable and to learn how to maintain network security. Ask about the following:

Firewalls
A firewall is your network's first line of defense against intrusion from the Internet. Firewalls protect your internal network from users on other networks by filtering or limiting inbound and outbound network traffic, such as websites, e-mail, videoconferences, instant messages and so forth.

Passwords
Learn how to create and secure your network's passwords to keep unauthorized users out.

Virus Protection
Viruses are malicious programs designed by hackers to damage computer files or slow the Internet. Most new computer systems come with virus protection software, but you will need to update it. Visit www.symantec.com/avcenter or www.mcafee.com for anti-virus downloads. Be sure to train employees to never open suspicious attachments.

Staying Current
Some potential network vulnerabilities reside within your network's software. Learn how to keep your software up-to-date and protected at www.cftech.org.

Some general safety tips that may apply in any office:
- Doors should remain locked if the office or an area is unoccupied. If the office has more than one entrance, only one door should be used by everyone to enter and exit. In large offices, it helps for employees to have security cards or keys to enter the building and the bathrooms.
- Purses, briefcases and other valuable items should be kept out of sight when possible, locked away in a desk or closet.
- Non-employees should not be allowed to go past the reception area without notice to co-workers by phone or intercom.
- Do not leave checks, petty cash or stamps in plain sight, within easy reach or in an unlocked desk drawer.
- Collect emergency contact information for all employees.
- Create a meeting spot outside of the office in case of evacuation.
- Hold regular training sessions with staff to review safety policies and procedures.
- Perform emergency drills.

Insurance

Some foundations hire a consultant to assess their insurance needs and recommend coverage. Others find a volunteer who is knowledgeable in this area or use an agent who represents a number of insurance carriers to recommend the best types of insurance.

Errors and Omissions

Community foundation professionals frequently help donors plan their giving. While donors should always seek independent counsel in connection with gifts, errors and omissions coverage (which is also known as malpractice coverage or professional liability coverage) protects the community foundation against liability for damages arising from the rendering of, or failure to render, professional services.

General Liability

Community foundations need to protect their assets with liability insurance. Liability insurance generally covers claims against the foundation for any bodily injury incurred on the premises. Community foundations may be perceived to have deep pockets and therefore are at risk of attracting civil suits. It's impossible to purchase enough liability insurance to cover every contingency. Most foundations carry enough to retain good legal counsel should the need arise.

Special Events Insurance

Sometimes also referred to as an event rider because it is usually an addition to the general liability policy, this is insurance for events that are outside the day-to-day operations of the community foundation, such as fundraising events.

Property

Property insurance protects your office against physical damage to, or loss of, your assets. Assets, broadly defined, include the area in which your business operates and the property housed there. In case of catastrophes like fire, explosion, theft or vandalism, property insurance helps cover the cost of repairing damaged property or replacing what is lost.

Bonds

A bond is a type of insurance that protects against loss from fraud, theft or embezzlement by staff. Banks, for example, routinely bond a number of their employees. Anyone who can withdraw or disburse funds on behalf of the foundation should be bonded, including those who keep the books, all signatories on the accounts and the asset managers. Such insurance can often be included as part of overall general liability coverage.

Workers' Compensation

Workers' Compensation, which is required by law, protects both employees and employer in the event of a job-related sickness, injury or death.

Director's and Officer's Liability

Community foundations are exposed to risks because people (staff, volunteers, board members) and organizations (grantees) act as its agents. Risk management policies and procedures may not adequately protect your foundation—or you—against liability.

Director's and officer's liability (D&O) insurance protects directors, officers and employees from legal liabilities that may be incurred while performing their duties. Some indemnification policies, including a policy offered through the Council on Foundations, also pay legal costs for claims related to board service. A good D&O policy will also reimburse the foundation for indemnification expenses it may incur.

Unlike general liability insurance (fire, theft, physical injury), D&O insurance covers only claims where there is no bodily injury or property damage. These types of claims include wrongful termination, discrimination in employment, sexual harassment, failure of fiduciary responsibility or failure to file a timely tax return.

Negotiate the best D&O policy for your organization. Each foundation has specific needs that should be addressed and spelled out in the policy. It is a good idea to carefully check what is excluded as well as what is included. All the people you want covered should be listed in the policy—even volunteers, if applicable.

For more information on D&O insurance, read Director's and Officer's Liability Insurance and Indemnification, Council on Foundations, www.cof.org, or visit Insurance Programs for Nonprofit Organizations at www.npo-ins.com. For more information on general insurance, visit the Nonprofit Risk Management Center at www.nonprofitrisk.org.

Maintenance and Service Contracts

Like most organizations, community foundations enter into a variety of contracts for goods, services and equipment. Some contracts are standard, pre-written documents that leave little room for negotiation (a service agreement on a copier, for example). Even so, it pays to shop around for the most favorable terms or the lowest price.

Other contracts can be quite complex. Those that involve large sums of money or risk should be reviewed by an attorney before they are signed. You should develop a policy with your attorney as to which contracts require legal review.

Whatever their nature, most service contracts contain the following elements:

- Goods and services to be provided
- List of parties involved
- Timeframe
- Dollar amount
- Conditions in which contract can be terminated by any party.

As a community foundation grows, it will likely enter into contracts more frequently. It helps to have one staff member negotiate terms and rates for contracts. If no one on staff has this expertise, the foundation might call on an experienced businessperson on the board or in the community who can act as an advisor.

What Is the Best Way to Manage Files and Records?

Records Retention

It is important—and legally required—for foundations to maintain good records of receipts, contributions, disbursements, assets and other financial data. Your foundation board should adopt a written policy setting forth standards for document integrity, retention and destruction. *For more on such a policy, see the "Governance and Accountability" chapter.*

A records management system helps you:

- Create, organize, maintain, use and retrieve records
- Identify and safeguard vital documents
- Preserve a historical memory of the foundation
- Assimilate technology as it relates to records
- Train personnel on the foundation's policy and procedures.

Some foundations parcel their recordkeeping to accountants, custodians and/or consultants. Regardless of whether you outsource bookkeeping or manage it in-house, it is your foundation's responsibility to ensure that records are kept in good order. Here are some tips for what to keep and what to toss.

Keep the following records **permanently** on file in your foundation's principal office:

1. **Certificate of incorporation/deed of trust** and bylaws including a record of changes.

2. **Board minutes** and resolutions.

3. **Tax documents** (recent returns—three years and less, audit records, state documents regarding tax status should be kept on site. Older returns may be stored elsewhere but should be retained).

4. **Foundation application for exemption/determination letter** IRS Form 1023 (required for all tax-exempts filing after July 1987).

5. **IRS correspondence.**

6. **Documentation for gifts of real property** made to community foundations.

7. **Legal correspondence,** including opinion letters of counsel.

8. **Property records, insurance policies and records** relating to pension and retirement plans.

In addition to its permanent records, your foundation will also want to keep certain files on hand for a **certain period of time:**

1. **Grant files**—Keep during the period in which the foundation might be audited (up to six years to be safe). Grant files might include a copy of the grantee's determination letter or documentation that the organization is a 501(c)(3).

2. **Records of contributions**—Documents relating to cash contributions must be kept until tax reporting is complete and the audit period has ended. Records relating to gifts of securities should be kept until the securities are sold, the transaction is reported on the tax return and the audit period has expired.

3. **Charitable solicitation**—Keep a record of efforts to comply with federal and state charitable solicitation laws (regarding provision of goods and services to donors). Keep records until the expiration of the audit period relating to the gift or solicitation campaign. Check with your attorney or the state attorney general regarding whether and how long solicitation records must be kept for state purposes.

4. **Personnel records**—Check with your attorney or accountant to determine the required length of time to retain these records. For example, records relating to wages and various federal employment taxes must generally be kept for four years.

5. **Financial records**—Records such as purchases of investment assets only need to be kept until the assets are sold or otherwise disposed of and for the duration of the audit period. Foundation transaction records, such as purchases of office equipment, need not be kept for longer than the time necessary for tax reporting and the audit period that follows.

6. **Contracts**—Contracts for services generally need not be retained forever, however, it is a good idea to keep them even a few years after the contract expires.

Excerpts of the above from "Keep, File, Toss," by Jane C. Nober, Foundation News & Commentary, *March/April 1998.*

Filing Systems

Every community foundation office needs a filing system. This helps you stay organized, but more important, it helps your foundation stay accountable—especially in the event of an audit or public questioning.

Filing systems make it easy to locate important documents with minimal time and effort. Some people find that establishing a filing system is complicated and time consuming, but it doesn't have to be.

First, decide what types of files the foundation will keep. It helps to file by categories that make sense to you, such as: financial records, donor files, grant files and personnel files. Once you have divided your files into categories, there are a number of ways to organize these documents.

You might store your grant files alphabetically by organization name, chronologically by year or numerically by a proposal number you assign. When designing your system, consider: *Where would users intuitively look for these files?* Filing primarily by organization name and secondarily by year makes it easy to access any given agency's grant history. On the other hand, filing by year might make for a smoother transition when archiving materials.

Again, the key is finding a method that makes sense to you—and will make sense to your successors. You might include an explanation of your filing system in employee manuals.

Paperless Office

Community foundations today accept grant proposals via their website, communicate with stakeholders by e-mail and file material electronically. More foundations today are moving toward a paperless office—reducing the amount of paper documents and taking advantage of technology.

Interested in going paperless? There are several low-cost solutions. The best tool to buy is a scanner. Scanner technology allows you to convert paper documents into computer files. Initially this can be time consuming, but if necessary, it is a task that you can outsource.

In addition to a scanner, you may want to consider conversion software, which converts electronic files into images. Having a conversion option saves staff time and eliminates the manual process of printing a document, scanning it and then coding it for the imaging software. Many companies sell imaging software, and you can find solutions that will handle thousands of documents per day down to a small number of documents per month.

Remember, your paperless office is only as good as your computer back up. Backing up your data is easy to do, but you must do it regularly. *For information on creating a paperless office, visit www.cftech.org.*

Archiving

At one time or another, all community foundations must clean house, clearing old files from storage and disposing of equipment and supplies that are no longer used. This isn't as easy as it sounds. For example, you might want to hold onto documents that preserve the foundation's history—but you just don't want to look at them everyday.

When in doubt, start an archive. As interest in American foundations continues to grow, many research centers urge foundations to establish archives and make them available for study. Archives not only are important from a public perspective, but also can be extremely valuable for the successors of the community foundation.

What should an archive contain? Here are some ideas:

- Minutes from board meetings
- Contribution files
- Grant files
- Annual reports
- Oral and/or written histories
- Press clippings
- Photographs
- Videos
- Correspondence.

Once you have your files, where do you store them? If the foundation is headquartered in a small office without much storage, consider scanning the material and storing it digitally. If you plan to keep hard copies of the archive, invest in archival supplies to preserve your records over time. A number of archival supply houses stock storage boxes, document folders, paper and mounting boards, plastic sleeves, conservation glues and more.

If you don't have the space—or interest—in storing the archive yourself, find storage space in an off-site warehouse, or donate it to a local library, repository or historical society. They will likely have tools to preserve your materials and can tell you what has historical value. *For more information on where to donate your archive, contact the Special Collections and Archives at Indiana University or the Society of American Archivists (see "Sources").*

Tips for Filing Documents

- Create a special cover sheet for vital statistics—something you can quickly review before you wade through the stack of papers.
- To quickly locate documents you use often, photocopy them onto colored paper.
- Make file names compatible between paper and electronic versions.

How Do You Set Up a New Office?

Setting up a new office involves more than mundane matters. It can directly affect how well you meet your mission. Some community foundations struggle with how to run the inner workings of an office—securing office space, allocating equipment and establishing administrative systems. Whether you are a new foundation, or simply relocating to a new office, the following tips will help:

Location

First, consider where your foundation offices should be. Remember, your location sends a message to the community. For example, if a foundation locates its offices in the midst of a traditional business and financial center, it may communicate to donors that it takes a business-like approach to its philanthropy. If a foundation resides in the middle of a neighborhood where it makes its grants, it may create an image of accessibility. Think carefully before you stake your spot.

Space

How much space will the foundation need, now and in the future? Consider whether you might expand staff in the next three to five years. Aside from floor space, what other features do you need or want? Examples include conference rooms, storage areas, closets, a copier/fax/mail room, a kitchen, security system, adequate parking and so forth.

Some community foundations share office space with another organization—a private foundation, nonprofit or business, for example. Shared arrangements can save time and money and allow more flexibility for the organizations involved. With any sharing arrangement, make sure you have a written agreement between all parties and have that agreement reviewed by your attorney.

Office Furniture and Equipment

Buying the right furniture and equipment means more than making the office look pretty. It involves careful placement of workspaces within the building and proximity to equipment. It requires configuring lighting, desk space, meeting areas, communal rooms and more. It sets the tone for staff morale, performance and interaction. Here are some main areas to consider:

- **Storage**—You will want to have plenty of cabinet and storage space for grantee files, financial and legal records and more. Make sure your file cabinets and storage units are fireproof.

- **Copy and fax**—Copy and fax machines come in a variety of sizes, price ranges and functions. Fax machines are generally easier to acquire. Many personal computers come with fax software already installed. Otherwise, you can download free programs online. Copiers can be more expensive, but many come with the option to lease. If you decide to lease a copier—or any other office equipment—make sure you have a strong service commitment from the company and get the leasing terms, service agreement and warranty in writing. Many community foundations invest in color copiers, giving them the option to print their own brochures and marketing materials.

- **Telephones**—Office phones today come equipped with features such as speed dial, multiple-line capability, speakerphone and more. You can purchase a basic or complex office phone system, depending on the size of the foundation, the number of staff and your communication needs. To save on costs, look to most any dealer to sell you refurbished equipment—previously owned equipment that has been inspected and restored to a sellable condition.

- **Conference calling**—Check with your local telephone company to see what conferencing options it offers or visit conference services online such as www.freeconference.com. If you hold many conference calls, you might consider a speakerphone for multiple users, called a conferencing unit.
- **Postage**—You have two options for eliminating inconvenient runs to the post office: a postage meter or an online postage service. Keep in mind it is always helpful to have a postal scale for weighing letters and packages.

4.

LEGAL AND FIDUCIARY RESPONSIBILITIES

> **WHAT YOU WILL LEARN**
>
> Legal issues surrounding community foundations are extremely complex. Read here to learn the basics on legal structure, governing documents, the public support test, tax requirements, material restrictions and state laws. Learn what potential liabilities to watch for and what policies your foundation needs. Find out how to manage foundation assets and track finances, as well as the basics of budgeting and investment. Finally, learn the requirements on audits and how you can prepare for them.

What Legal Rules and Requirements Do You Need To Know?

Your community foundation is subject to federal, state and local laws. Before you set up or run a foundation, you must learn the rules. It is important that both staff and board understand the legal parameters of their work; the implications of making certain decisions; and the need for policies, controls and knowledgeable legal counsel.

This guide assumes you have educated yourself on the legal and financial requirements for community foundations. The following chapter will remind you of these requirements. It is not meant to replace legal advice or other, more comprehensive resources in these areas. Be sure to contact your attorney or the appropriate government agencies for the laws—or any changes to the laws—pertaining to community foundations.

If you are just forming a community foundation, consult First Steps in Starting a Foundation, *Council on Foundations, 2001 and the* Legal Compendium for Community Foundations, *Council on Foundations, 1996, www.cof.org.*

Legal Structure: Trust or Corporate?

Community foundations can exist in a variety of legal forms. Some exist in the trust form with single or multiple banks as trustees; some exist as multiple trusts with an incorporated distribution committee; some exist as a single corporation with no trusts; and others operate as a combination of trusts with a corporation.

Most newer community foundations opt for the corporate form, either with or without trustee-bank involvement, because of the greater flexibility the corporate form provides for business operations. Some community foundations have added a corporate form or even converted from trust to corporate form.

Single-Entity Requirements

For community foundations in the form of multiple trusts, nonprofit corporations or unincorporated associations to be treated as a single entity for tax purposes, rather than as separate organizations, the community foundation must comply with six single-entity requirements. Failure to meet these single-entity rules may cause one or more of the trusts to be reclassified as private foundations.

To be classified as a single entity for tax purposes, community foundations must meet the following six requirements:

1. **Must be commonly known as a "community foundation," "community trust" or "community fund."**

2. **Common instrument.** All funds must be subject to a common governing instrument or a master trust or an agency agreement.

3. **Common governing body.** There must be a governing body that directs or monitors (in the case of a fund designated for a specific charity) distributions of all funds for charitable purposes.

4. **Variance power.** The governing body must have and must be prepared to exercise the variance power. This is the power to modify any restriction or condition on the distribution of funds for any specified charitable purpose or to any specified charitable organization if, in the sole judgment of the governing body, the restriction or condition becomes "in effect, unnecessary, incapable of fulfillment, or inconsistent with the charitable needs of the community." In other words, in appropriate cases, the community foundation must be able to redirect a fund away from the charity or cause that the donor initially selected.

5. **Reasonable return on investments.** The governing body must review the investment performance of participating trustees and investment managers. In addition, the governing body must have the power to replace trustees and investment managers for breach of their fiduciary obligations and for failure to produce a reasonable return on investment over a reasonable period of time.

6. **Financial reports.** The community foundation must prepare periodic financial reports that include all its funds.

Technically, these rules do not apply to community foundations that are organized as corporations and hold all their assets in the corporation's name. However, most community foundations (even those in the corporate form) include the single-entity requirements in their organizational documents and adhere to the rules, as they feel the rules embody what it means to be a community foundation. *For more information on these requirements, see the* Legal Compendium for Community Foundations, *Council on Foundations, 1996.*

What Are Governing Documents?

Certain requirements are necessary for community foundation status. Your organization must be recognized as tax-exempt under section 501(c)(3). It must satisfy the public support test under section 509(a)(1) and section 170(b)(1)(A)(vi). Your foundation must operate under one name, and you must have a permanent IRS ruling or an advance ruling letter for which the determination period has not expired.

In addition to these requirements, you should maintain the following governing documents.

For a corporation:

- The articles of incorporation, which contain clauses meeting state law requirements for a nonprofit corporation.

- The bylaws (sometimes called the code of regulation), which contain the rules the board has adopted for governing. These documents are subject to occasional change or modification by the board.

For a trust:

- A declaration of trust, meeting state requirements for a trust and listing the rules governing the foundation. Although it is not required, most foundations in the trust form also develop bylaws to use as a governing tool.

For both corporation and trust:

- Internal Revenue Service (IRS) ruling letters stating that: (a) the foundation is a 501(c)(3) tax-exempt organization and therefore will pay no federal income tax and all contributions from donors may be claimed by the donor as deductible gifts, and (b) the foundation is a public charity and not a private foundation.

- Other governing documents, such as instruments of trust or revocable trust or other agreements with donors, participating trustee banks or agreements for long-term financial support for a public/private partnership and so forth.

- IRS Form 1023 (Application for Recognition of Exemption) to the IRS seeking exemption from taxation as a nonprofit organization and the IRS determination letters granting tax-exempt status.

Every board chair, board member, CEO and senior staff member should familiarize themselves with these basic documents. The CEO should take inventory of all documents and notify the chair and the board of anything missing.

NATIONAL STANDARDS

C. A community foundation meets the public support test set forth in Internal Revenue Code Section 170(b)(1)(A)(vi) as modified by Treasury Regulation Section 170A-9(e)(10).

G.9. A community foundation's governing body ensures that the community foundation meets all laws and legal requirements.

What Should the Bylaws Include?

- Foundation name and location
- Required number of meetings annually
- Board member nomination, election and/or appointment process
- Board structure, including size, committees and responsibilities
- Terms for board service (e.g., two years, three years) and rotation policies
- Meeting guidelines (quorum, attendance policy)
- Evidence of variance power (if not included in the articles of incorporation or declaration of trust)
- Bylaw amendment process.

What Is the Public Support Test?

Although community foundations and private foundations perform very similar grantmaking functions, a community foundation is classified as a public charity and thereby has tax advantages that a private foundation does not have. To obtain these advantages, the community foundation must demonstrate to the IRS that it meets the "public support test" by attracting contributions from a diverse group of donors.

Community foundations follow a basic strategy to meet the public support test. They make sure a dominant portion of their revenue comes from sources **other than** (1) contributions primarily from a few related donors and (2) investment income. If most of their revenue comes from these sources, it could lead to classification as a private foundation.

Despite the complexity involved, the public support test is very generous and most community foundations have little difficulty passing the test.

Ways to Pass the Public Support Test

1) **The Mechanical Test**—This test relies on a mathematical formula. If, over the preceding four years, the amount of "public support" equals or exceeds one-third of "total support," then the community foundation has met the test and will continue to qualify as a public charity for the existing and following year. Public support includes the total amount of gifts by: (1) donors who contribute less than two percent of the community foundation's total support, (2) government entities and (3) other public charities. Gifts from other donors count up to two percent of total support.

2) **The Facts and Circumstances Test**—If the public support fraction described above is less than one-third but greater than ten percent, a community foundation must demonstrate that it is organized and operated to attract new and additional public support on a continuous basis. The IRS also considers other facts and circumstances to determine if the organization is really publicly supported. Thus, the IRS considers such issues as the range of support the community foundation receives. Does it have many donors or just a few? Does the board represent the broad interests of the public? The Facts and Circumstances Test is more subjective than the Mechanical Test.

Note: If the public support fraction falls below ten percent, the community foundation will be reclassified as a private foundation.

Once your foundation files for tax-exempt status and meets the public support test, it must maintain this status by continuously demonstrating that its activities are for charitable purposes. A community foundation does this by meeting the federal tax and state laws described in this chapter.

For more information on the public support test, read the Legal Compendium for Community Foundations, *Council on Foundations, 1996,* or How To Calculate the Public Support Test, *Council on Foundations, 1998.*

What Are Federal Requirements?

Tax Filing

Tax filing requirements may differ among community foundations, depending upon their foundation structure, the state in which the foundation resides and the activities of the foundation. Because of the complexity of the reporting and changing requirements, some foundations delegate the filing responsibility to either their auditors or attorneys. In other instances, foundation will draft the documents for review by external professionals before submitting them to the IRS.

Currently, under federal tax law, community foundations must file: Form 1023, filed at the time the community foundation is formed, and Form 990, which is filed each year and reports the foundation's income, expenses and changes in assets. Form 990 includes lists of grants, names and addresses of board members, compensation of top staff and the five highest paid consultants and ways the foundation meets the public support test.

The CEO and the chief financial officer (CFO) of every foundation should review Form 990 and other annual information returns before filing with federal and state agencies. Depending on state law, the CEO and CFO may be subject to additional requirements.

By law, community foundations must provide a copy of all Form 990s that your foundation filed in the last three years to anyone who requests them in writing or in person. Note that although you must provide Schedule B, you may redact the names and addresses of donors as well as any information that clearly identifies donors, before disclosing the schedule. Your foundation should create a written policy on how you make Form 990 available to those who request the document and other ways the foundation shares this information with the public, such as in your annual report or on your website. You can also refer inquiries to www.guidestar.org, the National Database of Nonprofit Organizations, but keep in mind that your most recent Form 990 will not be posted immediately on GuideStar. Although GuideStar postings may not be technically sufficient for those who want a complete copy, they may provide enough information to fulfill many inquires. You must also provide copies of Form 1023 to requesters. Contact the Council's legal department at legal@cof.org for additional disclosure requirements of these forms and information about permissible fees for copying.

Unrelated Business Income Tax (UBIT)

By law, your foundation's purposes must always be charitable. It may carry on activities that do not substantially further charitable purposes, as long as those activities do not override the foundation's mission. Income from activities that do not further a charitable purpose is generally referred to as unrelated business income. Unless an exemption or exclusion applies, this income must be reported on Form 990-T, and any owed taxes must be paid. Community foundations are also required to report this income to the state. The requirements for each state differ.

Excess Benefit and Intermediate Sanctions

Your foundation may not use its assets in any way that results in "private inurement"—unfair or unreasonable tangible or economic benefits to individuals or companies. Violating this rule can cause loss of tax-exempt status. A subset of this rule, called "excess benefit transactions," penalizes foundation insiders, such as the CEO, the CFO and all board members, who engage in unfair dealings with the foundation. Penalties can apply to the insider and also against substantial senior staff who knowingly approve such transactions. These penalties are called "intermediate sanctions" because they do not necessarily require revoking the foundation's tax-exempt status.

Gift Substantiation and Disclosure

Gifts to the foundation are generally tax deductible to the donor. However, if the gift exceeds $250, that deduction is not available unless the donor has a receipt from the foundation. *For the rules regarding gift acknowledgment, see the "Resource Development and Donor Relations" chapter.*

Source: The Guide for Community Foundation Board Members, *BoardSource and Council on Foundations, 2003.*

What Are State Requirements?

State Filings

In addition to federal filings, you must also generally submit state tax filings, unless you have obtained state tax exemption. Community foundations with corporation components usually must file a report annually or periodically with the secretary of state or other government office that regulates corporations. Failure to file this type of report can result in revocation of the corporation's charter. These requirements vary widely by state. Trusts may also have periodic reporting requirements to a court or other supervisory body.

To find out your state requirements, contact your state tax office.

State Charitable Solicitation Law

Most states require charitable organizations to register with their state attorney general or other designated state agency before they can solicit residents for charitable contributions. Community foundations serving a geographic region that includes more than one state may need to register annually in multiple jurisdictions. Registration in more than one state may also be necessary if the community foundation continues to solicit gifts from donors who have moved to another area.

If you hire professional fundraisers to assist your staff members with development projects, they may have to register with the state and annually comply with charitable solicitation laws as part of their business. Verify that your consultants are in compliance with any applicable state laws before signing a contract.

To find out the charitable solicitation laws for your state, refer to www.nasconet.org or www.multistatefiling.org.

Other Laws to Know

- State tax exemption
- Employment laws
- Intellectual property
- Securities laws (including the Philanthropy Protection Act of 1995)
- State and federal laws banning support of terrorism.

In working with a community foundation, legal issues may arise. Most foundations rely on the guidance of experienced legal counsel to watch for any potential problems. Regardless, board and staff should educate themselves on federal, state and local laws.

If legal violations do occur, the state or federal government can apply a variety of enforcement tools, including fines and civil or criminal actions against individuals or the foundation. In egregious cases, the organization could lose its charitable status.

Ask your attorney to advise the board and staff on these laws and to keep members abreast of all legislative changes.

What Policies Does Your Foundation Need?

Your board must create policies on foundation operations and practices. It is your job as CEO to implement these policies under the guidance of the board. Policies should include:

- Personnel policies
- Conflict of interest (*see the "Governance and Accountability" chapter*)
- Code of ethics (*see the "Governance and Accountability" chapter*)
- Indemnification of board members
- Investment and spending
- Confidentiality (*see the "Resource Development and Donor Relations" chapter*)
- Risk management
- Document integrity, retention and destruction (*see the "Governance and Accountability" chapter*)
- Whistleblower protection (*see the "Governance and Accountability" chapter*).

What Are the Material Restriction Rules?

Because community foundations have public charity status and special tax privileges, rules exist for how much donors can restrict a gift they make to the foundation.

The general rule is this: Donors may not impose a "material restriction." A material restriction is a condition that prevents a community foundation from using assets, or the income derived from assets, to further its exempt purpose. For a more detailed discussion of situations where material restrictions do and do not exist, consult the *Legal Compendium for Community Foundations*, Council on Foundations, 1996. *For a full list of material restrictions, see the "Resource Development and Donor Relations" chapter.*

How Do You Manage Foundation Assets?

Your board is legally responsible for investing money and acting wisely on behalf of the community foundation. Recent corporate scandals have created new expectations with respect to accountability, even for nonprofits. As CEO or senior staff, you are responsible for making sure your board fulfills its legal obligation.

The Fiscal and Administrative Officers Group

The Fiscal and Administrative Officers Group provides professional enhancement for the financial and administrative staffs of community foundations. Find more information on FAOG by contacting the Council on Foundations, www.cof.org, COF CODE: **FAOG**.

NATIONAL STANDARDS II AND IV

II.G.6. A community foundation's governing body reviews and adopts an annual operating budget.

IV.F. A community foundation ensures that the foundation's financial resources are used solely in furtherance of its mission.

As foundation staff, you have two primary roles in managing the foundation's assets:

- **Fiscal responsibility**—Developing and reviewing the foundation budget, monitoring the financial performance, making sure tax returns are filed correctly and on time, ensuring internal controls are in place and making sure an independent audit is conducted.
- **Investment responsibility**—Working with the board to develop investment policies, hire investment managers and review the foundation's portfolio performance.

In a foundation office, financial and accounting procedures involve everything from who signs checks and handles cash to who approves expenses and issues credit cards. The board and CEO clearly define job descriptions for staff in these roles.

Although this chapter gives a general overview, it does not document the intricacies of all financial and accounting rules. Consult your accountant and attorney to keep you informed.

How Do You Track Finances?

The accounting and financial reporting function of your community foundation measures your activities and overall performance. Accurate and timely financial reporting meets fiduciary standards and shows good stewardship before a variety of constituents—the board, grantees, donors, regulatory agencies, various media, the field and the general public.

A CEO's fundamental decision will be whether this function should be addressed internally or outsourced. Because this position requires a great understanding of nonprofit accounting, the staff or external professionals should be experienced in this area.

The primary method of accounting for community foundations requires that separate accounts be established for each of the various funds. Depending on the number of donors or funds established, this creates a fairly complex accounting and financial reporting structure that maintains the activity and balances for each of the donors. Much like a bank or mutual fund, the foundation is required to report on an individual level (i.e., customer/donor) and a combined level (i.e., the total for the foundation). In addition, since the foundation invests the assets, the foundation must have the financial data available to generate the necessary information concerning the investment performance of the foundation.

Financial reporting should be generated on a regularly scheduled basis, based on the operating environment of the foundation. There are a number of different types of financial reporting that may be required of the community foundation. These include general purpose financial statements that are issued annually, internal management and board reporting, donor statements, grant reporting and budget reporting. A community foundation should be capable of generating all of these kinds of reports through an automated system.

Accounting and financial reporting are best managed through the use of software designed specifically for fund accounting and reporting. The best solution involves an integrated approach that addresses all aspects of the operations of a community foundation. There are many vendors offering foundation management software, some that even specialize in products for community foundations. *For information on the latest software available, visit www.cftech.org.*

What Are the Basics of Budgeting?

Budgets are a financial tool most executives and boards use to help manage foundation operations. To comply with National Standards, you must demonstrate a board-approved annual budget that documents sources of revenues and the nature of expenditures.

An operating budget, as distinct from a grants budget, is your foundation's blueprint for yearly organizational objectives. It is both a planning tool as well as a fiscal control mechanism. As your staff routinely monitors the administrative budget throughout the year, it may be necessary to reallocate resources within that budget.

There are a variety of ways to develop the administrative budget, including zero-based budgeting, base-plus budgeting, departmental or cost center budgeting, and others. Each foundation will determine which of these makes the most sense for the organization.

Most foundations find it helpful to divide the administrative budget according to various areas. Examples of line items might include:

Revenue:

- Investment returns
- Administrative fees from component funds
- Administrative fees for services
- Unrestricted contributions
- Interest on income
- Grants (internal and external)
- Brokerage commission recapture
- Other.

> ### Is Your Foundation in Good Financial Health?
>
> - Does the budget support the overall strategy and goals of the foundation?
> - Is your cash flow projected to be adequate?
> - Do you have sufficient reserves?
> - Are your permanent funds growing?
> - Do you regularly compare financial activity with what you have budgeted?
> - What areas of the budget have the most flexibility?
> - Are your expenses appropriate? How do they relate to operations?
> - Do you have the appropriate checks and balances to prevent errors, fraud and abuse?
> - Do you have a process in place that ensures compliance with donors' intent?
> - What policies and practices do you have in place for approval of expenses, increase/decrease in administrative fees and use of reserves?

Expenses:

- Salaries and benefits
- Professional development
- Fees for professional services
- Occupancy
- Office expenses
- Programmatic expenses
- Communications
- Travel and conferences
- Funds available for grantmaking
- Other expenses.

In addition to the administrative budget, many foundations develop a separate capital budget each year for equipment, facilities and so forth.

The board must decide how best to meet or exceed operating costs. One method of doing this is to set administrative fees against component funds to generate revenue. Administrative fees, however, won't cover all foundation costs. Community foundations need to derive revenue from many sources—not only administrative fees. *For more information on operating funds, see the "Resource Development and Donor Relations" chapter.*

Working with a Finance Committee

Staff must report to the board regularly about the foundation's financial health. The staff or the accountant prepares monthly or quarterly financial statements, showing the annual budget, spending for the month just passed, total spending year to date and perhaps spending as a percentage of the total budget. Staff should inform board members about cash balances, significant amounts due to the foundation and any acquisition or disposal of property.

It is the board's responsibility to approve and monitor the administrative budget. To help the board do this, staff should provide board members with timely, reliable data and keep the board well informed. Staff should also explain every area of the budget to the board—for example, showing what kind of costs are incurred under certain line items like "travel" or "printing."

Some boards use a finance committee to monitor the details of foundation spending. The finance committee oversees the budget and annual operating plan and makes recommendations to the full board. It monitors the foundation's fee structures and accounting policies, and recommends financial guidelines for items such as an operating fund. The finance committee also reports any financial irregularities, concerns or opportunities to the full board. It oversees compliance with bylaws and board policies and, generally speaking, protects the foundation, board and staff from undue risk.

What Are the Investment Basics?

As staff of a community foundation, you are a fiduciary—responsible for seeking out the best return and risk tolerance on investments. Fiduciary responsibility does not mean that you actively manage the foundation's assets but that you actively manage the process. Most community foundations delegate asset management to an external professional or firm, which then monitors investment performance and adheres to the directives of the foundation. Your foundation will provide these directives through written policies and procedures developed by the board, investment committee, staff or external professionals—in most cases, investment consultants.

Developing an Investment Strategy

Community foundations manage investments differently depending on their size and structure. A variety of approaches and investment products may be used, including mutual funds, balanced portfolios, investments managers for specific asset classes, the use of passive indexed funds and investment collaboratives.

Your board needs to define its investment goals and understand its fiduciary responsibilities.

In carrying out oversight of the foundation's investment, the board should:

- Develop written investment policies
- Document the investment decisionmaking process
- Determine a reasonable amount to distribute for charitable purposes
- Establish a return required to support the spending policy
- Establish an investment strategy that minimizes risk
- Employ skilled investment consultants and/or managers, board and staff.

An **investment policy** is a written statement of the overall investment philosophy, describing what the foundation is trying to accomplish with its funds. The policy lists individual investment objectives and describes how these contribute to the overall goals of the foundation. It includes the foundation's asset allocation criteria and its spending policy. The policy should also describe what is expected day-to-day of managers, as well as the standards to evaluate a manager's performance.

Your financial professional or legal counsel should help develop the investment policy. Although every foundation's policy will be different, each should contain the same basic points. Investment policies should:

- Define general objectives (such as preserve and protect the assets; achieve aggressive growth, and so forth).
- Delegate day-to-day asset management.
- Describe asset allocation parameters and guidelines for diversification.*
- Describe asset quality (itemize quality ratings for stocks, bonds or short-term reserves based on your risk tolerance).

NATIONAL STANDARDS IV

A community foundation (1) has investment policies that include asset allocation guidelines, a spending policy, and criteria for measuring investment performance; and (2) makes available to the public upon request the names of its investment managers, fees charged (including investment and administrative fees), and the governing body or appointees responsible for investment oversight and investment.

- Define who reviews investment performance and managers, what the frequency and regularity of reviews should be and how the foundation will document such reviews.*
- Establish measures to evaluate investment performance.*
- Include a spending policy.*

A **spending policy** is the annual percentage of assets a foundation decides to spend on administration and grants. The policy describes restrictions on spending, spending calculations and the controls that are in place to ensure compliance with the governing instruments and the donors' intent. Many community foundations develop a grants budget based on their spending policy.

Typical spending rules combine calculations based on previous years' spending, the current year's income, investment return rates and the policy of the foundation covering grant commitments.

A good spending policy:

- Provides sufficient funds for operations and grants.
- Leaves sufficient funds for the assets to grow, at minimum, with inflation so that inflation-adjusted spending is perpetuated.
- Minimizes the impact of market volatility on year-to-year spending.
- Is clearly articulated and documented.
- Implies a challenging, but achievable, investment objective.
- Minimizes its own impact on the investment process.

Investment Committees

An investment committee ensures the board's investment policies are up to date and properly implemented. It proposes (but does not make) policies that support the foundation's mission, values and strategic plan. It is up to the full board to adopt these recommendations and make the appropriate policies. This committee also oversees investment performance, hires and fires investment consultants and managers, and watches for conflicts of interest or excess benefit transactions.

Investment Consultants

Although some community foundations rely on a knowledgeable board member, staff member or in-house investment committee to manage their assets, most go to the outside for help. Many foundations hire more than one manager, mixing their assets among different classes as well as retaining managers with different attitudes, outlooks, risk tolerance and more. With several managers and asset classes, how can a foundation keep track?

Who's Who in Investing?

Investment Consultant: Develops or refines investment, asset allocation and spending policies. In addition, the consultant can help select and evaluate the investment manager and report on investment performance.

Investment Manager: Implements the investment program and manages the day-to-day activity of the portfolio.

Investment Custodian: Holds and safeguards assets placed in its care. For a fee, custodians, typically a bank or trust company, settle transactions, invest cash overnight, handle accounting and provide reports.

*Required for compliance with National Standards

The answer is an investment consultant. Investment consultants can help foundations by:

- Developing or refining an investment policy
- Formulating an asset allocation policy and rebalancing decisions
- Formulating spending and gift policies
- Selecting, evaluating and—if necessary—terminating investment managers
- Monitoring and reporting on investment performance.

How do you find an investment consultant?
Ask your colleagues. Foundations near you may be able to help you identify someone. Read the Council's Foundation Management Series for a list of investment consultants your colleagues use. Visit www.cof.org.

What should you ask in an interview?
When interviewing investment consultants, ask:

- Is your firm independent/unaffiliated or a subsidiary of a larger organization such as a custodial bank or brokerage or money management or actuarial firm?
- How do you and your firm make money? Does the firm manage money? Do you or the firm accept revenue from investment managers (commissions, fees, etc.)?
- Are you the owner of the firm or an employee?
- What is your expertise and experience?
- For whom do you work/have you worked? How many foundation and nonprofit clients do you currently have?
- What is your work process and style? How will you work with the foundation to accomplish its goals?
- What are the characteristics and standards of your firm's manager search—how many firms, which types, which asset classes?
- Under a retainer contract, are there any limits on consulting hours or any additional fees?

Always ask for references—and check them. Speak with clients (other community foundations, if possible) who use that specific consultant so they can tell you about both the firm and the individual.

Source: "How to Select an Outside Investment Consultant," by William McCarron, Foundation News & Commentary, *May/June 1996.*

What Are Uniform Laws?

Uniform laws are statutes drafted by the National Conference of Commissioners on Uniform State Laws and submitted to state legislatures for adoption. They cover a wide range of subjects where uniformity in the law is desirable. Two uniform laws are particularly important to the work of community foundations. They are:

UMIFA—The Uniform Management of Institutional Funds Act (UMIFA) has been adopted in most states (the exceptions are Alaska, Pennsylvania and South Dakota). Although "uniform" implies that the law is the same across the states, some states have adopted UMIFA with substantial differences from the original. UMIFA governs issues such as the investment of assets, delegation of investment management,

> **NATIONAL STANDARDS IV.G**
>
> An annual audit (financial review when assets total less than $1 million) is performed by an independent public accountant, reviewed and accepted by the governing body and made available to the public upon request.

the use of both income and market returns in determining the spending permitted for endowed funds and the release of donor restrictions. UMIFA applies to all community foundations that are corporations and, in some states, to community foundations that are trusts. *For additional information, see the COF Analysis of UMIFA, May 2004 at* www.cof.org, or contact the Council's legal department at legal@cof.org.

Uniform Prudent Investor Act—Although not yet as widely adopted as UMIFA, the Uniform Prudent Investor Act governs the investment practices of trusts, including charitable trusts in those states that have adopted it. Community foundations that are trusts are subject to the Uniform Prudent Investor Act in adopting states, unless the state explicitly amended UMIFA to include trust-form community foundations.

"Asset allocation determines 90 percent of your investment return; who you choose as an investment manager only contributes to 10 percent of your return. The best investment we ever made was to hire an independent investment consultant who has given us direction and discipline—and we are reaping the rewards!"

—Peggy Ogden, President and CEO, Central New York Community Foundation

What Should You Know About Audits?

Audits ensure the accuracy of the foundation's financial statements and show donors the foundation is operated in an honest and efficient way. They confirm that the foundation exercises proper stewardship of funds placed in its care and that funds are being used as donors originally intended.

Most community foundations hire an outside firm once a year to conduct an independent audit. To comply with National Standards, your foundation must receive an annual audit with a management letter or an independent financial review. A financial review is less extensive than an audit, as it is a review of individual financial statements only. An audit examines the financial statements taken as a whole in relation to the organization's internal control structure.

The audit (or financial review) must include an unqualified opinion and be conducted by an independent public accountant. Once your foundation receives its audit or financial review, you must make the results publicly available, for example, in your annual report or on your website.

Your foundation board should develop a separate audit committee, with members who are completely independent of the foundation and who have demonstrated financial expertise. The audit committee recommends and works with an auditor, ensuring they have full access to financial and related records. The committee reviews the audit report and arranges for the auditor to meet with the full board once a year. Once the audit is complete, the committee presents it to the full board.

There are different levels of audits. Auditors might conduct a simple financial review—checking the books to see that they balance—or they may do a certified audit—testing income and expenditures, and in some cases, reviewing internal controls, investment policies, grantmaking and more.

Make sure it is clear at the start what the foundation will be paying for. Although some accountants give cost estimates for each aspect of the audit, others will simply give you one estimate for the audit and add on costs at the end for preparation. Here are a few tips to help keep costs down:

- **Keep records as automated as possible.** This makes it easier for the auditor to access the information.

- **Keep ledgers as clean and clear as possible.** If it is difficult for the accountant to decipher ledgers, it just means more time for them and more money out of the foundation's pocket.

- **Do your paperwork.** Have staff do the simple paperwork to avoid accumulating more costs during an audit.

The audit firm should provide a written report highlighting any weaknesses or areas for improvement. Many community foundations routinely publish the results of their audits in a financial statement, along with assets, liabilities, income and expenses.

To increase your accountability, your foundation should change audit firms periodically.

For more information on audits, visit the Standards & Effective Practices for Community Foundations site at http://bestpractices.cof.org. The American Institute of Certified Public Accountants (AICPA) has released an Audit Committee Toolkit for Not-for-Profit Organizations. The toolkit provides sample documents of best practices and is available to download at *www.aicpa.org.*

Management, Finance and Administration: Questions to Consider

- What does the foundation manage well? What can you improve?
- When is the right time to staff up?
- What functions can you fill in-house, and what do you need to outsource?
- When should you invest in technology?
- How aware are your board members and staff of their legal and fiduciary responsibilities?

Resources on Management, Finance and Administration

Publications

2005 Grantmaker Salary and Benefits Report. Council on Foundations, 2005. Also available on CD-ROM. www.cof.org

2004 Investment Performance and Practices of Community Foundations. Council on Foundations, 2005. Also available on CD-ROM. www.cof.org

Blau, Andrew. *More Than Bit Players: How Information Technology Will Change the Ways Nonprofits and Foundations Work and Thrive in the Information Age.* Surdna Foundation, 2001. www.surdna.org

Beckwith, Edward and Marshall, David. *Community Foundations and Agency Endowments.* Council on Foundations, 2001. www.cof.org

Creating and Using Investment Policies. BoardSource, 1997. www.boardsource.org

First Steps in Starting a Foundation, Fifth Edition. Council on Foundations, 2001. www.cof.org

Gast, Elaine. *The Guide to Small Foundation Management.* Council on Foundations, 2002. www.cof.org

Kibbe, Barbara, and Fred Setterberg. *Succeeding with Consultants: Self-Assessment for the Changing Nonprofit.* The Foundation Center, 1992. www.fdncenter.org

Konrad, Peter and Alys Novak. *Financial Management for Nonprofits: Keys to Success.* Regis School of Professional Studies, 2001. To order, call 800/798-4153 or 303/458-4150.

Nober, Jane C. "Hands On: Keep, File, Toss?" *Foundation News and Commentary,* March/April 1998: 47–49. www.foundationnews.org

Podolosky, Joni. *Wired for Good: Strategic Technology Planning for Nonprofits.* San Francisco: Jossey-Bass, 2003. www.josseybass.com

Spending Policies and Investment Planning for Foundations: A Structure for Determining a Foundation's Asset Mix, Third Edition. Council on Foundations, 1999. www.cof.org

The Wilder Nonprofit Field Guide to Developing Effective Teams. Amherst H. Wilder Foundation, 1999. www.wilder.org

Web

Association for Information Management Professionals (ARMA)—www.arma.org

CF Tech—www.cftech.org

Community Foundations Standards & Effective Practices—http://bestpractices.cof.org

Consortium of Foundation Libraries—www.foundationlibraries.org

Employee Benefits Institute of America—www.ebia.com

Employee Benefit Research Institute—www.ebri.com

HandsNet—www.handsnet.org

Investment Fund for Foundations (TIFF)—www.tiff.org

Management Assistance for Nonprofits—http://mapnp.nonprofitoffice.com

Martindale-Hubbell Lawyer Locator—www.martindale.com/locator/home.html

Nonprofit Software Index—www.npinfotechorg

Professional Records and Information Services Management—www.prismintl.org

Special Collections and Archives IUPUI—www.ulib.iupui.edu/special

Society for Human Resource Management—www.shrm.org

Society of American Archivists—www.archivists.org

Technology Affinity Group (TAG)—www.tagtech.org

Techsoup—www.techsoup.com

Transition Guides—www.transitionguides.com

World at Work—www.worldatwork.org

CHAPTER 4
GRANTMAKING AND COMMUNITY LEADERSHIP

"The proposal sounds good. Of course, I still have to run it by my people over at the Psychic Friends Network."

Grantmaking and Community Leadership

In This Chapter

Introduction 121

1) Managing the Grantmaking Program 123
    How Do Fund Types Relate to Grantmaking? 123
    What Kinds of Grants Do Foundations Make? 124
    What Other Ways Do Community Foundations Provide Support? 124
    How Do You Assess a Community's Needs? 125
    How Do You Develop a Competitive Grantmaking Program? 126
        Define Grantmaking Goals 126
        Develop and Publicize Grant Guidelines 126
        Solicit Proposals 128
        Review Proposals 130
        Conduct Site Visits 130
        Recommend Proposals 131
        Decline Proposals 132
        Approve Proposals 133
        Monitor Grants 134
        Evaluate Grants 135
    Who Staffs the Grantmaking Process? 137

2) Strategic Grantmaking 138
    What are Your Grantmaking Choices? 138
    Grantmaking Philosophy 139
        Responsive/Interactive/Proactive/Venture Philanthropy 139
        Types of Support 140
        Length of Support 142
        Geographic Focus 143
        Grant Size 144
        More Grantmaking Choices 145
    How Can You Help Your Board Make Choices? 149

3) Working with Grantees 150
    What is Due Diligence? 150
    How Can You Enhance Relationships with Grantees? 151

4) Working with Donors 153
    How Can You Involve Donors in Grantmaking? 153
    How Can You Monitor Fund Distribution? 154

5) Community Leadership 155
    Why Is Community Leadership Important? 155
    Who Leads? 156
    When Should Your Foundation Take on a Leadership Role? 157
    What are Community Leadership Activities? 158
        Convening 158
        Collaborating 159
        Public Policy 160
    How Do You Evaluate Community Leadership? 162

Questions to Consider 162
Resources for Grantmaking and Community Leadership 164

GRANTMAKING AND COMMUNITY LEADERSHIP: AN INTRODUCTION

"To whom much is given, much is expected. A community foundation is an institution to which much is given. Therefore, we must expect much of ourselves and have the courage to lead boldly—by taking chances, bridging differences, convening the hard conversations and opening doors for the greater good of the community."

—Donna G. Rader, Vice President of Grants and Programs, Winston-Salem Foundation, North Carolina

As a community foundation, you offer great value through your grantmaking and leadership. You are the hub that connects people—your donors, grantees, volunteers and the community. You bring the creativity, the strategy, the overview and the skill to causes that matter—making changes that matter.

Your community foundation cannot begin to make these remarkable changes until it articulates *how* it will do so. This isn't a task for the weary or those committed solely to maintaining the status quo: The world is big and there are infinite ways to change it. *What's important to your community? What are its most pressing needs, and who will define them? How will you help your donors and the community in meeting those needs?*

Grantmaking and leadership are at the heart of your community foundation work. In essence, they are why you do what you do. They show your commitment to make a difference in the community and the way you fulfill that commitment.

This chapter leads you—the community foundation CEO and program staff—through the steps in designing, or refining, a competitive grantmaking program (one in which you use unrestricted funds for grantmaking). In the following four chapters, you will learn about:

1) **Managing the Grantmaking Program**—Read here to learn about the different kinds of grants community foundations can make and how different types of funds play a role in determining those grants. This section walks you through the competitive grantmaking program—from setting priorities; establishing guidelines; and soliciting, accepting and reviewing proposals; to making site visits, communicating with grant seekers and monitoring and evaluating grants.

2) **Strategic Grantmaking**—What are your grantmaking choices? This section describes the many different approaches to strategic grantmaking according to grantmaking philosophy, type and length of support, geographic focus, grant size and more. It discusses the advantages and limitations of each and gives you information to help design the best program for your foundation.

> **NATIONAL STANDARDS**
>
> **V**
>
> A community foundation:
>
> A. Operates a broad grants program to multiple grantees that is limited neither by a single focus or cause nor exclusively to the interests of a particular constituency.
>
> B. Awards some grants from its discretionary resources through open, competitive processes that address the changing needs of the community.

3) **Working With Grantees**—Find out how to perform due diligence and how you can ensure good grantor/grantee relationships.

4) **Working With Donors**—In this section, find ways to engage donors in grantmaking, including newsletters and bulletins, customized services, meetings and events, and more. Learn how donors use their funds and how you can monitor fund distribution.

5) **Community Leadership**—Learn how to determine when your foundation should take a leadership role and how to evaluate and communicate results from such activities. This section helps you differentiate between different kinds of leadership, including convening, collaborating and public policy.

If your foundation has already established a grantmaking program, use the information here to review and improve your current priorities and methods or to stimulate new options. This chapter will offer you ideas and help you compare your work to the work of your colleagues.

Few, if any, of your activities will be as visible as the grants that you make and the leaders you become. Take the time to thoroughly define—and constantly redefine—these invaluable roles. Remember that grantmaking and leadership are acts of great generosity and at the same time, great privilege. They take the incredible courage, creativity and community knowledge that only your foundation can offer.

1.
MANAGING THE GRANTMAKING PROGRAM

How Do Fund Types Relate to Grantmaking?

Before understanding grants, you must first understand where community foundations get the money to make grants. Donors to community foundations establish funds for a specific or unrestricted charitable purpose. Assets are held in permanent component funds, which may be perpetual or time limited, and generate income then used to make grants. Donors may also establish time-limited funds, which are paid out completely in grants.

Donors can choose from many types of funds. The type of fund affects the kind of grant the foundation can make with money from that fund. Although the community foundation board has the ultimate control of all grants, the type of fund can influence the board's decision.

Each fund type has its own grantmaking component:

- **Unrestricted fund** (also called a general fund)—These are funds a community foundation can use freely, without stipulations or conditions or for which stipulations have expired or been removed. As used by community foundations, the term unrestricted fund includes endowed funds—those for which spending is restricted to the funds investment return—as well as those for which there are no spending restrictions.

- **Field of interest fund**—This type of fund supports grants in a broad area of interest (e.g., arts and culture).

- **Donor-advised fund (DAF)**—Legally an unrestricted fund, a donor-advised fund is a fund by which the donor, or designated advisor, may recommend grants to eligible recipients. These recommendations may not be binding, as they are subject to final approval by the foundation. DAFs may be established as temporary or permanent funds.

- **Designated fund**—A fund designated for one or more specific organizations by the donor at the time the fund is created.

- **Organization endowment fund**—A fund established by a nonprofit to use the income for its own purposes.

- **Scholarship**—Funds are awarded to individuals or educational institutions to support individuals who are pursuing a training or education opportunity.

- **Special projects fund**—A fund established for limited purposes or to support the work of a non-501(c)(3) organization. Generally not permanent.

For more on types of funds, read the "Resource Development and Donor Relations" chapter.

> **WHAT YOU WILL LEARN**
>
> Read here to learn about the different kinds of grants community foundations can make and how different types of funds play a role in determining those grants. This section walks you through the competitive grantmaking program—from setting priorities, establishing guidelines, and soliciting, accepting and reviewing proposals to making site visits, communicating with grant seekers, and monitoring and evaluating grants.

What Kinds of Grants Do Foundations Make?

A grant is an award of money to an organization or individual to undertake charitable activities. Community foundations may make a number of different grant types, each with a different purpose.

Grants are generally categorized according to the purpose they serve for the grantee. **Program/project grants** support programmatic activities of a grantee to achieve a defined projected outcome, whereas **general support grants** (also called **unrestricted or operating**) support an organization's overall activities including operating expenses and overhead. General support grants may be used at the discretion of the grantee. **Capital grants** support "bricks and mortar" projects such as purchasing land, constructing facilities or undertaking similar activities. **Research or planning grants** give organizations and/or individuals the time, support and leverage to plan ahead and gather information for a specific project. **Start up or seed grants** offer funds for new programs or organizations. **Demonstration grants** are a type of seed grant that may serve as a model for replication in the future. **Capacity building grants** (also sometimes called **technical assistance**) offer operational or management assistance to a nonprofit, such as paying for the services of a consultant to help improve the organization's ability to serve its purpose.

Other grants are not characterized by how the grantee will use them, but according to a certain condition. For example, a **matching or challenge grant** is given on the condition that the grantee raise additional funds (often the same amount, but sometimes more or less) from other donors for the same purpose. These grants help inspire a larger grant than the foundation could alone provide. **Contingency grants** also depend on a stipulation—hiring a financial officer, for example, or reforming a practice. A foundation can often encourage better practices among its grantees with these grants.

Still, other grants can be categorized by when or how they are paid. **Multiyear grants**, for instance, are those paid incrementally over a period of time. These can lend stability to organizations and maximize the return on the foundation's investment. They may also obligate a foundation's funds into the future.

Interim grants can be approved by the board or staff to address immediate needs that can't wait for the next board meeting. Sometimes interim grants are known as **emergency grants**, if they are in response to a natural disaster or other kind of crisis.

Not every community foundation offers the grants listed here. Foundations often customize their grants to suit their own program or community circumstances.

What Other Ways Do Community Foundations Provide Support?

Although grants continue to be the most common form of support, community foundations assist nonprofits in other ways as well.

In **program-related investments** *(PRI)*, the foundation makes a loan or other investment to a grantee at low or below-market interest for a period of time. Loans and PRIs recycle a foundation's funds, as they are generally repaid, and they almost always focus on projects related to the foundation's own charitable purposes. PRIs can be made from a foundation's income or assets.

Sometimes money doesn't even change hands for the community foundation to help nonprofits. For example, a community foundation might act as a **fiscal sponsor** or administrator of a fund to which multiple gifts are given. For a fiscal sponsorship a community foundation agrees, in writing, to be responsible for the fiscal management of a particular program or project that does not have its own tax-exemption status with the IRS.

How Do You Assess a Community's Needs?

No matter the size of a foundation, there will always be more community needs and grant requests than can be funded. To decide among funding opportunities, your foundation will set priorities. These priorities will be based on the community's current assets and needs, balanced with the resources your foundation can provide.

Before you can set grantmaking priorities, you must first assess your community—learning what assets and needs exist. *What resources does the community already have? Where are the gaps in service and resources? What concerns your community?*

Some foundations perform formal community assessments to answer these questions. They might hire outside surveyors or consultants to do the job; however, such endeavors can be costly. Before hiring a consultant, look to the data already available to you.

Staff can collect anecdotal and quantitative information through simple, ongoing activities: surveying newspapers and local newsletters, reviewing reports on your local community or field journals, joining e-mail lists and searching websites.

The people in the community are your best sources for information. Tap into local expertise at meetings, site visits, luncheons and other communication. Your foundation might convene focus groups of key individuals, experts and/or practitioners on a particular subject. Or you might conduct phone and written surveys followed by individual meetings.

Talk to other local grantmakers to learn what they fund and where any gaps in resources exist. This will allow you to avoid duplicating work, while at the same time fostering a cooperative spirit among peers. You can not only learn from each other, but also might identify opportunities to work together.

Once you do a broad community scan, you may want to narrow your research to include one or two priority areas. Here are some tips:

- Research the issue(s) by surveying literature and reviewing local and national statistics.
- Collect pertinent information from a variety of sources.
- Determine what is already being done and by whom.
- Identify gaps in current responses.
- Determine what action is needed, based on the data gathered.
- Assess the opportunities for how the community foundation can help.
- Determine what resources are available to help.
- Estimate the level of "risk" involved for the community foundation if it does or does not take action.
- Estimate the benefits to the community foundation if it does take action.

Look to national trends in the nonprofit sector, as well as the funding policies at the federal, state and local levels. You might also contact affinity groups in your foundation's area of interest. An affinity group is a coalition of grantmaking institutions or individuals interested in a particular funding interest area. *For a list of affinity groups, contact the Council on Foundation's Diversity Programs staff at inclusive@cof.org.*

There are many methods for community assessment. Your method will depend on how much time and staff your foundation can devote. Start with what you know and work from there.

Keep in mind: Your priorities may (and by all means should) shift over time. For example, demographic, technological and economic changes may trigger new directions and initiatives. As the CEO and/or program staff, you should constantly review grantmaking priorities and continually assess your community. This will help you stay in tune with changing needs.

How Do You Develop a Competitive Grantmaking Program?

Once you've established your grantmaking priorities, you can start planning your competitive grantmaking program. A good grantmaking program focuses on 1) making grant decisions and administering grants and 2) communicating to grantees, grant seekers and the public.

Grantmaking programs call for certain foundation elements to already be in place. For example, you need a grants budget that determines how much annually can go to grants, based on earnings from your various funds. You need a system for managing and tracking grants. You need job descriptions for staff, board and volunteers, defining the roles they play in grant approval and monitoring. And you need certain policies, such as conflicts of interest, due diligence and donor involvement. *Look to the other chapters in this book for more information.*

Depending on your foundation's size, operations and style, you can customize your grantmaking process. There are many ways to "do" grantmaking and not one way is necessarily better than the next. The steps described here are some of the most common:

1) Define grantmaking goals
2) Develop and publicize grant guidelines
3) Solicit proposals
4) Review grant proposals
5) Conduct site visits
6) Recommend proposals
7) Decline proposals
8) Approve proposals
9) Monitor grants
10) Evaluate grants.

Define Grantmaking Goals

Your community foundation board should adopt grantmaking goals that embrace its vision of the greater good. As a CEO, help your board establish grantmaking goals that describe what it wants to accomplish in the present to bring about your vision for the future. *What needs will your foundation's philanthropy meet?*

Without grantmaking goals, your foundation won't be able to communicate its value to the community. The clearer the goals, the better staff and board can make decisions, evaluate your successes and communicate with grantees and the community.

Develop and Publicize Grant Guidelines

What will you fund and not fund? What restrictions will you place on grants? Grant guidelines describe your foundation's grantmaking goals, priorities, criteria and procedures. They communicate to grant seekers what the foundation's areas of interest are and how they can apply for a grant.

Guidelines also help the community foundation with its internal grant review process. With guidelines in place, the foundation will receive proposals more suited to its program interests—saving staff from having to wade through a stack of ineligible proposals.

Guidelines can be short and simple, long and detailed—just as long as they are clear. Most are one or two pages, written with concise, jargon-free language.

What should guidelines include? There are no hard and fast rules on this; however, many community foundations include the following types of information:

- Brief history of the foundation.
- Values, vision, mission statements.
- Statement on the nature and size of grants.
- Any restrictions on grants—*What will the foundation fund and not fund?*
- Application process and deadlines—*What information should grant seekers provide and when?*
- A description of the selection process—*How will proposals be evaluated? How and when will the community foundation make its funding decisions?*
- Any special policies—*What rules, if any, apply for first-time grants, renewals, site visits, grant reporting or evaluation and so forth?*
- Contact information for the foundation—*How should applicants contact the foundation in case they have inquiries?*

As part of the grant guidelines, you will also want to establish a timeline for your grant cycle. Some community foundations make grants at set intervals (monthly, quarterly, semiannually, etc.) while others operate with an annual cycle.

When creating guidelines for your grantmaking, you might also think ahead to the grant review process. Consider the following questions:

- How will you determine if grants fall within your mission?
- What are the identified interests or fields of interest?
- Will the foundation fund a grant for the opportunity to raise its own visibility?
- What is the foundation's risk tolerance? How controversial is it willing to be?
- What is the foundation's interest in funding capacity building? Emergency requests?
- How can the foundation help leverage additional funding (for the foundation or the grantee)?
- Will the foundation staff provide technical assistance in addition to funding?
- Will the foundation fund a grant when no one else will?
- Will the foundation fund organizations or activities to which you've given previous support?

> **NATIONAL STANDARDS**
> **V.C**
> A community foundation widely disseminates grant guidelines to ensure the fullest possible participation from the community it serves.

Some community foundations combine their guidelines with grant application forms. To comply with National Standards, you should make guidelines widely available, such as in your annual report, in your mailings and on your website, if available.

Solicit Proposals

There are many ways to solicit proposals. As explained in the previous section, the first step is to widely distribute grant guidelines. Your foundation should publicize as much as it can about its funding interests, goals and application process. This will spare grant seekers the trouble of writing proposals that have little chance of approval. Some community foundations welcome pre-proposal e-mails, phone calls or meetings to offer guidance to grant seekers. Others organize "meet the foundation" sessions that help prospective grant seekers learn about the foundation's interests and grantmaking process.

Many foundations have recurring set deadlines for grant applications, based on their periodic grant cycles. These deadlines serve as an informal and ongoing "call for proposals."

If your foundation initiates a specific project, you might consider issuing a **request for proposals (RFP)**. An RFP solicits proposals from potential grant seekers, clarifying the goals of the specific project and defining what is expected. A clearly written RFP sets the tone for good communication between the foundation and potential grantees. You can mail the RFP to nonprofit organizations in your community and advertise the RFP online and in your publications.

Although community foundations often customize their RFP documents, they typically include the following:

- Foundation's values, vision and mission statements
- Description of the project and its desired outcomes
- Range of amounts available for grants
- Grant guidelines, including who is eligible to apply

What Should Be Included in a Grant Application?

Community foundations differ in what they require for a grant application package. Depending on the size and scope of the grant, your foundation might even have different requirements for different grants. Foundations usually require some, if not all, of the following in their application packages:

- Applicant name and amount of request.
- Statement of need.
- Goals, objectives, key tasks and anticipated outcomes of the proposed project.
- Project budget, with a narrative description of how the funds will be used.
- Evaluation measures and plans to demonstrate impact.
- Description of organization's background and credibility.
- Background and expertise of key board and staff members.
- Diversity report describing demographics of board and staff.
- Previous grants by the community foundation and other funders.
- Plans for future funding.
- Financial statements, including an organization-wide budget, recent financial statements, a copy of a recent audit statement, Federal Form 990 and Schedule A to Form 990.
- 501(c)(3) determination letter, if applicable.

- Application form (if used)
- Description of required application materials
- Deadline and proposal review timeline
- Contact information.

Rather than accept a full proposal from grant seekers, some community foundations prefer a **letter of inquiry** first. Also referred to as a query letter, this is a brief letter outlining an organization's activities to determine if there is sufficient interest to warrant submitting a full proposal. Some provide a specific letter of inquiry form. Letters of inquiry can save time for both foundation staff and the applicant. Once the foundation fields letters of inquiry, it can then invite those that fall under its guidelines to submit a full proposal. As a courtesy, if your foundation asks for letters of inquiry, be prepared to answer all inquiries—not just those that have potential to become a proposal.

Many foundations ask grant applicants to submit a **common grant application** (**CGA**), rather than the community foundation using its own format. In many areas of the country, grantmakers have jointly created common application forms. These simple but effective forms make it easier to apply for grants and easier for the foundation to review proposals. CGAs also help the grantee report more easily to the foundation, as most include common reporting requirements. CGAs usually cover one specific geographic region and are typically developed through the regional association of grantmakers. *For examples of CGAs, visit the Forum of Regional Associations at www.givingforum.org.*

What will you require when grant seekers apply? Consider these questions:

- What format should the proposal or letter follow?
- What is the page limit?
- What legal and financial documents should the applicant include?
- To whose attention should applicants send proposals?
- What is the deadline?

Regardless of the method you choose for accepting proposals, your foundation may have different requirements for different applications, depending on the size and scope of the grant. Always be respectful of what you ask of applicants, considering the amount of time and cost they will spend preparing the proposal.

You might consider making the application forms available to grant seekers in a standard word processing format. This can come at a small cost to the foundation but a *big* savings of time to grant seekers. Here's a tip: If you do create a template, avoid putting lines on the application form, as it will be hard for applicants to maintain the format when filling in their response.

■ FROM THE FIELD: PRE-PROPOSAL MEETINGS

Some foundations hold periodic meetings for grantseekers, calling them "pre-application meetings" or "nonprofit information sessions." These meetings are open to any organization that wants to apply for a grant, allowing them to meet one-on-one with foundation staff. In the first half of the meeting, a community foundation staff member may talk about the foundation—what it is, what the funding areas are and how to apply. The second half can be open to questions. As one small community foundation CEO said, "Because of the communication that takes place at these meetings, we find ourselves saying no a lot less."

Review Proposals

Many community foundations form a grants committee (also called *distribution committee*) made up of board members and/or community volunteers from various backgrounds. The board and/or staff should nominate or appoint members of the community to serve on this committee, with careful attention to diversity.

In reviewing proposals, it is usually this committee and/or program staff who review applications to see if they are compatible with grant guidelines. As a part of this initial review, they will send acknowledgment letters to all applicants describing the process and timeline.

There are many ways to review proposals. One common way is to sort proposals into two or possibly three categories, such as (1) recommended, (2) not recommended and (3) interesting and worthwhile but not as important as those recommended. The committee or staff then prepares proposal summary sheets for board review.

When initially reviewing proposals, committee members and/or staff should search proposals for these signals:

- **Credibility**—The proposal will indicate in many ways whether the organization appears credible. *Does the organization know what it wants to accomplish? What evidence is there that it currently achieves its goals? What kind of reputation does it have within its community and beyond?*

- **Capability**—Your foundation is not merely in the business of supporting good ideas. You invest in groups who can turn those ideas into reality and in organizations that have the structure and systems to do so. *What skills do the organization's staff and board bring? Has the organization succeeded in similar endeavors of equal size and scale? Has the group gone as far as possible with their own resources before seeking grants?*

- **Feasibility**—Consider the project on its own terms, apart from the sponsoring organization. *Can the project be done? Has the organization allotted sufficient funds and time? Is the budget clear and justifiable?*

- **Leverage**—*How can this grant leverage dollars or impact? If the applicant is only requesting partial support, what is the likelihood of raising the balance from other donors/funders?*

- **Importance**—*Should this project be done? Is it significant? Is there evidence that the proposal will trigger action or work the community wants?*

By these standards, the strongest proposal candidates include those with the most compelling goals, with a clear ability to achieve those goals, and with eventual results that will be the most tangible and lasting.

Conduct Site Visits

Site visits enhance the grantmaking process and provide much information on potential grantees. They help you and your board understand the organization behind the proposal. They show your foundation's interest in the applicant's work and demonstrate your commitment to due diligence.

Most foundations use site visits as part of their grant application process or for grant monitoring and evaluation. Site visits can be interesting and rewarding for all involved. They introduce you to the people doing the project—key staff, board members and those whom the organization serves—and introduce them to your foundation. They help you assess the commitment of those involved and the breadth of support that exists for the proposed project. They also offer a professional development opportunity, as you will learn about the field in a way you might not be able to from sitting behind your desk.

Before you go on a site visit, be sure to:

- **Be prepared**—If applicable, read the proposal carefully and analyze its strengths and weaknesses, and note any key points you want to cover during your visit. Prepare questions you think your board might ask, and if you involve volunteers in the visit, be sure they are trained. Write down your questions in advance. Learn enough about the field so that you can participate intelligently in the conversation.

- **Be flexible and respectful**—Call the organization to set up an appointment that is mutually convenient. Never catch an organization off guard by just showing up.

- **Create a non-threatening tone**—Site visits are conversations, not inspections. Set a specific timeframe for your visit (usually no more than two hours, unless needed). Tell the executive director exactly what you hope to learn and stipulate who you would like to meet.

- **Include a board member and program staff from the organization**—If possible, include others than just the executive director and development staff from the grant seeker organization to gain a bigger picture of the organization.

- **Set an agenda**—Perhaps include introductions, a tour of the facilities, a brief presentation of the proposal by the grant seeker, a discussion and question/answer period.

- **Explain your process**—Let the grant applicant know your proposal review process and timelines.

In addition to site visits, foundation staff often perform additional research on the organization. This might include talking to other funders, organizations who are doing similar work, recipients of the organization's services or others who may have a useful perspective on the proposed project.

Recommend Proposals

Once the grants committee or staff reviews all proposals, they will recommend choices for the board's review. Sometimes, the staff will prepare summary sheets for the board. Proposal summaries can be relatively simple—a one- or two-page abstract is typical—and provide the board with pros and cons of the proposal, as well as additional information learned from site visits and research. Although summaries will differ based on the size and scope of the grant, most include:

- Applicant name and amount of request.

- A brief statement of how the funds will be used.

- Previous grants—A summary of the foundation's history with this grant seeker.

- Background—A brief paragraph that establishes the grantseeker's credibility.

Good Site Visit Questions

When visiting potential grantees, ask them the following:
- How will this project meet the needs of the community?
- What do you see as the new trends or movement in your field?
- What success story can you share about this program or your organization?
- Who wants this project—one person, a group, the community?
- How will you sustain this work after the grant ends?
- What questions do you have about the foundation and its grantmaking processes?

- Need—What need will be met with this grant?
- Specific objectives—Key tasks and anticipated outcomes.
- Evaluation—Highlights of the grant seeker's plans to document the process and demonstrate impact.
- Finance—Brief statement as to the grant seeker's financial stability. (Note: In some cases, financial documents may be attached to the summaries.)
- Personnel—Background and expertise of key board and staff.
- Diversity report—Regarding the composition of board and staff.
- Analysis—Description of how the grant would fit within the foundation's goals and priorities, as well as a list of potential benefits and risks involved.

The committee or staff brings proposal summaries before the board. In some foundations, the entire board will review proposal summaries; in others, a small committee will do the review. Regardless, once the board has proposal summaries, it holds a board meeting to:

- Review the proposals in each category, and if need be, reconsider any on the "not recommended" or "less important" lists.
- Review and discuss requests one at a time.
- Reach consensus or take a vote on approval and the amount given.
- Periodically review the grant selection criteria to make sure it still meets the foundation's mission.

Once the board makes its final decisions, staff will send award or declination letters to all applicants. At this time, the staff might also send proposal summaries, or full proposals, to donor advisors who might be interested in funding them.

Decline Proposals

By the nature of the business, grantmakers must frequently say no to grant seekers, and most will agree it is a hard part of the job. A typical foundation turns down proposals for any number of reasons. In some cases, grant proposals are simply ineligible—they don't meet your competitive grantmaking guidelines. In other cases, proposals might conform to your guidelines, but suggest a policy, strategy or competence level that the foundation doesn't favor.

Sometimes, regardless of how good a proposal is, there just isn't enough money to go around. If your foundation doesn't fund a proposal it thinks worthwhile, you might see what other funding sources are available in your community to do so. In many cases, community foundations have found donor advisors to fund projects they have had to turn down.

How to Say No—and Mean It

When turning down proposals, remember these helpful tips:

- Articulate your goals and guidelines to discourage applications with little chance of approval.
- Be prompt with your rejection so you don't give grant seekers false hope.
- If it is a policy of your foundation, explain why you've rejected the proposal so that grant seekers can make use of your feedback in the future.
- Be polite but firm in your response.

When you *do* have to turn grant applicants away, what is the best way to do it? How much to say, to whom to say it and toward what end makes for awkward, and sometimes complicated, conversations.

There are two general rules to consider. First, notify the applicant as soon as you know the answer is no. Second, the better your relationship to the grant seeker, the more you personalize your response.

These rules follow simple common courtesy. Even so, the range and method of declining proposals is wide. Here are some suggestions for how to say no:

Postcard. If a proposal is clearly ineligible, a quick and simple reply allows more time for the grant seeker to try its luck somewhere else. In some cases, you may want to send this response without taking the proposal to the board.

Letter. If the proposal is eligible but falls short of a grant award, your foundation should consider sending a letter. You might also include a copy of grant guidelines with the letter.

Although nonprofits appreciate a personal letter as opposed to a form letter, many community foundations avoid listing the reasons for the denial in writing. If a rejection letter goes into too much detail, nonprofits will often assume that, with the appropriate changes, their proposal is guaranteed for funding come the next grantmaking cycle.

Conversely, if you offer no feedback, you might be inviting another ineligible proposal as well, thus wasting your and the applicant's time. It doesn't help the grant seeker, for example, if you focus on "their score" in your decline letter. If you do score proposals, be sure to summarize the meaning behind the score and how their proposal fell short of the selection criteria.

Depending on your foundation's style and intention, how much you communicate to grant seekers will vary. Some foundations include the contact information for the program staff, should the grant seeker need additional information.

It's a good idea to tell applicants outright whether they should resubmit an amended or new proposal for future consideration. If there isn't enough interest to warrant any future proposal from the organization, state that clearly as well. Being open about this will save both the applicant—and your staff—valuable time and resources and build respect among both parties.

Phone Call. If the proposal goes through some revisions and/or receives strong consideration by the board, the staff may consider a phone call. A simple conversation on how applicants can improve their proposals or why they didn't get funded can mean the world to nonprofits. It offers them technical assistance and builds relationships for the future. However, your foundation should decide in advance how much feedback is too much.

Approve Proposals

If the board chooses to fund a particular proposal, staff will send a grant award letter and a grant agreement to the applicant (the letter and agreement are sometimes one and the same). The award letter states that the community foundation has made the grant. Occasionally, some foundations send a check with the award letter; most, however, send the check once they receive a signed grant agreement.

The grant agreement lists the terms of understanding between the foundation and the grantee. This agreement affirms the tax status of the grantee, includes any contingencies the foundation has placed on the use of the funds and lists its requirements for grant reporting. A good grant agreement explains how the foundation will measure success and how grantees can show their progress along the way.

Grant agreements will vary based on the size and scope of the grant. When drafting agreements, consider the many options that can be included. Most grant agreements should:

- Clearly establish the purpose for which the grant funds are to be spent.
- State the amount and timing of payments.
- Clearly state the time period for the grant and steps that must be followed to alter that time period.

- Contain language that requires grantees to request permission to alter the use of the funds.
- Include any conditions imposed upon grants that need to be met to secure the entire amount of funding (e.g., for matching funds).
- State the process for repaying any remaining unspent or misdirected funds.
- Describe conditions under which the grant may be terminated and the consequences of such termination.
- Outline the reporting requirements—some attach a model or a report form customized for the specific grant.

Depending on the situation or the grant, some foundations also include the following in their grant agreements:

- Restrictions on re-granting, including grants to individuals.
- Information about the foundation's own evaluation process.
- Instructions for grantees to acknowledge the community foundation in any/all printed materials or news releases related to the grant (some foundations attach a sample news release for the grantee's use).
- Copyrights and other rights on materials produced as a result of the grant.
- Expectations on the grantee's organizational behavior—for example, a commitment to nondiscrimination in employment and services.

Some community foundations hold "pre-funding meetings" with their approved grantees. The community foundation and the grantee collectively review and discuss the grant agreement and any concerns or questions involving the grant. Foundations find this clarifies information and improves communication with grantees right from the start. As one small foundation CEO said of these meetings, "It helps them and it helps us. And we find that they perform better on the grant as a result."

Monitor Grants

Grant monitoring is the means by which you watch how grantees implement the grant. You can monitor grants through site visits, grantee reports or other methods.

Some foundations monitor grants at the end of their cycle; others monitor periodically. If your foundation monitors grants on an ongoing basis, you may uncover trouble areas and if needed, modify the grant midway.

Grant reports can be relatively simple and short and usually require grantees to attach an income and expense budget. One cost-effective way to monitor grants is through grantee self-reporting forms, a do-it-yourself model that often works well. This is a good way to build self-assessment skills within grantee organizations. You can also rely on common grant report forms available though your regional association of grantmakers (www.givingforum.org).

On a grant report form, you will want to ask grantees certain questions, such as:

1) What were the outcomes relating to the goals and objectives of the proposal? What has changed, improved or happened as a result of your efforts?

2) How were the funds spent in comparison to the proposed budget?

3) What significant changes, if any, did you make in the content of the project or expenditure of the grant? What caused these changes?

4) How has the project affected or related to other community-wide initiatives addressing this need?

5) What have you learned about your audience, community resources or the issue you are addressing through this project? How will this information affect your organization?

6) If you have plans for continuing this project, how will you secure future funding?

7) If this project has been ongoing for a number of years, how have you monitored its effectiveness? What are the indicators that the project is making a difference?

8) Are there ways, other than funding, that the foundation could be helpful to your organization or project?

If the grant calls for periodic or end-of-project reports, your foundation should always acknowledge receiving reports and review them in a timely way. You might send a simple post card or form letter to the grantee, or in some cases, make a phone call. As always, be respectful of grantees, both in what you request of them and how you acknowledge their efforts.

Evaluate Grants

Although similar in nature, grant evaluation is very different from grant monitoring. Grant monitoring involves the grantee setting goals and reporting to the foundation on the degree of success or failure along the way. Evaluation describes what has changed because of the grant or, to a larger degree, how it has affected the overall grantmaking program.

Evaluation involves taking a more in-depth look at the results and accomplishments of grants. Your foundation should plan ahead for how you will evaluate the grant.

The board establishes policy on how the foundation will conduct its evaluations and who will be responsible for the task—for example, the staff, board or an outside evaluator. If you are the CEO, you can help your board understand the importance of evaluation by explaining that it:

- Increases the knowledge and impact of a foundation's grantmaking
- Increases the knowledge of the community and area agencies

Why Do Evaluation?

Evaluation helps your foundation:
- Be accountable to the public trust
- Improve your foundation's grantmaking
- Assess the quality or impact of funded programs
- Plan and implement new programs
- Disseminate innovative programs
- Increase knowledge
- Inform future grant decisions
- Inform the direction the foundation takes in the future.

Evaluation helps grantees:
- Articulate their progress
- Improve their work
- Demonstrate accountability.

Parts of the above adapted from "Seven Reasons to Evaluate," Foundation News & Commentary, *January/February 1993.*

- Helps determine future grantmaking emphasis
- Brings credibility to grant programming.

Once your board is "on board" with the evaluation process, where do you begin? Not all of your grants will require the same level of evaluation, and your criteria will vary from grant to grant. The key is to define—or have the grantee define—what determines "success" for a particular grant or initiative.

Evaluations can be simple or elaborate. In simple evaluations, community foundations ask grantees for a final report and interview the grantee or clients of the grantee. If a community foundation has the resources, it might conduct a formal evaluation—especially if the grant is part of a large-scale initiative.

Formal evaluations can be costly and time-consuming, but they don't have to be. You might only evaluate grantees that received above a certain dollar amount, for example. For some grants, you might look at quantitative data as to how many people were served and how that made a difference. With others, you might examine the qualitative results of the grant, answering questions such as, "How do clients feel about their circumstances as a result of the grant?" In any case, criteria should relate to the grant or program purpose and, again, should be defined at the onset of the grant.

When developing an evaluation process, consider these questions:

- What do you want to know in a year from now that you don't know today?
- What are the three most important things to learn from this grant/initiative?
- What success stories have come from the grant(s)?
- How should you receive evaluation results?
- How will you use the information from the evaluation?
- How can you gain feedback on the granting process from grantees?

A good rule for evaluating grants? Keep it simple. Collecting data takes time and work. The fewer questions you ask grantees, the more effective staff will be in giving you answers.

"A good rule for evaluating grants? Keep it simple."

Sample Grantmaking Flow Chart

Foundation distributes grant guidelines and, if applicable, RFPs
▼
Foundation conducts pre-proposal meetings
▼
Foundation receives proposals
▼
Proposals entered in files/grants management system; staff sends acknowledgment letter to grant applicants
▼
Proposals may go before grant/distribution committee for initial fielding; staff sends declination letters and identifies other potential funders for declined proposals
▼
Committee, staff and/or board members do site visits
▼
Committee and/or staff prepare proposal summaries, make recommendations to board
▼
Board votes on which proposals to fund; staff sends declination letters and sometimes seeks potential funders for declined proposals
▼
Staff sends award letters and grant agreements; grantees sign and return agreements
▼
Staff monitors and evaluates grants

Who Staffs the Grantmaking Process?

Every foundation manages its grantmaking through different staff, board and volunteer positions. Below are some of the possible staff positions and duties within the grantmaking function. In smaller organizations, one person may fill all four functions. Titles and responsibilities for staff positions may vary.

Vice President, Program

- Directs the program activities of the organization, including grantmaking, special projects or other programs operated by the organization.
- Establishes policies and procedures to manage programs.

Program Director

- Manages the grantmaking program of a particular subject area or geographic region.
- Recommends (or has the authority to approve in some cases) distribution of grant dollars within budget for the program area.

Senior Program Officer

- Supervises other program staff in implementing grantmaking or in-house programs in addition to performing the duties of the program officer.

Program Officer

- Investigates and evaluates grant proposals and/or implements in-house projects.
- In organizations with several paid staff members, this position may involve one subject area or geographic region. In organizations with few paid staff, program officers are usually responsible for most aspects of the grantmaking process (including program research, proposal evaluation, grant tracking, post-grant evaluation).

Program Associate

- Evaluates grant proposals, conducts background research and prepares proposals for funding.
- In organizations with several paid staff members, this is often an entry-level position.

Program Assistant

- Assists the program officer(s) with duties previously outlined and provides some administrative support.
- May also keep track of grants if there is no grants manager/administrator.

Grants Manager/Administrator

- Tracks grants made by the organization.
- Obtains and maintains reports required from grantees.

2.

STRATEGIC GRANTMAKING

> **WHAT YOU WILL LEARN**
>
> What are your grantmaking choices? This section describes the many different approaches to strategic grantmaking according to grantmaking philosophy, type and length of support, geographic focus, grant size and more. It discusses the advantages and limitations of each and gives you information to help your board design the best program for your foundation.

What Are Your Grantmaking Choices?

Strategic grantmaking describes the way your foundation approaches its grantmaking. It means taking a look at your community's needs and making choices as to how you will use grantmaking to bring about change. It requires your board to thoughtfully plan and establish goals for the outcomes you seek, the funding programs you establish and the types of grants you make. As a CEO, you can help bring these choices before your board.

If you compared different community foundations, you would find that all have different answers to what works. As you read through the following section, keep in mind that no approach to grantmaking is black and white. The choices listed here are not exhaustive, nor is each approach mutually exclusive. Most community foundations do not fall into an "either/or" category, but use different approaches at different times for different purposes.

Although this section cannot capture every approach, it does reflect the broad spectrum of choices available to you. It will give you a start for understanding various grantmaking options and for presenting those options to your board.

The biggest choices your foundation will make regarding grantmaking include:

- Grantmaking philosophy
- Type of support
- Length of support
- Geographic focus
- Grant size.

Your foundation will make other choices as well, including:

- Kinds of organizations funded
- Grants to individuals
- Interim grants
- Ways to leverage and collaborate
- Degree of risk
- Level of community involvement.

As you read the descriptions of these approaches, think about your own foundation and the choices it has made. Again, remember that no approach, or variation of that approach, is right or wrong. Community foundations can—and should—fall anywhere along the spectrum. Encourage your board to consider these questions:

- What decisions have you already made in your grantmaking approach?
- What is the rationale for those decisions?
- What new choices should you consider?
- How often should the board revisit these approaches to see that they continue to serve the foundation's mission and goals, as well as match resources you have for grantmaking?

Grantmaking Philosophy

Responsive, Interactive, Proactive, Venture Philanthropy

What kind of grantmaker do you want to be? Will you respond solely to community requests or create your own agenda and initiatives? The answers to these questions shape your grantmaking philosophy. For the sake of discussion, there are four common models that describe grantmaking philosophy:

A **responsive** model reacts to the needs of its community and programs that grant seekers initiate. A responsive foundation is concerned with today's needs and the ways its support can meet those needs. A foundation under this model might have an open-ended deadline for grant applications and award grants based on those proposals received. Its focus is generally on the activities funded and the ways those activities solve problems in the short term. It awaits proposals and is less likely to take the initiative, preferring to be completely responsive to nonprofits.

An **interactive** model funds new ideas and initiatives for what "could be." An interactive foundation hopes to change the status quo and improve services in the community, e.g. prevention and outreach. It might solicit grantees to submit a proposal for a particular grant.

A **proactive** model seeks a new way of doing things, often a result of studying the most promising grantmaking techniques. Foundations that take a proactive stance will either seek out the organizations or programs they want to fund or develop their own initiatives. Many times, those who follow this model are interested in systems change and policy and/or development work. Proactive foundations will often issue an RFP to solicit proposals targeting the change they seek.

The **venture philanthropy** model intends to fundamentally change the sector and the way things are done. In this model, the foundation may become highly involved in the grantee organization, try to influence outside systems and structures and experiment with new forms of organizations or initiatives.

The four models listed here are just that—models. Most community foundations choose a middle ground, while others take a variety of approaches for different circumstances. As you consider what your foundation is doing today and what it hopes to do in the future, remember this: No answer is right or wrong.

How Can Your Community Foundation Be Proactive?

- Use unrestricted funds to respond to unmet needs by soliciting appropriate grant proposals from certain organizations.
- Initiate and participate in joint projects by several organizations.
- Serve as a convener for community-wide discussions to address unmet needs.
- Provide technical assistance to grantseekers to assist them in formulating better projects and solutions.

Types of Support

Project Support and Operating Support

The discussion on project and operating support has existed for close to a century—almost as long as grantmaking itself. Community foundations question whether to concentrate on specifics—such as single project or program support, special initiatives or other discrete, short-term endeavors—or to focus more on general operating grants that support the overall work of a grantee organization.

What are the advantages and limitations of these two different grantmaking strategies?

Project Support

Advantages:
- Foundation can respond to new, innovative cutting-edge projects.
- Foundation can better control how the money is spent.
- Grantees don't rely too much on one funding source.

Limitations:
- Nonprofits may "mold" their agencies around available grants.
- Grantee does not have the ability to use grant money as it knows best.
- Many funded projects are not sustained.

Operating Support

Advantages:
- Organizations are strengthened—builds infrastructure so that they can stay focused on their mission.
- Grantees decide where dollars are spent, which establishes trust.
- Sustainability is enhanced.

Limitations:
- Operating grants may not keep the interest of the community foundation board.
- Project grants are easier to track and measure.
- Grantees may rely too much on one funding source.

No single solution may work when it comes to project or operating support. The merits of both should be considered in terms of the program objectives of your foundation and the potential grantee. Many times, a community foundation will offer a mix of different types of support to different organizations. Although it may be true that nonprofits grow to rely on operating support funds, you can avoid this with a mutually understood exit strategy by the foundation and grantee.

Questions to consider:

- What is more important to your foundation—investing in new ideas or sustaining an organization over time?
- Would a shift in the level of project or operating support have an impact on your program goals?
- Could your budget be apportioned fairly between operating and project support?
- If you fund project or operating grants, what is your exit strategy? How can you engage grantees in this conversation from the onset?
- How will you evaluate the results of an operating support grant?
- In what ways can you encourage grantees to be more outspoken about their needs? In what ways can your foundation be more supportive?

Capacity Building

Whereas project support makes grants for specific projects, capacity building strengthens the organizations behind those projects.

Government and foundations mostly make **project-specific grants**, which can lead nonprofits to have weak infrastructure. Although they may have a strong sense of mission and service, few nonprofits have the staff or resources to take their organization to the next level. A growing number of community foundations establish grants programs specifically for capacity building, developing strong organizations that can support strong programs.

Capacity building efforts can take many forms and can be through grantmaking or non-grantmaking activities. Examples include funding for:

- Consultants
- Professional development
- Leadership training
- Strategic planning
- Evaluation
- Facility purchases or renovation
- Board or staff retreats
- Advocacy training
- New equipment/technology
- New staff positions
- General operating grants, if in combination with one or more of the above.

Non-grant capacity building might include:

- Help with grantwriting/fundraising
- Advice on marketing and communications
- Nonprofit gatherings for networking and information exchange.

When considering capacity-building grants, consider these questions:

- In what kinds of capacity building will the board be willing and eager to invest?
- What criteria would an organization have to meet before it would be eligible for a capacity-building grant?
- How should you work with nonprofits to determine their needs and readiness for capacity building?
- How engaged should you be when working with nonprofits? How close is too close?
- How long would it take to see the results of capacity-building efforts? Are you willing to wait that long?

Length of Support

Short-term and Long-term Funding

Once you decide on the kinds of grants your foundation will make, the question then becomes: *How long should that funding last?*

Grants usually fall under two categories: **short-term funding** is a single year or single grant period of project funding support; **long-term funding** (also called multiyear funding) is three years or more of continued funding, often for operating or project support, or as seed money for a new organization. Here are some advantages and limitations of each:

Short-term Funding	Long-term Funding
Advantages: ■ Encourages grantee self-reliance by broadening funding base. ■ Enables the foundation to share resources among many organizations over time. ■ Allows the foundation to plan ahead. ■ Typically requires a minimal investment. **Limitations:** ■ Pushes grantee focus toward fundraising, rather than serving the community. ■ Limits long-term impact for grantees. ■ Requires grantees to constantly create new (or the impression of new) projects. ■ Restricts real impact.	**Advantages:** ■ Encourages grantee self-reliance by building organizational capacity. ■ Enables foundations to build significant partnerships with organizations over time. ■ Allows grantees to plan ahead. ■ Creates long-term impact. **Limitations:** ■ Limits short-term support for the community as a whole. ■ Restricts resources to only a few organizations. ■ Ties up foundation funds for years. ■ Requires a greater investment of time and money.

Not sure about short-term or long-term grantmaking? Consider these questions:

- What is the rationale for a time limit on grants?
- Do you have a written policy on how long you will support organizations? Should you include exception clauses in those policies?
- If you decide on a policy to allow long-term funding, what criteria would an organization have to meet before you would support them for many years (longer than three) or even indefinitely?
- How can you reduce support over time to keep the grantee from relying too much on your foundation?
- In what ways can you assist organizations when you do reduce support?

For many community foundations, the best answer seems to be a mix of both approaches. Seeing the benefits both ways, foundations combine short-term and long-term grants to reflect their program objectives. This way, they are free to decide the better strategy for each grant. For a mix of approaches, foundations can

- Fund a variety of short- and long-term projects.
- Offer long-term funding but limit the number of successive years an organization can apply for a grant.

- Collaborate with other funders to support multiple-year funding. For example, foundations can alternate funding every two years, over a ten-year period. That way, the organization will receive the benefit of long-term support, without burdening one foundation.
- Offer a challenge grant to organizations when the foundation decides not to fund long term.
- Offer step-down funding in future years to wean long-term grantees.

Geographic Focus

Local, National and Global Funding

Community foundations historically made grants within a defined geographic area—typically no larger than a state. Although most continue to do just that, a growing number of community foundations have entered the national and international grantmaking arena. Individual donors are increasingly turning to donor-advised funds through their community foundation as a mechanism to support national and/or overseas work.

Taking a broader, global perspective doesn't necessarily mean making grants to organizations outside the United States. Some community foundations choose to channel international support through intermediary organizations based in the United States. Giving through an intermediary organization is often the simplest way to make grants internationally. Advantages to working with intermediaries include:

- Staff expertise to help explore issues, identify beneficiaries and screen projects
- Help in bridging linguistic and cultural differences
- Familiarity with social, political and cultural contexts, including local risks and conflicts

---

■ FROM THE FIELD: *IDENTIFYING COMMUNITY NEEDS*

One small New England community foundation wanted to become more responsive about its grantmaking. The foundation sent a simple questionnaire providing information on demographics and charitable interests to donors, grantees and the foundation's general mailing list. In a follow up after the questionnaire, the foundation held focus groups and one large-scale donor forum to discuss the issues facing the region. At the forum, the board led discussion groups based on the information gathered in the surveys and asked participants to go into more detail about their concerns for the region. Based on the survey and the focus groups, the foundation revealed primary needs in the community and established a new initiative to meet those needs. The staff feels the process improved its grantmaking effectiveness and at the same time, helped donors feel more connected the community and the foundation's work.

■ FROM THE FIELD: *SHORT VERSUS LONG-TERM FUNDING*

One community foundation makes long-term grants of ten or more years, providing not only unrestricted money but also advocacy, technical assistance, convening, evaluation and communication strategies. With this level of support, grantees can improve their own operations and programs and eventually sustain themselves. According to the vice president of programs, "By funding long-term, we care about not only changing an organization, but changing an overall system."

After trying long-term grants several years ago, another community foundation decided that short-term funding was the way to go. They found their hands tied when they made long-term grants. Since then, the foundation only makes grants for a single-year period. According to the associate director of finance, "Long-term grants can make a big difference in an organization; however, it is unfair to other agencies that have pressing needs as well." To this foundation and many others, being fair means being inclusive and being inclusive means awarding many grants to many worthy recipients—albeit short-term.

- Access to relevant networks
- Savings in staff time or administrative expenses
- Local accounting and reporting infrastructure
- Knowledge of local laws and regulations.

Some American community foundations have found it helpful to collaborate with community foundations in other parts of the world. For example, one community foundation hosted a delegation from Poland, which attracted the interest of new donors from the local Polish-American community. The interest of those new donors in supporting projects in Poland led the foundation to amend its articles of incorporation to include international grantmaking.

Foundations considering direct grantmaking abroad should take into account the government's prohibitions on funding terrorism. *See* International Dateline *Second Quarter 2004 at www.cof.org, COF CODE:* **International** *for more information.* Using an intermediary can help with this issue as well.

Grant Size

Few Large Grants, Many Small Grants

Community foundations of all sizes and types find that small grants ($10,000 or less, for example) can be an innovative tool in their grantmaking. Because relatively little money is at stake, foundations can free themselves from a traditional mode of operations and explore a creative way of doing work.

Some feel that small grants give them a "bigger bang for the buck," allowing them to see tangible results with quicker turnaround. This can appeal to donors who want to see the immediate impact of their dollars. Small grants are generally less complicated in the application process and allow for quick grant decisions.

With small grants, your foundations may be more likely to:

- **Open the grant decisionmaking process to the community**—In some cases, foundations have turned the entire process over to community members.

- **Take more risks**—With smaller amounts of money, you might be more experimental, looking beyond the traditional public charity organizations that receive the majority of grants. For example, some foundations give small grants to start-up nonprofits with no track record.

The USA PATRIOT Act

In 2001, Congress enacted the USA PATRIOT Act to enhance penalties for those who commit acts of terrorism or who support terrorism. Although the act's requirements with respect to financial institutions do not apply to U.S. philanthropic organizations, they are subject to Executive Order 13224 and could, in extreme cases, face stiff criminal penalties for funding charities designated as supporters of terrorism. The Office of Foreign Assets Control (OFAC) of the U.S. Department of Treasury issues lists of Blocked Persons or Specially Designated Nationals (www.ofacsearch.com). The question of what steps community foundations should take to ensure they are in compliance with these new restrictions is complex. At a minimum, foundations should check all potentials grantees against the GuideStar database, as well as the official IRS Publication 78, because GuideStar more quickly identifies organizations placed on one of the terrorist watch lists.

For additional guidance on compliance, read "Grantmaking in an Age of Terrorism: Some Thoughts About Compliance Strategies," by Janne G. Gallagher, International Dateline, Second Quarter 2004, www.cof.org. For information on technology solutions to list checking, read "Seeking a Safe Harbor," by Martin B. Schneiderman, *Foundation News & Commentary*, May/June 2004, www.foundationnews.org.

- **Have quick turnaround on decisions**—Some community foundations issue checks within 48 hours after receiving grant proposals.
- **Streamline grant applications**—Some community foundations have shortened, or even abandoned, grant application forms for small grants. Others provide more hands-on assistance to applicants to break down the usual barriers between the grantmaker and grant seeker.
- **Create a mini-grants pool**—You can establish a pool of funds to keep on-hand for small grants and/or emergency requests.

Some foundations steer away from small grants, finding them too labor intensive for staff. Consider the following benefits of small versus large grants programs.

Many Small Grants:

- Allows the foundation to serve more of the community
- Enables many recipients to benefit from the community foundation
- Increases board and committee awareness to a wide range of community organizations
- Creates opportunities for publicity through multiple human-interest stories.

Few Large Grants:

- Offers more possibility of affecting one area of need
- Involves less paperwork and administrative management
- May attract more media attention.

Many community foundations vary their approach to grant size, choosing to award some large, some small, depending on the circumstances.

More Grantmaking Choices

Kinds of Organizations Funded

Most community foundations require the majority of their grantees to be public charities recognized as exempt under section 501(c)(3) of the Internal Revenue Code. Those that do often ask potential grantees to provide a copy of their determination letter from the IRS. However, community foundations should also verify that the organization continues to hold that status by checking IRS Publication 78 or its electronic equivalent. Houses of worship—such as churches, synagogues and mosques—are automatically exempt under section 501(c)(3) and are classified as public charities. They do not need to seek a determination letter from the IRS and often will not be listed in Publication 78. Community foundations also frequently make grants to governmental entities such as schools, public libraries and park departments. For these purposes, a

---

• FROM THE FIELD: FAX GRANTS

One West Coast foundation has developed a specialty in "immediate response grantmaking," sending checks 24–48 hours after requests are received. With these "Fax Grants," teachers fax in a one-page letter requesting up to $500 for field trips, books, supplies or whatever else they need for their class. This has a profound effect on teacher morale, as teachers in the public school system often have little ability to make changes happen quickly.

governmental entity is the equivalent of a section 501(c)(3) public charity as long as the grants further a public purpose.

Many community foundations also make grants to organizations that aren't incorporated as 501(c)(3)s and also to individuals for study, travel or research; in times of disaster or economic hardship; or for prizes and awards.

Unlike private foundations, community foundations are exempt from the expenditure responsibility rules, which require private foundations to follow specific procedures to make grants to a non-501(c)(3) organization. However, community foundations making such grants are responsible for assuring that their grants further a charitable purpose.

When considering grants to non-501(c)(3) organizations or individuals, community foundations should:

- First, determine whether their organizing documents permit the foundation to make such a grant. Some community foundation charters, articles of incorporation, deeds of trust or bylaws restrict grantmaking to 501(c)(3) public charities.

- Determine whether the funds will be used for a charitable purpose—which includes religious, scientific, literary and educational activities, as well as the relief of poverty and distress, the promotion of amateur sports and the prevention of cruelty to children and animals.

- Determine whether the grant-funded activities will serve the public or provide benefits to private interests. Only a grant that serves the public can be a charitable expenditure.

- Once your foundation makes the grant, collect documents that demonstrate the charitable nature of the expenditure to IRS auditors or others. In some cases where it is unclear, it may be wise to get a legal opinion from your attorney who should be well versed in community foundation rules and practices.

You should require follow-up reporting from the non-501(c)(3) grantee organization that details the progress made toward achieving the charitable goals of the project, just as you would with a grant to a 501(c)(3). Keep these documents in the grant file.

Grants to Individuals

From time to time, community foundations may be called upon to make grants to individuals, which they may legally do. Sometimes these grants are in response to a disaster or other tragedy and may be called **emergency grants**. All community foundations receive emergency requests that may be difficult to resist. Your foundation should have a policy in place for handling such requests. Some community foundations have a fund from which the CEO or program director can make small grants without prior board approval. Others use a pool of donors as an emergency resource, which allows donors to see the immediate effect of their gift.

More commonly, community foundations make grants to individuals in the form of **scholarships** (although scholarships can also be paid to an institution rather than the individual student). Scholarship programs are a big part of what community foundations do. Many times, scholarships manifest through memorial funds, in response to a tragedy, death or other immediate circumstance. Donors find scholarship programs particularly meaningful at a difficult time in their life. Community foundations are able to serve these donors, reacting swiftly to establish the scholarship fund and quickly connecting other donors to the cause.

Scholarships are a good sell to donors, allowing them to support educational advancement, encourage traditional and nontraditional students and, many times, leave a legacy in their name.

These programs benefit community foundations as well. Scholarships usually focus on youth and education—two central concerns of most communities, which can bring good publicity and create more awareness about the foundation. Scholarships can also generate new contributions from diverse segments of the population and can help you bring new volunteers into the foundation's activities.

Scholarships, however, are complicated. They require a lot of administrative work on your foundation's part. Among other tasks, the staff must publicize the existence of the program, collect applications, coordinate review committees, determine financial need and academic merit, disburse funds and track recipients.

Traditionally, community foundations have estimated that administrative costs run from 5 to 20 percent of the programs. If administrative costs are to be deducted from the particular scholarship fund to which they are attributable, donors should be made aware of such charges from the start. Similarly, if the community foundation opts to levy a fixed administrative fee on scholarship funds, the donor should be aware of the amount.

When designing or reviewing your scholarship program, consider these questions:

- What are some of the value-added reasons for starting or growing a scholarship program at your community foundation?
- What cautions exist in starting or expanding a scholarship program?
- How can you meet donors' needs and interests with alternatives to scholarship programs?
- Do your governing instruments authorize grants to individuals for educational purposes?
- What academic or achievement standards will you apply to the program?
- How can you simplify administering the scholarships program?
- Does your scholarship conflict of interest policy disqualify committee members and their dependents?

- How can you make the scholarship application more "user friendly?"
- Will you offer loans in the scholarship program?
- Will you award scholarships to the institutions or to the students themselves?
- What combination of evaluations should you use in the selection process?
- What issues do you need to consider when designing or revamping your scholarship award process?

Once you've decided to implement a scholarship program, the best advice is to keep it simple. Here are some ideas:

- Consider one standard application form for all scholarship funds
- Limit reporting requirements from students and institutions
- Limit administrative details and responsibilities
- Form a scholarship selection committee to choose the participants
- Engage and outsource local experts in identifying awardees and acting as scholarship program officers.

For more information on grants to individuals, read Grants to Individuals by Community Foundations, *Council on Foundations, 2004, or Scholarship FAQs, at www.cof.org.*

Interim Grants

Interim grants include funds that are distributed at the discretion of board or staff members, without the approval of the full board. These grants usually fit within the foundation's mission, but in some cases, do not. Some foundations use interim grants to incubate new program areas or to respond to immediate needs.

Generally, interim grants are small in size, requiring a shorter application process and a quicker turnaround. Often, interim grants require speed in delivering the award to the grantee. For example, they might be used to respond to emergencies that cannot wait until the next board meeting.

Ways to Leverage and Collaborate

Leveraging is sometimes called the "multiplier effect." It occurs when an amount of money is given with the express purpose of attracting funding from other sources or of providing the organization with the tools it needs to raise other kinds of funds.

If your foundation is interested in leveraging funds, it can start by helping grantees access additional community resources. Some do this by:

- Suggesting other funders
- Making phone calls to other funders on behalf of grantees

- **FROM THE FIELD:** *SCHOLARSHIPS*

    Scholarship programs can bring your foundation good publicity and possibly new donors. One Midwest foundation continues to facilitate media coverage of scholarship recipients, initiating at least two feature stories per year on successful graduates. The foundation has also developed an alumni program, encouraging past scholarship recipients and families to stay connected and involved with the foundation.

- Attending and/or scheduling meetings with other funders
- Securing funding through matching grants or another means.

Foundations can leverage grant dollars by collaborating with other funders. Although some foundations see the value in being the sole supporter of a program, many will also engage in joint funding. They find that by working with others in the community, they make the most of available resources.

Community foundations can approach leveraging differently. Some seek out already established programs in the community, to which they match their grant dollars. Others prefer to be the first supporter of a program, working then to attract other grantmakers and donors.

Level of Community Involvement

How involved should the community be in your grantmaking decisions?

Some community foundations operate with limited community involvement, establishing all grantmaking priorities and making all grant decisions in-house. Staff might assess the community before grantmaking to inform their work, but when it comes to doing the work itself, they rely on their own knowledge and people to get the job done.

Other community foundations take an entirely different approach and involve community members directly. They may actively solicit community advice on needs, priorities and grant decisions. Some might form a grant review committee composed entirely of members from the community, who field initial grant proposals and prepare recommendations for the board. They might also use community members as volunteers or consultants who bring technical assistance to the foundation and/or its grantees.

Like so many of these choices, foundations don't necessarily fall to one extreme or the other. Many times, they will engage the community at different levels depending on the nature of the grant or initiative.

How Can You Help Your Board Make Strategic Grantmaking Choices?

As the CEO, how can you help your board make choices for its grantmaking program? Here are some tips to spark a good board discussion:

- Help the board understand its various grantmaking options. Provide educational materials for pre-reading.
- When considering options, remind the board to situate your foundation in the current environment as well as in the desired future.
- Use a visual voting system such as a number scale or colored dots for each of the choices. This will provide a quick image of what the board perceives.

Remember, long-lasting changes sometimes happen gradually. Help the board make its choices mindfully and over time. Remind them that the work doesn't end with one decision, but requires continual review and reassessment for grantmaking to meet changing needs.

3.
WORKING WITH GRANTEES

> **WHAT YOU WILL LEARN**
> Find out how to perform due diligence and how you can ensure good grantor/grantee relationships.

> **NATIONAL STANDARDS V.D**
> A community foundation performs due diligence to ensure that grants will be used for charitable purposes.

What Is Due Diligence?

Due diligence describes the practices one applies to reviewing grant requests before approving them. Due diligence means that, before making a grant, your foundation investigates prospective grantees to determine that they qualify to receive the grant, manage their fiscal resources in a prudent manner, have the capacity to fulfill the terms of the grant and are willing to furnish your foundation with any reports you require. The National Standards require that community foundations perform due diligence to ensure that grants will be used for charitable purposes, consistent with the nature of the fund from which the grant is made.

Your foundation should develop and maintain a good due diligence policy. Due diligence helps you:

- Ensure donors that grants will be used for the purposes intended and that the foundation complies with applicable laws and regulations.
- Develop a process for when there is doubt about a grant recipient's eligibility. *How will you communicate that to the grantee? How will you communicate that to the donor who suggested the grantee?*
- Give your grants the seal of approval.
- Work to improve the effectiveness of your grants.

How to Do Due Diligence

For each potential grantee, ask these questions:

- Do they comply with applicable laws and regulations?
- Do they deliver the benefits they claim to provide?
- Do they have the capacity to fulfill grant requirements?
- Can they provide IRS letters or their equivalents?
- Are they financially stable?

At the very minimum, you will want to verify that the organization is recognized by the IRS as a public charity. You can check GuideStar (www.guidestar.org), the National Database of Nonprofit Organizations, for information on the grant seeker and to view a copy of its Form 990. Throughout the course of the grant period, you might ask grantees to provide you with progress reports and a final narrative and financial report.

For more information on performing due diligence, Council members can refer to the Standards & Effective Practices for Community Foundations website at http://bestpractices.cof.org.

How Can You Enhance Relationships with Grantees?

In the eyes of grant seekers and grantees, foundations often have an aura of mystery about them. Many find it difficult to understand how community foundations work, where the money comes from and how to access the foundation. Others may associate foundations with power and authority and therefore feel intimidated.

Your relationship with grantees is based on mutual respect, candor and understanding. For that reason, you should be as open, honest and accessible as possible, through the grant process and beyond.

Here are a few rules to follow for good grantee relations:

- Be clear about what you ask for. Define the purposes of the grant, your expectations and the ways you will evaluate and publicize the results.
- Return phone calls.
- Be truthful, compassionate and considerate.
- Admit error and be willing to apologize.
- Listen to grantees and help them feel comfortable.
- Offer feedback when it is appropriate.
- Don't withhold information that is important to give.
- Ask for advice from grantees on how the foundation can improve its process.

Remember that as funders, any advice your foundation offers carries tremendous weight with nonprofits. Before giving advice, consider whether it was requested, whether it's appropriate and how it will be used.

Beyond providing financial support, some foundations offer the following to enhance their grantee/grantor relationships and to learn how to better serve the community:

Grantee Advisory Committees—To get continual constructive advice, appoint grantee advisory committees as sounding boards for your policies, priorities and practices, and in some cases, for specific program areas.

Inviting Grantees—Invite your grantees to board or other meetings to speak on subjects of mutual interest. Your board will likely find these presentations both stimulating and helpful in determining where to focus resources.

More Frequent Site Visits—Foundations should take the time to give grantees a quality visit, with adequate time and participation. Site visits shouldn't be limited to program officers; executives and board members benefit from doing site visits as well.

Foundation Evaluations—Many foundations evaluate the work of grantees, but seldom put their own foundation practices under the microscope. Although it isn't required by law, more community foundations are seeing the value in self-assessment to improve their effectiveness and demonstrate accountability. Some foundations have hired consultants and sent questionnaires to grantees.

There are many creative ways to improve your practices, learn from your grantees and strive for a better process:

- Conduct surveys, focus groups and/or informal interviews with grantees and colleagues.
- Develop a feedback program (such as an appointed or hired ombudsman) that would be a vehicle for those dealing with your foundation to make both positive and negative comments.
- Bring in teams of outside evaluators, including representatives from the larger nonprofit sector, who look at the foundation's internal processes and conduct confidential interviews with foundation staff and board members, as well as applicants and grantees.

One of the most common ways to assess your own work is through grantee surveys. Surveying your grantees can provide your foundation with information to understand better its choices and operations. Grantee feedback not only helps the grantmaking staff improve its process, but also provides stories and anecdotes for the development and communications staff to highlight in their work.

Most grantee surveys cover issues such as the selection process, interactions during the grant and perceived foundation impact. When surveying, assure grantees of the confidentiality of their answers, so that they will give you honest feedback.

Here are some ideas for what to ask grantees:

- How would you describe your encounter with the foundation?
- How well were you kept informed during the funding process?
- What could the foundation have done to better support you?
- How comfortable are you approaching the foundation with problems?
- How responsive were the staff members?
- How fairly do you feel you were treated?
- How did you hear about the foundation?
- What factors influenced your decision to apply?
- What comments do you have on the application process itself—including the application form, site visit, interview (i.e., was it difficult, manageable, helpful, hurtful and why)?
- Do you think the foundation's strategies and priorities are on target with community needs?
- What advice would you give about the future of the grantmaking process?

For more information on grantee/grantor relationships and foundation self-assessments, and to learn about the Grantee Perception Report management tool, visit the Center for Effective Philanthropy at www.effectivephilanthropy.org.

■ FROM THE FIELD: DUE DILIGENCE

For one small foundation with limited staff, it was important to use volunteer resources to ensure due diligence. With staff guidance and oversight, the foundation solicited volunteer committee members to individually rank grants and research grant applicants. These rankings were then discussed at a committee meeting and final grant recommendations were brought before the board. This is an effective way for a small foundation to get the work done and still involve community members. According to one foundation staff member, "This practice has made our grantmaking well-rounded because the review committee members come from different perspectives—both geographically and by area of interest."

4. WORKING WITH DONORS

WHAT YOU WILL LEARN

In this section, find ways to engage donors in grantmaking, including newsletters and bulletins, customized services, meetings and events, and more. Learn how donors use their funds and how you can monitor fund distribution.

How Can You Involve Donors in Grantmaking?

More and more community foundations are involving donors in their grantmaking. The more you can inform donors of your grantmaking practices and opportunities, the more effective and satisfying their philanthropy will be. As donors feel engaged and enthused about suggesting certain grants, they might apply that enthusiasm to their continued giving, both current and deferred.

When it comes to grantmaking, every donor is different. Some have very particular ideas of what they want to support; others are open to suggestion or advice. Some will place no restrictions on their gift; others desire more involvement. Some will want to be part of the process; others will leave the job to the foundation.

Donor-advised funds are one way community foundations involve donors in grantmaking. With these funds, donors are able to recommend how funds are spent. Community foundations are also trying to find ways to educate donors on a range of needs in the community. The more community foundations involve donors, the more likely the donors' interests will broaden to new areas for giving.

There are many ways to involve donors in grantmaking. Here are some ideas:

- Brief donors on areas of community need, either in person or in printed materials (such as newsletters, fund statements, your website).

- Periodically meet with donors to provide customized information services.

- Provide information to donors about grants made from unrestricted or field of interest funds.

- Distribute grant opportunities in newsletters/bulletins.

- Invite donors to foundation and/or community meetings or grantee presentations.

- Invite donors on site visits/bus tours.

- Invite donors to serve on foundation advisory committees and advise on community needs and/or recruit new donors.

- Determine and track donor interests over time.

- Give donors the opportunity to learn about or become involved in community issues.

By identifying the donors' interests at the time they establish their funds, you can make them more aware of issues and opportunities that would appeal to them. Some foundations use donor intake forms at the time donors establish funds, asking them to identify their areas of interest and their preferred method of contact should grant opportunities arise.

To comply with National Standards, you should document examples of how donors respond to your education activities and how they become involved in the community as a result of your efforts.

How Can You Monitor Fund Distributions?

Just as it monitors all of its grants, your community foundation must monitor those distributions that donors recommend. You will perform due diligence on grantee organizations and rely on your policies and processes to show accountability.

As a reminder, you should know the legal and financial requirements as established by the IRS and federal and state law. When developing a process to monitor funds, here are some questions to consider:

- How can you make donors aware of their privileges and limitations with regard to advising?

- How will your foundation perform due diligence on potential grantees recommended by the donor?

- Who is responsible for ensuring that donor-advised distributions are made properly?

- How will you document situations in which the foundation declines or changes a donor recommendation?

- Does the community foundation monitor distributions from donor-advised funds?

- Does the foundation clearly state that the distribution is from the ABC FUND of the Community Foundation XYZ?

For more information, refer to the "Management, Finance and Administration" chapter, or read the Legal Compendium for Community Foundations, *Council on Foundations, www.cof.org.*

> **NATIONAL STANDARDS VI**
>
> A. A community foundation informs and educates donors about community issues and grantmaking opportunities
>
> B. A community foundation involves donors in identifying and responding to community issues and opportunities.

■ FROM THE FIELD: INFORMING DONORS

One large West Coast foundation created an opt-in donor service—one that provides local funding ideas for donors within their areas of interest. It customizes the service for donors, presenting them with funding ideas at in-person meetings and sending them summary proposals monthly. The foundation recently started to provide access to these prescreened funding ideas online as well. The foundation asks donors for a 30-day turnaround on their response. Within a period of three years, the program has identified more than $10 million dollars in local grants that might not otherwise have been made. Donors appreciate access to prescreened funding ideas, and nonprofits appreciate the foundation spreading the good word about their work.

5. COMMUNITY LEADERSHIP

WHAT YOU WILL LEARN

Why should you consider a community leadership role? Learn how to determine when your foundation should take a leadership role and how to evaluate and communicate results from such activities. This section helps you differentiate the different kinds of leadership, including convening, collaborating and undertaking public policy work.

Why Is Community Leadership Important?

Leadership is one way for community foundations to contribute to their communities. Your foundation shows leadership when it brings people together, when it collaborates on initiatives with other organizations and when it serves as a catalyst for positive change. Community leadership gives foundations the opportunity to be more than a problem solver; it lets them become a "convener of solutions."

Few institutions enjoy the vantage point of community foundations. Your foundation sees into many aspects of the community, holding a great amount of knowledge without a biased interest. It has "the big picture" knowledge to form partnerships with many of the key local players.

With this ability comes great responsibility but also great rewards. By showing leadership, community foundations must meet challenges and rise to opportunities, making change for now and for the long term.

By taking on the role of community leader, community foundations can accomplish many outcomes. If you have the staff and financial resources, as well as board approval, your foundation may want to get involved with at least one major community leadership activity. But what does community leadership entail? The following will give you some ideas of what your leadership can accomplish.

Leadership can help your foundation:

- **Build community capacity**—Nurture and build your community's strengths and assets. Help others respond to challenges and opportunities, develop local leadership, promote self-reliance, emphasize prevention and mobilize civic participation and resources.

Top Ten Reasons to Become a Community Leader

Why should your foundation consider becoming a community leader? Because you can potentially:

1. Have a greater impact on major community issues.
2. Make a difference on a limited grantmaking budget.
3. Increase the effectiveness of grantmaking.
4. Bring together community factions that may not otherwise meet.
5. Address issues of common concern.
6. Increase the incidence of donors jointly supporting projects.
7. Enhance the stature and reputation of your community foundation.
8. Increase skill and expertise of community foundation board and staff.
9. Attract new donors.
10. Increase giving.

Source: National Standards & Effective Practices for Community Foundations website at http://bestpractices.cof.org

- **Understand the changing nature of your communities**—Leadership helps you get to know your community even better. Spend time consulting with members of the community, make yourselves available for discussion, be active participants in the community, monitor local and national trends and be aware of change.

- **Create opportunities for dialogue**—Bring together people with different ideas and points of view and create opportunities for respectful dialogue on important issues in your community.

- **Develop partnerships**—Form, encourage and support partnerships among individuals, nonprofit organizations, neighborhood and community groups, service clubs, foundations, professional advisors, businesses, government, the media and others.

- **Reflect diversity**—Bring together different points of view and engage the broader community in your decisionmaking.

Source: Community Foundations of Canada, www.community-fdn.ca

Who Leads?

When a community foundation staff commits to a leadership role, they must have the support of the foundation's board and senior staff. This is particularly important when large amounts of resources are required to support the activity and where the foundation's image and prestige may be placed on the line.

The more you involve the board and senior staff in leadership, the more it can:

- Send a clear message that the entire foundation is behind the work
- Improve your credibility on the issue in the eyes of the wider community
- Attract other key community leaders to work with your foundation
- Ensure sustainability for the work
- Provide a broad cross-section of resources to support the work.

To determine who plays the lead role in leadership, consider who has the most expertise, credibility and experience on the issue. Sometimes it's necessary for the CEO to be the visible leader. Where the issue has to do more with grantmaking or program issues, the senior staff person might take the lead.

Leadership Ideas

Why should your foundation consider becoming a community leader? Because you can potentially:

- Get behind initiatives that address a priority issue
- Create initiatives that address foundation or community priorities
- Develop partnerships with other funders
- Join other community leaders already working on an issue of importance to the community
- Collaborate with others for cross-section public policy changes
- Build community capacity
- Create opportunities for dialogue—convening, conducting meetings
- Reflect diversity of the community—be inclusive
- Evaluate and share results.

Excerpt from Center for Community Foundation Excellence Community Leadership Curriculum. For more information visit www.cof.org (CF CODE: **CCFE***).*

If the board is in the best position to provide leadership, the CEO should inform and engage them in the leadership activity. How can you, as the CEO, promote an important initiative among board members? Here are some suggestions:

To engage the board in leadership:

- Include relevant material on the issue as an information item in board meeting handbooks (short and succinct) and offer to answer questions.

- Engage a subcommittee of the board (e.g. a "Community Leadership" Committee) in discussions about the issue and provide additional information between meetings.

- Begin to identify and recruit advocates among board members for the work you want to undertake.

- Connect the issue to the priorities of the particular committee and begin to build a case for your foundation's involvement. Allow a board member to become the spokesperson for the issue.

- When the time comes for the board to vote on getting involved, let the board speak.

Once the actual work begins, one or more staff members become a liaison between the initiative and the board, providing updates on progress, accomplishments and the final outcomes for the work.

When Should the Foundation Take on a Leadership Role?

"Before stepping forward into a leadership role, assess what it will mean to your foundation."

Sometimes community foundations take leadership on an issue before exploring possible consequences. Before stepping forward to take leadership on a community issue or to resolve a problem, the CEO or senior staff should assess the issue and how it might affect the foundation. A strategic assessment helps you understand the issue or problem and determine whether it is the right time for you to address it.

To assess a leadership opportunity, take the time in advance to:

- Determine whether or not the work is consistent with your mission and vision

- Research the issue at hand

- Assess options for the kind of leadership the foundation can provide

- Determine what resources—financial, staff, expertise—are available to sustain your participation

- Determine the level of commitment from your board and staff

- Determine who is already doing something on the issue

- Explore potential partnerships

- Determine the risks in doing/not doing this work

- Consider the impact of this work on your image/prestige in the community.

To comply with National Standards, your community foundation should document how it identifies community issues and sets objectives to address those issues and, similarly, how it identifies and selects opportunities for leadership and convening.

> **NATIONAL STANDARDS**
> **V.E**
>
> A community foundation works to identify community issues and opportunities and acts as a leader and convener, using its human and/or financial resources to address immediate and long-term community issues and opportunities.

What Are Community Leadership Activities?

Convening

Convening brings people together around a common cause or goal. A simple meeting such as a luncheon or a half-day seminar can be surprisingly effective for many purposes, including:

- Information sharing
- Discussing best practices
- Enhancing relations
- Encouraging partnerships
- Coordinating responses.

By consulting with the community, your foundation can learn where it is needed the most. Convening creates the opportunity to bring people together for dialogue—whether it is a group of grantees, donors, other funders, civic leaders, professional advisors, community members or a combination.

Convening can take many forms, from informal meetings to the most elaborate of events. Some examples of convening include:

- Meetings
- Brown bag presentations
- Workshops
- Social events
- Luncheons
- Focus groups
- Listening sessions
- Open houses
- In-service training
- Facilitated panels/discussions/debates.

As a convener, your foundation introduces people who otherwise may not meet. This can create partnerships among individuals, donors, nonprofits, neighborhood and community groups, service clubs, foundations, businesses, governments, the media and more. By bringing different points of view together, you engage the broader community and manifest an opportunity for change.

Convening enhances your relationships with grantees and grant seekers. For most nonprofits, the only contact they have with the community foundation is through the grant application. Only rarely are nonprofits asked to join their foundation counterparts in discussions about serious policy issues, the challenges to philanthropic institutions or the big questions that face the independent sector.

Many communities convene regular meetings of grantmakers to discuss programs and possibilities for joint ventures. Others have formed local associations of grantmakers and/or state and regional associations of grantmakers (www.givingforum.org).

Focus Groups and Listening Sessions

One way to convene people around an issue is to organize a **focus group**—an informal session to gather information and learn perceptions about a specific issue. Rather than define one area of discussion, some foundations also hold what they call **listening sessions**—an opportunity for open dialogue on what community members have to say.

If you are considering one of the above, these tips may help:

- Choose participants randomly to gain a diversity of opinion.
- Invite—never require—participants to attend.
- Include 10 to 20 participants who interact with the foundation—grantees, colleagues, employees and so forth.
- The goal is to gather information—not to educate or influence opinion. The facilitator might pose a set of questions to which participants respond. In listening sessions, the facilitator will simply moderate the discussion.
- Explain that there are no wrong answers or opinions and no need for participants to reach consensus.
- If possible, hold more than one meeting for any one topic. This way, you will gain a wider spectrum of opinion.
- Be sure someone takes notes at the gathering. If you would like to record the session, you should (and according to some state law, you must) get permission from each participant.

For more information on focus groups, see the InnoNet website at www.innonet.org and click on "Resources."

Collaborating

Your foundation alone cannot solve every community issue or problem. At a time when resources are limited and the challenges facing communities are increasingly complex, more and more organizations see the value in collaborating.

What is collaboration? Simply stated, collaborations are well-defined, mutually beneficial relationships you enter with one or more organizations to achieve common goals. These partnerships create new energy and ideas and many times result in increased resources.

Successful collaborations entail a commitment to:

- Having mutual goals and a clearly defined relationship
- Jointly developing a structure
- Sharing responsibility
- Having mutual authority and accountability for success
- Sharing resources and rewards.

By forming partnerships with others in the community, you can make the best use of your available resources. There are other benefits as well.

Collaborations bring buy-in from many sectors in the community. When groups and organizations play a role in the decisionmaking on an issue, they are more likely to involve themselves in the work to be done.

Second, collaborations open channels of communication. Many times, different groups are working on the same issue, sometimes without even knowing it. Collaboration centralizes the effort and avoids duplicating the work others have done.

Third, collaborations allow input from diverse voices in the community (racial, cultural, socioeconomic) that otherwise might not be heard. This can create a richer and more lasting response to community problem solving.

So how do you start collaborating? There's more than one way to do it, and your strategies will vary depending on the issue or task at hand.

In any collaboration, consider the following steps:

- Identify and approach potential partners.
- Take time to understand the vision and mission of those partners.
- Collectively define the goals, actions and outcomes of the collaboration, so that all parties are clear and committed to the plan.
- Carefully develop agreements with all partners to the collaboration, outlining duties and expectations for the work.
- Design an exit strategy so that each organization knows when it has fulfilled its obligation.

Keep in mind that collaborations are hard work. Whenever you work with other organizations or people, you might encounter challenges, such as organizational and/or personal egos, others taking too much credit for the work, misunderstandings or unexpected twists and turns. In most cases, if all parties communicate clearly and gain a mutual understanding of what is expected, you can avoid potential conflicts.

The benefits of collaborating usually outweigh any challenges. Collaborations create a valuable forum where community partners can come together for the greater good. That might sound simple, but when funders and community leaders bring their collective expertise and perspective to an issue, they are more likely to burst forth with breakthrough ideas.

Public Policy

As a leadership organization, you have a powerful voice that can be used to benefit your community through public policy change. Often, your public policy work will create more impact than any one grant or program you offer.

Public policy is any legally appropriate activity aiming to affect or inform government laws, administrative practices, regulations or executive or judicial orders. It can comprise a wide range of activities including:

- Legislative lobbying
- Administrative or regulatory advocacy
- Judicial advocacy
- Public interest research
- Public education efforts
- Community organizing
- Voter and candidate education

- Public information dissemination and access
- Facilitating and building partnerships
- Coalitions and negotiations among nonprofits and government.

Although lobbying is only one form of public policy activity, it is often the most important step toward changing laws that affect the groups and people you serve.

Community Foundations Can Lobby

Community foundations are governed under the same federal tax rules for lobbying as public charities, under section 501(c)(3). Unlike private foundations that are generally restricted from lobbying except on those issues affecting their own operations, community foundations may lobby to the same extent as other public charities.

Lobbying, as defined by federal tax law, is any attempt to influence a specific legislative proposal. This means a bill that has been introduced, or a draft bill that may be introduced in any legislative body such as a city council, state legislature or Congress. Lobbying occurs, for example, when you or another staff person call or meet with legislative staff, stating your organization's position on a bill. Lobbying also occurs when you urge others to make those contacts. This is called grassroots lobbying.

Lobbying and public policy work benefit the community and can benefit your foundation as well. For instance, it can:

- Raise awareness of your mission.
- Mobilize members, volunteers, donors and board members.
- Attract favorable media attention.
- Establish and expand government investment in important social programs.
- Reform laws and regulations that govern the operation and evaluation of your foundation's operations.
- Benefit the citizens of your community beyond that of any one direct service program.

Support Lobbying in Other Ways

Some community foundations may not engage in lobbying themselves, but may make general support grants to public charities that do. A general support grant that is not earmarked for lobbying will not be considered lobbying by the foundation.

Community foundation staff can educate donors about organizations that engage in public policy work on causes they care about. When foundations inform donors about opportunities to support public policy, it expands the pipeline of usually scarce dollars for public policy activities. When donors give to public policy, it makes them feel a part of the effort for social change.

There are also multiple opportunities to work with government departments and agencies to advance good public policies. Partnering on policy issues helps foundations initiate pilot programs that may later attract government funding.

Guidelines for Public Policy Work

Community foundations have traditionally shied away from public policy work for fear it might alienate donors or create an impression of partisanship. However, this work enables you to make a significant difference on issues you are already addressing through grantmaking. It helps maximize grantmaking dollars while creating lasting change. Community foundations that plan to lobby should consider making the election under section 501(h). This allows them to measure lobbying by their expenditures rather than a test based on their activities, which can be vaguer. Be sure to obtain and review a publication that explains lobbying—what it is and what it is not—and the expenditure limits. For more information, contact the Council on Foundations Government Relations Department at govt@cof.org, the Alliance for Justice at www.allianceforjustice.org or the Center for Lobbying in the Public Interest at www.clpi.org.

Here are some lobbying suggestions for community foundations:

- Make the election under 501(h)
- Communicate clearly with legislators
- Build local coalitions that support the particular policy/legislation
- Be prepared with facts and figures to support your effort
- Avoid "grassroots lobbying" beyond the permitted limits, which is stating your position to the general public and asking them to contact legislators
- Pick your issues carefully and on a nonpartisan basis
- Make sure that you don't alienate your strong supporters.

Public policy work requires strategic leadership, an ability to convene a broad cross-section of people together to work on the issue and access to resources to support the work. Most community foundations are advocates for improving their local communities and are in the right position to lead this work.

How Do You Evaluate Community Leadership?

When your community foundation invests staff and other resources in a community initiative, you will want to know—and show—how you made a difference. Unfortunately, evaluating leadership isn't always easy. Often there is no quantitative value associated with leadership. Its value, instead, is in long-term change.

Nonetheless, as the CEO and staff, you must report on the outcome of your activities. To do this, you should establish objectives at the very onset of activities. Define what will constitute a realistic "success" for the foundation and the community. As with any evaluation, define how you will measure objectives and within what timeframe. Always aim for realistic outcomes—those that are possible within the limits of available resources, including time, personnel, expertise and finances.

Grantmaking and Community Leadership: Questions to Consider

- How do your grantmaking priorities and process match your mission?
- Which current grantmaking strategies work well? Which could work better?
- When will you be ready for more proactive grantmaking?
- How do you define your leadership role?
- Do you have the resources (capacity, credibility, money) to take on community leadership?
- How will you select the issues on which to lead?
- Should you focus more on long-term or short-term interventions?
- How will you handle controversial issues when taking leadership?
- What process will you use to decide whether to lead "out front" or "behind the scenes"?
- How do you keep the board informed and involved? How do you keep donors, prospects and key opinion leaders informed and involved?
- How does your grantmaking and leadership work toward your vision?

Evaluation methods will vary, depending on the nature of the issue at hand and the type of leadership activity with which you're involved. Your approach to evaluation should be more than documenting activities, events and programs, as in "We convened X amount of community members." Instead, it should speak to the changes you've made—or changes you anticipate—that will make a positive difference in people's lives. For example, you might describe the outcome of the activities, the relationships built and any plans for future work on the issue. You might also observe the community's agenda to see if issues you've worked on are reflected there and/or if they have been funded by others.

Still, how will you know if your leadership activities have made a difference? Look for the following signs of success:

- Strong commitment from the leadership of all organizations involved.
- Open and effective communication among those involved.
- Participation from relevant sectors of the community's diverse population.
- A clear statement of goals, objectives and measurable outcomes for the initiative.
- An action plan that has the consensus of all partners and that outlines roles and responsibilities for each.
- Realistic expectations regarding outcomes.
- Benchmarks to monitor progress, maintain focus and measure impact.
- A clear exit strategy that specifies when and how your foundation will close out its work in the leadership effort.

Communicating the Results

Once you've evaluated the success of your leadership activities, you will want to share the results. Communicating your successes:

- Provides information to the community about a particular issue.
- Builds awareness and support for further work on that issue.
- Shows your foundation's accountability for its investments in the community.
- Helps your community foundation market its accomplishments to attract additional resources.
- Helps others see what remains to be done.

For more information on communication strategies, read the "Communication, Marketing and Public Relations" chapter.

Resources for Grantmaking and Community Leadership

Publications

Avery, Carrie. *Guide to Successful Small Grants Programs: When a Little Goes a Long Way.* Council on Foundations, 2002. Visit www.cof.org

Best Practices in Grants Management. Grants Managers Network, Council on Foundations, 2001. www.cof.org

Community Foundations and Public Policy: A Primer. Council on Foundations and the ProNet Public Policy Group. www.cof.org

Connor, Joseph A. and Stephanie Kadel-Taras. *Community Visions, Community Solutions: Grantmaking for Comprehensive Impact.* Amherst H. Wilder Foundation, 2003. www.wilder.org

Grantmaking Basics: A Field Guide for Funders. Council on Foundations, 1999. www.cof.org

Edie, John. A. *Foundations and Lobbying: Safe Ways to Affect Public Policy.* Council on Foundations, 1991. www.cof.org

Evaluation for Foundations: Concepts, Cases, Guidelines, and Resources. Jossey-Bass Publishers, 1993. www.josseybass.com

Gallagher, Janne G. "Grantmaking in an Age of Terrorism." Legal Dimensions of International Grantmaking, *International Dateline*, Second Quarter 2004. www.cof.org

Gast, Elaine. "The Long and the Short of It," *Foundation News & Commentary,* May/June 2002. www.foundationnews.com

Gast, Elaine. "Project vs. Operating Support: Which is the Better Strategy," *Board Briefing,* Council on Foundations, 2002. www.cof.org

Gray, Sandra Trice and Associates *Evaluation with Power: A New Approach to Organizational Effectiveness, Empowerment and Excellence.* Jossey-Bass, 1997. www.josseybass.com

Handbook on Counter-Terrorism Measures: What U.S. Nonprofits and Grantmakers Need to Know. Download at www.cof.org

Meeting the Collaboration Challenge Workbook: Developing Strategic Alliances Between Nonprofit Organizations and Businesses. Leader to Leader Institute. 2002. www.pfdf.org

Nober, Jane. *Grants to Individuals by Community Foundations.* Council on Foundations, 2000. Visit www.cof.org

Nober, Jane. "Legal Brief: Faith-Based Grantmaking: A Basic Guide for the Perplexed," *Foundation News and Commentary,* May/June 2001. www.foundationnews.com

Nober, Jane. "Legal Brief: Community Foundations and Grants to Non-Charities," *Foundation News and Commentary,* September/October 2001. www.foundationnews.com

Saying Yes/Saying No to Applicants. GrantCraft. www.grantcraft.org

Scanning the Landscape: Finding Out What's Going on in Your Field. GrantCraft. www.grantcraft.org

Schneiderman, Martin B. "Seeking a Safe Harbor," *Foundation News & Commentary,* May/June 2004. www.foundationnews.org

Using Competitions and RFPs. GrantCraft, www.grantcraft.org

When Community Foundations and Private and Corporate Funders Collaborate. Council on Foundations, 2000. www.cof.org

Winer, Michael and Karen Ray. *Collaboration Handbook: Creating, Sustaining and Enjoying the Journey.* Amherst H. Wilder Foundation, 1994. www.wilder.org

Working Better Together: How Government, Business, and Nonprofit Organizations Can Achieve Public Purposes Through Cross Sector Collaboration, Alliances, and Partnerships. Independent Sector, 2002. www.independentsector.org

Web

Alliance for Justice—www.allianceforjustice.org

Charity Lobbying in the Public Interest—www.clpi.org/community_foundations.html

Community Foundation Fundamentals Course, The Center for Community Foundation Excellence, www.cof.org, COF CODE: **CCFE**

Community Foundations Standards & Effective Practices database—http://bestpractices.cof.org

Congressional Yellow Book—www.leadershipdirectories.com

Congressional Quarterly—www.cq.com

Council on Foundations International Programs—www.cof.org or e-mail internatl@cof.org

Council on Foundations Legislative Network—www.cof.org

Council on Foundations-sponsored Affinity Groups—www.cof.org or e-mail inclusive@cof.org

Foundation Giving—www.fdncenter.org

Grant Benefit—www.grantbenefit.org

The Community Foundations of Canada website featuring free tools and resources

Grantcraft— www.grantcraft.org

Offers practical wisdom and publications for grantmakers

Grantmakers for Effective Organizations— www.geofunders.org

Advances the effectiveness of grantmakers and their grantees

Grantmakers Without Borders— www.internationaldonors.org

Aids international funders by organizing workshops, study trips, information sharing and collaborations

Innovation Network, Inc.—www.innonet.org

Offers information on ongoing program evaluation

National Taxonomy for Exempt Entities (NTEE)—http://nccs.urban.org/ntee-cc/

(You need to click on the icon that says NTEE.) Features useful information for coding and categorizing grants if you are reporting data to the Foundation Center

Planning Congressional Meetings: A How-To Kit—

www.cof.org/files/Documents/Government/Plan.Cong.pdf

Thomas—http://thomas.loc.gov

Up-to-date information on federal legislative proposals

U.S. International Grantmaking Project, Council on Foundations—www.usig.org

Offers information on guidelines governing international grantmaking

U.S. House of Representatives—www.house.gov

U.S. Senate—www.senate.gov

White House—www.whitehouse.gov

CHAPTER 5
RESOURCE DEVELOPMENT AND DONOR RELATIONS

"By God, gentlemen, I believe we've found it—the Fountain of Funding!"

Resource Development and Donor Relations

In This Chapter

Introduction 171

1) Building a Climate of Giving 173
    Who Are Potential Donors to Community Foundations? 173
    Why Do People Give? 173
    What Are the Advantages of Giving through Community Foundations? 175
    What Choices Do Donors Have for their Philanthropy? 176

2) Creating Funds 179
    How Do Community Foundations Build Permanent Unrestricted Funds? 179
    What Gifts Can Donors Make? 180
        Assets for Giving 180
        Gifts That Produce Lifetime Income 182
        Special Giving Options 183
    What Funds Can Donors Create? 185
        Major Types of Funds 185
        Benefits of Various Funds 187
    What Should You Consider When Seeking And Accepting Gifts? 187
    What Policies Do You Need for Gifts and Funds? 189
        Gift Acceptance Policies 190
        Fund Agreements 191

3) Designing a Development Plan 192
    What Should Your Resource Development Plan Include? 192
    What Is the Best Way to Identify and Approach Donors? 193
    How Do You Build Relationships with Donors? 194
        Using Different Approaches for Different Donors 194
        Individuals 194
        Corporations 195
        Private Foundations and Charitable Organizations 196
        Government Agencies 196
    What Activities Can You Use to Attract Donors? 197
    How Can You Build Relationships With Diverse Donor Groups? 198
    What Communication Strategies Help in Development? 198

What Ongoing Activities Make for Good Donor Relations? 200
    Distribute Gift Guidelines 201
    Acknowledge Gifts 201
    Report Back to Donors on their Funds..201
    Keep Donors Informed and Engaged..202
How Can You Build Operating Funds?...203
How Do You Measure Success?...204

4) Legal Considerations for Resource Development 205
What Are the Tax and Legal Implications of Various Gifts and Funds? 205
What Are Donor Restrictions? 205
How Can You Remove Donor Restrictions? 207
What Are Confidentiality Policies? 208

Questions to Consider 208
Resources for Resource Development and Donor Relations 209

RESOURCE DEVELOPMENT AND DONOR RELATIONS: AN INTRODUCTION

"In the foreseeable future, community foundation donors will want more control, more information from staff, fewer constraints on grants, a wider range of services, a higher level of professionalism and more trust than ever before."

—Todd Lueders, President/CEO, Community Foundation of Monterey County

Developing resources is one of the most important functions of your community foundation. Without the resources to thrive, your foundation couldn't exist to serve its community. It might have the most altruistic mission in the world. However, without the money backing it, it won't be able to make that mission a reality.

As a resource development and/or donor services staff, how can you attract contributions? What are your potential markets and how can you reach them? What are the basic motivations for giving and what "selling points" can you offer prospective donors? This chapter will give you answers for these questions and more.

The strategies for developing community foundation funds have changed in recent decades. Originally, development work meant encouraging donors to will money to the community foundation. The public support test changed all this, requiring community foundations to develop new contributions on a regular basis. Community foundations still seek permanent funds to meet changing community needs. However, more community foundations today turn to donor services as an important development strategy. Why the shift? Perhaps because community foundations realize that they must first serve donors to secure the resources to serve nonprofits.

In the following four sections, you will find:

1) **Building a Climate of Giving**—This section discusses the world of donors—who they are, why they give and why they give specifically to community foundations. It discusses the choices donors have for their philanthropy and the value that community foundations bring them.

2) **Creating Funds**—Find out what gifts donors can make and the funds they can choose. Learn how to build permanent unrestricted funds and what policies you need for accepting and rejecting gifts.

3) **Creating a Development Plan**—This section will help you develop a plan for resource development. Learn how to identify and attract donors, build relationships with diverse groups and understand what affects a donor's decision to give. Find out what communications strategies will help you in development and how you can make presentations to potential donors and advisors. Discover what ongoing activities make for good donor relations.

4) **Legal Considerations for Resource Development**—You and your board must know the tax and legal rules on various gifts and funds. Learn the basics here, including information on donor restrictions and how to remove them, as well as why confidentiality policies are important.

This chapter leads you through the process of creating development and donor relations strategies. If your foundation has already established a development program, use the information here to review and improve upon your current priorities and methods. Look for new ideas and compare your work to that of your colleagues.

"The generational transfer of wealth is underway, and community foundations are increasingly well-positioned to offer the options people need to make their dreams come true in the community. It's one thing to talk about the numbers and statistics; it's another to work with folks who are tremendously excited about putting their passion into action through philanthropy."

—Sheryl Aikman, Vice President, Development,
The Community Foundation of Western North Carolina

NATIONAL STANDARDS III.A

A community foundation has, or works to develop, broad support in the form of contributions from many separate, unrelated donors with diverse charitable interests in the community served.

1.
BUILDING A CLIMATE OF GIVING

> **WHAT YOU WILL LEARN**
>
> This section discusses the world of donors—who they are, why they give and why they give specifically to community foundations. It discusses the choices donors have for their philanthropy and the value that community foundations bring them.

Who Are Potential Donors to Community Foundations?

Behind every dollar raised, there is a donor. They are the heart and source of your resource development program. For your community foundation to cultivate donors, you must first understand their needs and motivations.

As development staff, the first thing you must do is identify possible donors. Who are they and how can you find them? Generally, donors fall into the following categories:

- Individuals
- Corporations
- Private foundations
- Nonprofit organizations and civic groups
- Government agencies.

Individual donors will be your biggest source for funds. You will want to consider different types of individuals and reach out to many groups. Think about the demographics you would like to attract—both today and in the future. Potential groups include:

- African American, Asian American, Latino and Native American individuals and families.
- Individuals and families with disposable wealth.
- Youth.
- Women.
- Farmers and land owners.
- Venture philanthropists, entrepreneurs and small business owners.
- Gay/lesbian individuals and families.

Once you have identified key prospects, you can research what motivates them to give.

Why Do People Give?

Most donors give for altruistic reasons. They want to do something good for the community. They want to help others. They want to make a difference. As altruistic as motives may be, donors also give out of self-interest. They want to feel good about themselves. They want their gift to be effective, to see their dollars well spent. They also hope to get the largest possible tax deduction for their gift.

Why do individual donors give? Although some have strictly personal reasons why they give, many donors say they give to:

- **Give back.** The "give-backers" believe in generosity and were perhaps raised in a culture of philanthropy. They give to show thanks to the community that helped them succeed at their own business or personal venture.

- **Create a legacy.** The "legacy-creators" hope to immortalize a part of themselves. They want to perpetuate their memory and values after their death, and they want their own name, or family name, to live on.

- **Memorialize someone.** The "memorializers" give in honor of someone else—parents, a spouse, a deceased loved one. Groups of people might establish a fund to honor an inspiring individual—a teacher, pastor or coach, for example. Memorial gifts may also be in response to a tragedy or disaster.

- **Gain recognition.** The "socialites" want to be grouped in a certain social standing. They give because their peers give and because they want to feel generous.

Other reasons why people give:

- To honor a milestone, such as an anniversary
- For a specific cause or organization to which they feel connected
- For estate or current tax benefits
- Because they have no heirs and don't want the government to be their main beneficiary.

Learning these common reasons why people give will make your job as development staff easier and more effective. Once you understand how to appeal to their motives, you will be able ask potential donors the right questions—and provide the right answers.

The likelihood of prospects becoming actual donors depends on many circumstances. It helps to know these reasons as you approach prospects, so that you can appeal to their interests. Some of these circumstances include:

- Closeness of the relationship with your foundation
- Personal and financial circumstances
- Age and work/retirement status
- Family change
- Financial windfall
- Involvement in the community and with your foundation
- Giving history—both to the foundation and to other organizations
- Interest and involvement in multiple organizations
- Passion for the community
- Relationship to the person who referred them to the community foundation.

What Are the Advantages of Giving through Community Foundations?

Community foundations are in the business of persuading people to give. Community foundations offer potential donors a variety of outlets for their charitable goals.

Everyone involved with your foundation must be able to communicate the specific value of community foundations over other vehicles. As development staff, you can help board and staff colleagues understand this value. For example, you might give them talking points for when they speak in public and provide them with the "Top Ten Reasons" why people give to community foundations.

Top Ten Reasons People Give through Community Foundations

Community foundations:

- Are **local organizations** with deep roots in the community.
- Offer a staff with **broad expertise** regarding community issues and needs.
- Provide highly **personalized service** tailored to each individual's charitable and financial interests.
- Help people invest in the **causes they care about most**.
- Accept a wide **variety of assets** and can facilitate even the most complex forms of giving.
- Partner with **professional advisors** to create highly effective approaches to charitable giving.
- Offer maximum **tax advantage** under state and federal law.
- **Multiply the impact** of gift dollars by pooling them with other gifts and grants.
- Build **permanent funds** that benefit the community forever and help create personal legacies.
- Are **community leaders**, convening agencies and coordinating resources to create positive change.

Institutions give through community foundations for many of their own reasons. Some of these reasons are listed here.

Private foundations give to:

- Leverage funds for specific charitable interests.
- Distribute grants in locations where the foundation has an interest, but limited local knowledge.
- Give outside the private foundation's defined philanthropic area of interest.
- Eliminate the administrative burden by transferring an existing foundation into a donor-advised fund or supporting organization.
- Transfer to a designated, field of interest or unrestricted fund when the family is no longer interested in participating in the foundation.

Corporations give to:
- Involve employees in philanthropy
- Reduce or eliminate the need for a staffed corporate giving program
- Gain good public relations
- Receive information on community needs.

Nonprofit organizations and civic groups give to:
- Expand their marketing exposure
- Gain expert stewardship on permanent funds
- Give donors choices in ways to support the organization.

What Choices Do Donors Have for Their Philanthropy?

Your board and staff should understand the choices donors have today, as well as the advantages and limitations of each.

In today's giving market, donors have many choices. As the demand has grown for giving vehicles, so too has the supply. More organizations now provide ways for donors to exercise their philanthropy, creating a competitive market for philanthropic dollars.

Your board and staff should understand the choices donors have today, as well as the advantages and limitations of each. By learning about a donor's many options, you can distinguish for them the community foundation's value above all the rest.

The Value of Community Foundations

With so many choices for their philanthropy, why should donors choose your community foundation? Community foundations offer donors the following bang for their buck:

- Permanence
- Flexibility
- Local control
- Connection to place/home
- Knowledge of local community
- Donor recognition (named funds)
- Vehicle to establish a legacy through a named endowment fund
- Investment management for assets
- Maximum investment returns for pooled funds
- Maximum tax advantage allowed by the law
- Minimal red tape
- Ability to accept complex gift types
- Various fund types to fill donors needs
- Ability to leverage contributions for maximum benefit
- Support of the whole community
- The chance to be part of a national movement.

Donors might choose the following philanthropic vehicles:

- Funds at community foundations
- Funds at other host organizations
- Direct gifts to nonprofits
- Supporting organizations at community foundations
- Private foundations.

Funds through Community Foundations

Community foundations are skilled at receiving and managing gifts of cash, real estate and assets such as privately held business interests, including venture capital and intellectual property. By creating a fund through a community foundation, donors receive the knowledge and wide range of services from a staff that knows and lives in the community it serves.

Community foundations offer a variety of funds to meet donors' needs. A **designated fund** allows a donor to identify which specific public charity to support. A **field-of-interest fund** enables donors to specify a general area of interest, such as education or healthcare, trusting in the community foundation to select individual grantees. Donors also have the option to give general gifts of support to the community foundation, called **unrestricted funds**, which can carry the donor's name

Donor-advised funds have become one of the most commonly used vehicles for giving and for good reason: They offer a relatively easy, low-cost alternative to private foundations, with greater tax benefits. Donors can give cash, stock or other assets; claim a charitable deduction on their income tax returns; and recommend how the money in the fund should be granted to charity. The donated funds are invested in the financial market. Donor-advised funds vary in minimum investment level and administrative fees.

Funds through Other Host Organizations

Donors now have a choice among many organizations for donor-advised funds. Universities and colleges, religious organizations, hospitals and some public foundations offer donor-advised giving options for their supporters. Charities sponsored by financial institutions such as Fidelity Investments and Charles Schwab also offer donor-advised funds. These funds may not offer the same level of donor education or variety in funds that a community foundation does. Let donors know that if they are looking for peer networking and broad community knowledge, a community foundation is the right choice for them.

Direct Gifts to Nonprofits

One of the most common ways people give is by writing a check to one of the hundreds of thousands of charities in the United States. Giving directly to charities can be easy if donors already know which organizations they want to support and if they want the charities to receive gifts immediately. But direct giving can have drawbacks for a donor. It requires them to conduct their own research, evaluate each charity and keep records of gift receipts for tax-reporting purposes. Community foundations do this work for the donor.

Supporting Organizations at a Community Foundation

A supporting organization qualifies as a public charity without having to meet the public support test. A supporting organization remains a separate entity from the community foundation—it has its own board of directors, makes its own investment and grantmaking decisions, and has its own tax-exempt status from the IRS.

Supporting organizations give donors a separate identity from the community foundation and more control over grantmaking and investment. For example, donors can establish different grant criteria from the community foundation and make independent investment policies. A supporting organization makes an attractive alternative to those considering a private foundation, as they offer more involvement without the administrative burden.

For more information on the legal rules for supporting organizations, read Supporting Organizations and How They Work, *by John A. Edie, Council on Foundations, 2003 at www.cof.org.*

Private Foundations

Some individuals and families establish **private/independent** or **private/family foundations** to have maximum control over grantmaking and to create a legacy of giving. Private foundations make grants based on charitable endowments. Because of their endowments, they are focused primarily on grantmaking and generally do not actively raise funds or seek public financial support.

Others establish **private operating foundations**, using the bulk of their resources to provide charitable services or run charitable programs of their own. They make few, if any, grants to outside organizations and, like independent and family foundations, they generally do not raise funds from the public.

Establishing a private foundation can be expensive and time-consuming, however, and donors generally need the assistance of lawyers, accountants and administrators. Private foundations are subject to an excise tax on net investment income, including net capital gains. Moreover, after the donor's death, the foundation may pass to heirs or others who may not have the time, skills, resources or interest to continue the donor's original intent.

For donors with the ability to make substantial gifts, community foundations offer a significant cost savings over establishing a private foundation. With a community foundation, administrative costs are shared among all funds and kept to a minimum. Donors can also make smaller gifts through a community foundation than they would a private foundation. *To learn how community foundations can market to private foundations, see the Private Foundation Portfolio on www.cfmarketplace.org.*

2. CREATING FUNDS

WHAT YOU WILL LEARN

Find out what gifts donors can make and the funds they can choose. Learn how to build permanent unrestricted funds and what policies you need for accepting and rejecting gifts.

How Do Community Foundations Build Permanent Unrestricted Funds?

To serve its community over time, the National Standards imply that a community foundation must build long-term, preferably unrestricted, permanent funds. Community foundations build permanent funds to address changing needs over time. In short, permanent funds ensure a flow of money for grantmaking.

Community foundations have the most control over unrestricted permanent funds. In addition to permanent funds, however, community foundations also seek non-permanent funds that support community programs and provide operating funds.

The most common way to build permanent funds is to accept gifts from many separate donors and place those gifts into component funds. From these funds, community foundations invest the principal and use a portion of its earnings to benefit the community.

Community foundations use permanent funds by:

- Investing the principal (gift) for the long term to preserve the historical gift value and the real gift value.

- Distributing a percentage of the fund's assets in grants.

- Charging investment and administrative fees.

Building unrestricted permanent funds can challenge community foundations. It has been said that community foundations must be "in it for the long haul," meaning the results of their development efforts will likely be seen over time rather than overnight.

As a development staff, the more strategies you develop, the better your chances. Most find that good old-fashioned relationship building brings the best results. If you can form long-term trusted relationships with donors and their professional advisors, they will be more likely to give to the foundation in their lifetime and beyond.

To begin the work, consider the following tips:

Make a commitment to persist. Building permanent funds requires time and patience, as community foundations acquire knowledge, build skills, implement new practices and develop relationships.

Develop a comprehensive plan with realistic timelines and measurable outcomes. As part of planning, think about communications and evaluation of strategies in advance

Ask your fellow community foundation colleagues, other funders, consultants and experts about strategies and lessons they have learned from building unrestricted permanent funds.

With a successful strategy and the staff and financial resources to implement it, your community foundation can build permanent funds while generating visibility, new partnerships and new ideas.

What Gifts Can Donors Make?

Community foundations are versatile both in the gifts they can receive and in the types of funds they establish. Donors can contribute almost anything of tangible value to the foundation—cash, securities, real estate, jewelry, art and more.

These contributions can be used to establish a new fund or augment an existing one. Donors may let the board decide how to use the proceeds of the funds they establish, or they may advise the board of their wishes. They can also name the fund or choose to remain anonymous. With so many ways to give, community foundations offer donors a flexibility that they can't find through other giving vehicles.

> **NATIONAL STANDARDS**
> **I.A**
> A community foundation [has] a long-term goal of building permanent, named component funds established by many separate donors.

Assets for Giving

Donors can make gifts of:

- Cash
- Publicly traded securities (stocks or bonds)
- IRA accounts or other retirement plans
- Life insurance
- An interest in a residence or farm
- Real estate
- Closely held business interests
- Charitable bequest
- Charity as alternate beneficiary.

Gifts can be outright or of a remainder interest. They can be made during a donor's life or as a bequest in the donor's will.

Gifts of cash

Donors first think of giving cash. Cash gifts can be in the form of currency, money orders, checks or credit card charges. Some donors may contribute to a specific fund within the community foundation, the income of which is used to make charitable grants in the community. Other donors establish a named fund and contribute to it over the years. Donors usually receive full income tax deduction for the contribution in the year they make it; however, if the gift is unusually large—that is, it exceeds 50 percent of the donor's adjusted gross income—the donor will need to carry over the excess to the next year. Excess deductions can be carried over for up to five years if necessary. Such a gift has great flexibility and gives the donor immediate and maximum tax deductibility. Community foundations know the value of cash gifts upfront, and the funds are immediately available for use.

Gifts of securities (stocks or bonds)
Appreciated securities are stocks or bonds that are now worth more than when the donor bought them. When donors make gifts of securities, they can give more at a lower cost than giving cash. In addition to receiving an income tax deduction, they also avoid paying capital gains tax on the appreciated value of the securities. Publicly traded securities are easy to value and sell, directing the proceeds to the fund of the donor's choice. As in the case of large gifts of cash, donors who make substantial gifts of securities, or any other property, may need to carry forward excess distributions to future years. Donors are permitted to deduct gifts of property in any one year up to 30 percent of their adjusted gross incomes.

Gifts of IRA accounts or other retirement plans
Donors can make lifetime gifts of retirement plan assets, or they can name the community foundation as the beneficiary of their retirement plan assets in their will. Because the proceeds of the retirement account are taxable to the beneficiary, good estate planning often dictates leaving retirement amounts to charity at death while bequeathing other assets to heirs. The gift may also reduce the donor's estate taxes as well.

Life insurance
Donors can name the community foundation as the owner and beneficiary of a life insurance policy. If the policy is not paid up, the donor can either make remaining payments directly or give the foundation the funds with which to make payments. Donors receive an immediate tax deduction—usually in an amount approximately equal to the cash surrender value. The annual premium the donor continues to pay qualifies for a tax deduction. The proceeds pass to the community foundation, free of estate tax. Donors must obtain a qualified appraisal to substantiate gifts of life insurance valued at more than $5,000.

With gifts of life insurance, community foundations should also develop a procedure for keeping the policy in effect, or surrendering it, if the donor discontinues paying premiums. Some life insurance gifts can be complex. Community foundations should develop gift acceptance policies that address which gifts the community foundation will accept and those it will not.

An interest in a residence or a farm
Often referred to as a life estate, donors may make a gift of their homes or farms, but retain the right to use them during their lifetime. Donors gain an immediate tax deduction for the value of the charity's remainder interest. Because the property will pass to the charity upon the death of the donor, it will not be subject to estate tax. The community foundation will usually sell the property and use the proceeds to establish a permanent fund in the name of the donor. Before accepting a life-estate gift, the community foundation should negotiate a clear agreement with the donor covering such issues as who will be responsible for expenses such as maintenance and repairs and property taxes and what documentation the community foundation will require to show that the donor has made required payments. Donors must obtain a qualified appraisal to substantiate the value of the gift.

Real estate
When giving real property, a donor can avoid capital gains on appreciation of assets and receive an immediate tax deduction at market value. At the time of the donor's death, there will be no estate taxes on the gifted portion. When the property is eventually sold, the proceeds are used to establish a permanent fund in the community foundation.

Community foundations should develop gift acceptance policies for real estate that cover such issues as the value of the gift, whether it is readily marketable, the circumstances under which an environmental scan will be required and who will be responsible for carrying costs if the property cannot be liquidated immediately. Donors must obtain a qualified appraisal to substantiate the value of the gift.

For more information on gifts of real estate, see "Tools of Giving" on www.cfmarketplace.org.

Closely held business interests
Donors who own a closely held business can transfer ownership, in whole or in part, to the community foundation, thereby minimizing tax liability. Donors can claim a charitable deduction for the fair market value of the stock. Usually, the business itself or the other owners will repurchase the contributed share, but this cannot be required or compelled as a condition of the gift. Donors must obtain a qualified appraisal to substantiate the value of the gift. If liquidation is likely to take some time, donors should be asked to contribute sufficient cash to permit the fund to make grants at a level that is commensurate with the fund's assets.

Charitable bequests
Charitable bequests enable donors to provide for their community after their death. Donors can make a bequest in their will to a community foundation for a specific amount, a particular asset or a remainder interest. They can request that the bequest be used to establish a fund in their name, or be used for unrestricted purposes, designated charities or a particular field of interest. Bequests allow donors to make larger gifts without having to part with assets during their lifetime. They also significantly reduce estate taxes. Bequests are not available until estates are settled after the donor's death; and values may change during that period. Some gifts make better bequests, such as tangible personal property (e.g., art, antiques, jewelry) and IRAs.

When a donor voluntarily informs your community foundation that a bequest has been planned, be sure to thank the donor in advance. Statistics show that some 30 percent of bequest gifts to charity are changed during a person's last few months of life—unfortunately, because they were ignored by the designated charity.

Charity as an alternate beneficiary
Some donors write a "common disaster" or contingent beneficiary clauses in their wills. If the named beneficiaries in the will die in a common disaster or do not survive the donors, the assets go to the community foundation.

Gifts That Produce Lifetime Income

Some gifts produce **income for life** or for a fixed term (and are also called split-interest gifts):

- Fixed Income
- Variable Income
- Charitable gift annuity
- Pooled life income fund.

Fixed income
Donors can create deferred gifts to receive lifetime income for themselves or their designees. A charitable remainder annuity trust may reduce income taxes for up to six years, reduce estate taxes and generate a lifetime income with the same amount each year. At the end of the term, usually the death of the first beneficiary, the remainder of the trust passes to the community foundation to create a fund for whatever charitable purposes the donor specified. These funds are deferred, meaning they are not immediately available for grants, and they are not recorded as gifts until the termination of the beneficiary's interest.

Variable income
Donors who receive an income that may grow over the years can arrange for a charitable remainder unitrust instead of an annuity trust. Donors specify a percentage (i.e., five percent) of the fund's assets that will be paid to them each year, instead of a fixed number of dollars. If the assets grow, their income grows. However, if assets decline, so does the beneficiary's income.

Charitable gift annuity
A charitable gift annuity is a contract between the donor and the community foundation, guaranteed by the foundation's assets. In exchange for the gift, the foundation pays the donor (and the spouse, if designated) a fixed amount for the term of the annuity—usually the beneficiary's life. Be sure to check your state laws regarding charitable gift annuities, as regulations may differ.

Pooled life income fund
Some community foundations maintain a pooled income fund, which pools gifts from many donors of a minimum contribution (such as $5,000). Donors receive income during their lifetime, with the option to have the income go to their spouse upon death. Upon the death of the last beneficiary, the funds transfer to the foundation for the purposes specified by the donor.

Planned gifts generally afford donors an immediate tax deduction for the predicted value of what will remain for charitable use, discounted for present value. For charitable gift annuities, the deduction is based on the difference between the total amount paid to the charity and the value of the annuity. Income donors will receive will be taxed at varying rates depending on the gift vehicle and whether the income is considered return of principle, capital gain or ordinary income.

Special Giving Options

In addition, community foundations offer **special giving options**, which include:

- Charitable lead trust
- Transfer of a private foundation
- Giving option for private foundation
- Corporate giving in the community
- Estate or trust—gift to charity
- Charitable organization closing.

Charitable lead trust
Charitable lead trusts allow donors to use a portion of their assets to create a trust, the income from which will go to the community foundation for a designated number of years. After a set number of years, the remaining principal of the trust and any accumulated appreciation returns to the donor's estate. Lead trusts often are used to minimize estate and generation-skipping taxes.

Transfer of private foundation
Private foundations that want to terminate can transfer their assets to the community foundation, creating a fund in their foundation's name or a supporting organization. Community foundations provide professional and cost-effective ways of administering private foundation assets. They can be an attractive alternative for private foundations that wish to continue their philanthropy without the administrative burden. The community foundation provides the private foundation with professional management and

investment practices, and ensures the foundation's purpose will be carried on in perpetuity.

Giving option for private foundation

Private foundations that don't want to transfer their entire assets to the community foundation can establish a named fund. This allows the private foundation to contribute part or all of the current year's income to the fund. Some private foundations establish funds with their community foundations to make anonymous gifts, to fund outside of mission or to make small gifts. Others do so to build relationships with the community foundation.

Corporate giving in the community

Corporations can also establish a named fund in the community foundation. Some do so to make anonymous gifts or for those outside their corporate giving program mission. Others do so to support the work of the community foundation. Corporations may also use their community foundation as a way to manage corporate contributions, as community foundations can help identify grantees and in some cases, provide administrative services.

Estate or Trust—gift to charity

Donors who are the executors or trustees under a will may be able to establish a fund with the community foundation in the name of the person who died. Depending on state law and with the approval of the court, if necessary, they may be able to distribute testamentary charitable trusts to the community foundation. The foundation is usually fully qualified to receive the charitable portion of the estate, and the burden of carrying out the charitable provisions would remain under the guidance of the foundation.

Charitable organization closing

Charitable organizations that are closing can transfer their assets to the community foundation, creating a fund in their organization's name. This allows the organization to continue its charitable mission into the future without the administrative burden of operations.

Excerpts from the above adapted from the Community Foundation Academy for New Trustees and Staff, "Characteristics and Roles" and the Central New York Community Foundation at www.cnycf.org.

> **NATIONAL STANDARDS III.D**
>
> A community foundation accepts and administers a diversity of gift and fund types to meet the varied philanthropic objectives of donors.

What Laws Do You Need to Know?

Your community foundation is subject to federal, state and local laws. It is important that both staff and board understand the legal parameters of their work; the implications of making certain decisions; and the need for policies, controls and knowledgeable legal counsel. For information on material restrictions for funds, UMIFA, Financial Accounting Standards Board (FASB) and more, see the *"Management, Finance and Administration"* chapter.

What Funds Can Donors Create?

Community foundation assets are held in many named component funds established by donors or the foundation for specific or unrestricted purposes. A fund designates resources for specific activities or charitable aims. Community foundations offer a variety of funds, enabling donors to achieve their charitable objectives.

Major Types of Funds

- Unrestricted fund
- Field-of-interest fund
- Donor-advised fund
- Designated fund for one or more organizations
- Organization endowment fund
- Scholarship fund
- Group memorial fund
- Supporting organizations
- Special projects fund/other fund types.

A discussion of the most common types of funds follows. Some funds may be a combination of the following types (such as designated and field of interest) within the same component fund.

Unrestricted

The donor allows the community foundation the discretion to use available grant dollars for a broad range of community issues. This provides the foundation the opportunity to respond to changing community needs that often cannot be anticipated at the time the gift is made.

Field of Interest

The donor instructs the community foundation to use the available grant dollars in a particular program area, such as education, health, youth, the environment and so forth, rather than restricting the money to one organization. The foundation determines the specific recipient. Field of interest funds are flexible enough to meet changing community needs in a specific interest area.

Donor-Advised

Establishing a donor-advised fund allows the donor to actively participate in the grantmaking process by periodically recommending how to use the gift. The community foundation verifies that the donor's recommendations meet its grantmaking policies and that the grantee organization is a qualified public charity or governmental entity. The foundation's board of directors has final approval of these recommendations. Grant awards are issued to charities in the name of the fund (or anonymously if the donor prefers), and contributions to the fund qualify for income tax deduction in the year they are made.

Designated

The donor instructs the community foundation to pay available grant dollars to one or more specific named charitable organizations, usually in perpetuity. Donations are then sent in the donor's name each year. Because the gift is given through the community foundation, the organization also receives services for planned giving and investment. The foundation monitors how donations are used to be sure a need always exists.

Organization Endowment

Public charities can establish an organization endowment fund at the community foundation. These funds offer community organizations a simple and efficient way to build an endowment and create sustainability. The community foundation helps the organization with planning, investing and administering the funds, as well as distributes grant dollars to the organization, as available for general purposes.

Scholarships

Scholarship funds allow donors to invest in the community's future and help deserving students—from preschool to postgraduate—achieve their lifetime dreams. These funds provide support for individuals pursuing a training or educational opportunity. As part of the fund, donors can specify certain eligibility criteria, such as the school(s) students must graduate from or be admitted to. Grants may be awarded to the individuals themselves, provided the foundation does the required follow-up, or to the educational institutions.

Memorial Fund

In the event of a tragedy, disaster or death, donors can establish a fund in the name of those who lost their lives. A group of people contributes to the fund, which is a permanent living memorial. Often these funds are dedicated to a particular field of interest.

Supporting Organization

A supporting organization is a separate charitable organization, a 509(a)(3) that attaches itself to the community foundation and enjoys its favorable public charity status. Donors who establish a supporting organization select some of the board members, maintain personal involvement and support their chosen causes. The community foundation appoints one or more board members; manages the investments; and administers the startup costs, grants and reporting.

Special Project/Other Fund Types

Some community foundations have additional types of funds such as pass-through funds, project funds, disaster relief or emergency hardship, acorn funds and so forth. These funds are generally established for limited purposes or to support the work of a non-501(c)(3) organization. They are generally not permanent.

Considerations for Donor-advised Funds

Community foundations have offered donor-advised funds since at least 1931. Even so, these funds have boomed in the last decade. Although most community foundations agree that unrestricted money is their most valuable asset, almost all now accept advised gifts and actively seek them. Some do so as a strategy to build permanent funds over time. For example, most donors want to participate in the grant process to see their dollars at work. Advised funds attract these donors and establish long-term relationships with them.

What are some ways your community foundation can accept donor-advised gifts while building an unrestricted endowment? Some community foundations:

- Place a limit on the advisory relationship of successive generations. At the end of a certain period, they ask the donor to let the gift evolve into a non-advised fund or part of the unrestricted endowment.
- Accept advised funds on the condition that donors commit a percentage of the total amount given to non-donor-advised use.
- Accept advised funds only from donors who agree to make a testamentary gift of unrestricted funds.

Most community foundations have an explicit policy guiding the acceptance of advised funds. Some require a minimum contribution of $10,000 to set up a fund; others have higher minimums.

Keep in mind: The fund minimums you set may have implications on your operations and your image. Community foundations should understand the costs associated with their activities. The Foundation Strategy Group (FSG) has developed a set of free tools to help community foundations do a cost-revenue analysis by better understanding their current economics and the implications of potential strategic and operational changes.

For more information and to access this tool, visit www.foundationstrategy.com.

Benefits of Various Funds

Type of Fund	Benefits to Donors	Benefits to Recipients
Unrestricted	Supports a wide spectrum of the community in perpetuity; casts donors as charitable visionaries; allows support to change as communities change	Addresses issues that may not be supported by restricted funds; provides for changing community needs; enables strategic grantmaking initiatives; funds innovative ideas; offers maximum flexibility
Field of Interest	Matches grantmaking with donor interest; recognizes donors for their interest; allows flexibility to provide grants for new organizations and programs in the future	Provides more resources for a particular field; narrows competition for grants from other fields; funds a variety of organizations; focuses community attention
Donor-advised	Attractive alternative to private foundations; flexible; actively involves donors and successors in grantmaking; teaches younger generations; builds relationship with the foundation	Provides support for select nonprofits; actively involves interested donors with specific nonprofits
Designated	Allows guidance during and after lifetime; gives donors an identity with nonprofits	Provides ongoing support, financial security and non-competitive funds; connects donors and nonprofits forever
Organization Fund	Smaller funds enjoy professional management at low fees, exposure and flexibility in the community	Provides operating support, financial security and non-competitive funds for an organization
Scholarships	Allows donors to recognize outstanding students; can establish a memorial to loved ones; sets example for younger generations	Provides needed funds for education; recognizes recipients and the institution; exposes recipient to philanthropy

Source: "Endowment Options," The Winston-Salem Foundation, www.wsfoundation.org

What Should You Consider When Seeking and Accepting Gifts?

With great flexibility and versatility, community foundations accept many types of gifts to meet the needs of their donors. Some community foundations initiate development programs by focusing on specific kinds of funds, such as donor-advised funds. Others focus on specific gift vehicles such as bequests or charitable gift annuities.

The gifts your community foundation accepts, however, can directly affect your operations. Before you accept a gift, always consider the added administrative responsibilities and stewardship requirements of each gift.

First things first: Will it cost the foundation money?

Your community foundation must be wary of accepting gifts with little or no cash value or those that will cost the foundation money. Property, for example, is one gift that can benefit the donor, sometimes at little or no benefit to the foundation. Donors sometimes attempt to unload property that is worthless or troublesome, or perhaps overvalued, in dispute or somehow unusable. Before you accept a gift, make sure it in fact has the value it appears to have—and that it won't cost your foundation more than you get.

When can the gift be used?

Before a community foundation accepts a gift, it should consider when the gift will actually be received by the foundation. This affects the grant cycle, as well as when funds will be recorded as income to the foundation.

Outright gifts permit the immediate use of the gift assets. Examples include cash, appreciated assets, tangible personal property and a charitable lead trust.

Deferred gifts require the foundation to wait, sometimes for many years, until it can access the funds. There are two types of deferred gifts—those that provide income back to the donor or a person the donor designates, and those that a donor has promised to make at a future time, such as a promised bequest in the donor's will. Usually the donor may have a change of heart with respect to the second category.

By knowing when a gift will actually be available, you can budget and plan your grant calendar in advance.

How much staff time will it require?

Some funds require more staff time than others. Scholarships, for example, take a lot of work to establish and administer. Donor-advised funds can also be labor intensive, as staff will process donor recommendations for grants sometimes several times a year. Field-of-interest funds may entail advisory committee meetings, sometimes in outlying areas, that must be staffed. Other funds (such as organization endowment funds and scholarships) may become involved in fundraising campaigns and events, and may generate numerous small gifts. You should know what your staff can handle before accepting the gift.

How will it affect the community foundation's image?

Certain funds might affect your image in the community and your ability to attract potential donors. For example, if a foundation allows too many field-of-interest funds, its mission might appear "all over the map." As an unintended result, this might dilute attempts at effective fund development. In contrast, a foundation with too few field-of-interest funds may appear too "single interest" instead of viewed as supporting the whole community. Most community foundations seek a balance in funds and constantly work to keep their public image in good standing.

■ FROM THE FIELD: TWO VIEWS ON DONOR-ADVISED FUNDS

Q: What does your foundation consider a higher priority—being a "community endowment builder" or a "philanthropic facilitator"?

A: We consider our job cultivating future philanthropists, building family around philanthropic values and providing research/information to make charitable giving a positive, life-changing experience. With that premise, 99 percent of our donor-advised funds are non-endowed and may recommend grants of any size as often as weekly, without geographic restrictions. In most situations, we encourage unlimited successor advisors and allow donors to recommend numerous investment manager options."

A: "We now primarily speak of our role as a center for philanthropy rather than an endowment builder, but our policies are still biased toward endowment building. We encourage donors not to have more than one generation of successor advisors. Our guidelines urge that after the first generation of advisors, the fund becomes an endowment. Regarding trust administration, we provide an incentive (a fee reduction) to charitable remainder trust donors who allocate at least 50 percent of the remainder for unrestricted purposes; trust remainders must be endowed.

Excerpt from "Donor-Advised Funds: A Tale from Two Cities," by Stuart Appelbaum and Bryan Clontz, Foundation News & Commentary, *May/June 2002.*

What is the charitable intent?
When accepting a new gift, a community foundation should always consider the intent behind it. Why does the donor want to give? Is it for altruistic reasons, or is it purely for the self-benefit it will bring? Self-interest alone should not be a sufficient reason for a donor to give to a community foundation. Although most donors do give for tax reasons, they should also intend for their gift to benefit the community.

Be aware that donors may ask the community foundation to do something illegal or unfavorable with their gift. To avoid such circumstances, your community foundation should consider developing standards on the gifts it accepts and the donor intent that is—and is not—appropriate.

What is the minimum size for funds that donors can create?
Finally, the foundation needs to decide and set policy on a minimum fund size. This isn't always an easy decision as there are pros and cons on both sides. If a community foundation sets too high a minimum, it may create an impression that philanthropy is only for the wealthy. Setting low minimums will attract smaller scale donors, creating an image of inclusiveness and accessibility. However, smaller funds may require more staff time, and fees may not cover administration costs.

Should you ever agree to hold a gift?
Most foundations follow a policy that calls for prompt liquidations of gifts. Generally, the foundation should never agree to a donor's request to hold onto a gift. Such an agreement violates the material restriction rules and could lead to the reclassification of the donor's fund as a private foundation. It also will lower the value of the gift and the value of the donor's tax deduction. The only exceptions to this rule are when the gift consists of property that the community foundation will keep and directly employ in furtherance of its mission, such as a historic property that will be the foundation's office, or if the asset is subject to governmental restrictions on sale, such as pre-IPO stock.

What Policies Do You Need for Gifts and Funds?

Your community foundation should be clear on which gifts, grants and funds it will accept and reject. By creating clear and consistent gift acceptance policies and fund agreements, you promote your accountability to donors and the community, and protect the integrity of your community foundation.

Gift Acceptance Policies

Gift acceptance policies are important for many reasons. They protect community foundations from accepting gifts and assets that could put it at substantial risk. They help the community foundation avoid accepting gifts that have excessive service costs. Moreover, they ensure donors receive consistent and fair treatment.

To comply with the National Standards, gift acceptance policies should include the following:

- Types and specifications of funds offered.

- Types and specifications of gifts and asset types accepted (or not accepted).

- Procedures for accepting gifts and establishing funds, including any necessary approvals.

- Conditions under which board approval is required to accept a gift or asset type or establish a fund.

- Minimum amount to set up a new fund.

- Procedures for disclosing to donors during the gift planning process the names and relationships of all parties involved.

> **NATIONAL STANDARDS**
> **III.E**
> A community foundation adopts gift and fund acceptance policies that address minimum fund size, types of fund options, types of gift mechanisms, and policies and procedures for accepting various types of assets and makes these policies available upon request.

Your foundation should customize its own policies based on what you want to provide and can handle internally. You might include, for example, information about the purpose of the development program, the roles of board and staff in promoting and accepting gifts, and guidelines for gift stewardship—including donor recognition and a description of the period in which gifts are to be acknowledged.

Some foundations create two versions of their written policies—a full version they keep on hand and a second, user-friendly version they share with donors and advisors that is simple and pertinent to the transaction or inquiry.

Gift Acceptance Checklist

Consider the following questions before accepting gifts:

- Does the gift remain true to the foundation's mission?
- What is the charitable intent behind the gift?
- How many restrictions are placed on the gift?
- Are the restrictions legally allowable or do they violate the material restrictions rules?
- How much staff time will it require to administer?
- Will the gift cost the community foundation money? (e.g., liens, gifts that are subject to taxes)
- How much administrative support will the gift require?
- What will be the minimum size of funds?
- How easy is the gift to liquidate?
- If a gift may take time to sell, what carrying changes and risks will the foundation incur?

Fund Agreements

Fund agreements define expectations for donors on what the community foundation will do with gifts. To comply with National Standards, fund agreements should include:

- Terms and conditions for each fund.
- Language consistent with the status of all gifts as irrevocable.
- Language consistent with the community foundation board having legal and fiduciary control over gifts.
- For any fund that specifies a particular charitable purpose or names a particular charitable organization as beneficiary, including organization endowments, designated funds, field of interest funds and scholarship funds, language stating that the board possesses variance power with respect to that fund.
- Language that does not suggest excessive donor control or otherwise give rise to material restrictions.

Fund agreements for donor-advised funds require additional explanations. Donor-advised fund agreements or guidelines for donor advisors should clearly state:

- Process for how the foundation will communicate to donors the limits on their authority and about board control.
- A description of the board's role in advised fund distributions.
- Prohibition against donor-advised funds being used to fulfill pledges and/or to secure benefits from the distribution recipient.
- List of any geographic constraints to donor-advised distributions.
- The process for acting on donor recommendations.
- Policies regarding naming successors to provide donor recommendations.
- Policies regarding whether principal and/or interest can be distributed.

Note that explicit reference to variance power is *not* required for donor-advised funds, unless they are restricted to support for particular purposes or charities. Always ask your attorney to review fund agreements before you give them to donors.

Where to Find Samples

When developing gift acceptance policies and fund agreements, be sure to review sample policies from your colleagues. You might identify areas where you do not have an existing policy or practice, such as gifts of unusual assets. Ask your neighbor community foundations to share their policies, or Council members can visit the Council on Foundation's Standards & Effective Practices database for samples at http://bestpractices.cof.org, or the Council's Center for Community Foundation Excellence courses. www.cof.org, COF CODE: **CCFE**.

3.
DESIGNING A DEVELOPMENT PLAN

What Should Your Resource Development Plan Include?

As development staff, the gifts you secure provide your foundation with the resources to help the community. But how do you begin?

Good resource development starts by increasing the community foundation's visibility and reputation within the community. To raise your visibility, you must have a plan—one that looks to both long- and short-term goals and guides your day-to-day work. Your plan will help the public see your foundation not just as a fundraiser, but also as an advocate that makes the community a better place to live.

Elements of a Strategic Development Plan

- **Long- and Short-term Goals**—*Where will the foundation be in five or ten years?*

- **Objectives**—*What does the board hope to achieve? Be sure to include more than monetary objectives.*

- **Target Audiences**—*Who are the groups of current donors? Who are potential donors? What market segments will you focus on?*

- **Strategies**—*How will you communicate with target audiences (initially and ongoing)? What tools will you use (campaigns, direct mail, websites, presentations)?*

- **Roles**—*Who will do what? What are the responsibilities and expectations of individual board members, staff members and/or volunteers?*

- **Timeline**—*When will you accomplish your objectives?*

- **Evaluation Measures**—*How will you measure your progress?*

You should develop a resource development plan that will attract the most prosperous markets of your community. To do so, you must get to know your community well. For example, where is most of the wealth concentrated? Is it held by a few individual estates or spread among individuals, corporations and private foundations? Once you have a picture of your community, you can focus your approach.

WHAT YOU WILL LEARN

This section will help you develop a plan for resource development. Learn how to identify and attract donors, build relationships with diverse groups and understand what affects a donor's decision to give. Find out what communications strategies will help you in development and how you can make presentations to potential donors and advisors. Discover what ongoing activities make for good donor relations.

> **NATIONAL STANDARDS**
>
> **III.C**
>
> A community foundation has a long-term goal of securing resources to address the changing needs of the community it serves.

What Is the Best Way to Identify and Approach Donors?

Identifying Donors

Start your development with the people closest to the foundation—those who know and care about it. These people include current and former board and committee members, as well as current donors and their family. They are your "inside" audience and can be your best bet for finding donors.

Ask your board, staff and even current donors who they know. For example, board members with corporate backgrounds might be able to identify sources of corporate wealth and motivate their business associates to give through the community foundation. Similarly, staff might have contacts from their former professions or from their university or religious institution.

From there, look to prospects outside the foundation, including:

- Professional advisors.
- Community leaders.
- Elderly long-time residents.
- People without heirs.
- Entrepreneurs/business owners.
- Board members of other nonprofits.
- Corporations.
- Private foundations.
- Charitable organizations.
- Government agencies.
- Parties representing judicial settlements (e.g., tobacco industry, utility overpayments)

Tips for Attracting Gifts

The following are some ways successful community foundations attract gifts and build permanent funds over time. They:

- Create a well-conceived development plan
- Build long-term trusted relationships with donors
- Build a relationship with and market to professional advisors
- Provide quality services and market products to donors and their advisors
- Build credibility in the community
- Emphasize personal visits and small gatherings rather than direct mail or special events
- Offer multiple and flexible options for donors and their advisors
- Demonstrate gifts that make a difference over a long period of time
- Offer donors an option of permanent recognition or anonymity
- Look to the long term rather than the immediate.

- People who were born and raised in your community and now live elsewhere.

This list is more than any foundation can cultivate at one given time. Pick one or two groups as your priority targets each year.

For more information on identifying donor audiences, see the "Communications, Marketing and Public Relations" chapter.

How Do You Build Relationships with Donors?

Using Different Approaches for Different Donors

You will vary your development strategies for each market segment. Soliciting gifts from individuals, for example, requires a different approach than soliciting gifts from corporations. Individuals often have personal reasons for giving, while institutions give for objective reasons.

Although your approaches will vary for different donors, your basic goals remain the same. Resource development is about building relationships. This means building relationships directly with potential donors, as well their peers, associates and advisors. As in any situation, a personal one-on-one approach creates the best impression and often brings the most success.

Individuals

When cultivating individual donors, patience and tenacity are key. The more visible your foundation, the more people will learn of its services and motivate others to give.

To reach potential donors directly, work through your board members. Encourage the board to talk to friends and business associates about becoming donors. Some community foundations hold special events, such as dinners, receptions and open houses, and ask board members to invite their peers. After the meal, the CEO and development officer makes a brief presentation, explaining what the foundation is

---

Talking Points for Individual Donors

With older donors of wealth, discuss:
- Estate plans and charitable interests
- Inheritance tax advantages
- Planned giving and income enhancement vehicles
- Range of options for charitable interest
- Donor-advised fund for lifetime of donor, spouse and maybe children
- Tools for educating next generation about philanthropy
- Named funds to keep family giving in perpetuity.

With younger donors of wealth, discuss:
- Donor-advised funds
- Supporting organizations.

With individual donors of smaller gifts, discuss:
- Insurance vehicles to dramatically increase gift potential
- Gifts from professional practices
- Pledges over three to five years
- Planned giving vehicles that enhance income in retirement, such as pooled income funds, charitable trusts, life estate gifts.

and how it functions. They then give a general overview of donor options and describe the good that grants have done in the community. No request for contributions is made at the dinner, but within a week, the community foundation sends attendees a thank-you letter and contact information should they like to learn more.

You might also look to current donors to speak on behalf of the foundation. Donors "put their money where their mouth is," and for that reason, they can often motivate their peers to give. Profile donors in foundation reports or newsletters and encourage them to talk with their associates, friends and family. Ask donors to tell stories about why they gave and the impact of their gift in the community.

As you identify potential donors, invite them to serve on advisory committees or to volunteer in other ways. This will engage them in the community foundation and hopefully encourage them to become even more involved.

One of the best ways to reach individual donors is through professional advisors (for example, trust officers, estate or financial planners, attorneys and accountants). With the right guidance, these professionals educate their clients about your community foundation and can help gain testamentary and other deferred gifts. For more on professional advisors, see *Presentations to Professional Advisors* in this chapter.

For tools on how your community foundation can market to professional advisors, such as the Charitable Giving Kit for Professional Advisors, visit www.cfmarketplace.org or customize your own e-newsletter for professional advisors at www.cfmarketplace.org.

Corporations

Peer-to-peer solicitations can be as effective with corporations as with individual donors. Ask board members to encourage fellow executives to make company contributions to the community foundation. Because corporations are both competitive and publicity conscious, this strategy often works.

Most corporations will not give to a permanent fund. The best approach may be to ask for contributions for operations or for funding a special project. Present the corporation with a concise proposal (either in writing and/or in person) stating the foundation's case and specifying a dollar amount. Answer their number one question: What's the bottom line? This approach mirrors the way they like to do business.

Talking Points for Corporations

- Discuss advised funds for their charitable giving.
- Ask for challenge gifts.
- Request pledges over three to five years.
- Ask for operating support.
- Ask them to consider employee matching gift contributions.
- Ask for gifts of stock from employees.
- Present at a local corporate-giving roundtable session.
- Find the local or regional corporate grantmakers association and share information with members about corporate-advised funds.

■ FROM THE FIELD: SEVEN TIMES A CHARM

As part of its donor cultivation plan, one community foundation in the Midwest develops a communications calendar listing their top prospects. On the calendar, they tally how many times the foundation makes contact with each prospect—either in person, by publication or mail. Their goal? To contact each person seven times per year.

Private Foundations and Charitable Organizations

When it is in the best interest of all involved, charitable agencies and private foundations will transfer their assets to the community foundation. This usually occurs only after years of cumulative experience and trusted relationships.

Instead of waiting for these asset transfers to perhaps "one day happen," you can take an active approach. First, identify those organizations where there is potential for a transfer of assets. Cultivate board members, directors and anyone else with influence from that organization.

Your best prospects in private foundations are those with:

- Aging donors and board members
- One or two generations removed from the founder
- No heirs to perpetuate the foundation
- Board members who have diverging funding interests or who are geographically dispersed
- Those with a grantmaking pattern similar to the community foundation.

The best prospects in charitable organizations are those:

- With substantial endowments
- That rotate board members frequently
- That need investment expertise.

Often, you can approach private family foundations in much the same way you do individuals, as they are sometimes personally connected to the assets. Identify private foundation prospects through professional advisors, board members, local community events and regional/national philanthropy workshops. You can also find lists of private foundations through your state's attorney general's office or website, or the Foundation Center at www.fdncenter.org.

Government Agencies

Few community foundations target government gifts. Still, it helps to maintain contact with government agencies, especially at the state and local level. From government sources, you can learn about current pass-through funds and other programs that may be of benefit. Keep in mind that government grants may come with significant strings attached. Carefully weigh whether to accept such grants.

Talking Points for Private Foundations and Charitable Organizations

With private foundations, discuss:

- Outright grants in the form of a permanent unrestricted fund or for operations
- Matching gifts
- Opportunities for joint ventures in grantmaking
- How you might help them achieve their objectives
- How your community foundation might provide them with back-office administrative services (if applicable)
- Possible termination of their foundation by transferring assets into a component fund or a supporting organization.

With charitable organizations, discuss:

- Your endowment management services
- Existing organization endowment funds.

Start by familiarizing the following officials with your community foundation. Consider contacting the:

- State attorney general.
- State official responsible for overseeing charitable trusts and foundations.
- Heads of state administrative committees and legislative committees responsible for any activities related to the community foundation's programs.
- Mayor and members of the city council.
- Heads of city departments whose activities are related to the community foundation.

Send these officials your regular mailings. You might also meet key local players in person and invite them to your foundation's events. If you do, be clear in the invitation what you are asking of them, however. State whether they are invited as an attendee or whether you would like them to be part of the agenda.

What Activities Can You Use to Attract Donors?

Community foundations cultivate relationships with potential donors in countless ways. The list below is not exhaustive, but will give you plenty of ideas:

- Gatherings in board and committee members' homes
- Annual luncheon
- Guests at board meetings (especially attorneys and CPAs)
- Newsletters
- Acknowledgment/recognition events
- Roundtable discussions about community issues
- Community tours/site visits
- Informational breakfasts
- Volunteer opportunities, including foundation's grant committees
- Get-acquainted sessions at previously scheduled meetings
- Presentation of the foundation's "story" at monthly meetings of civic and social organizations
- Handwritten notes thanking people for their gifts of time or money
- Outreach to former residents and retirees.

How Can You Build Relationships with Diverse Donor Groups?

Although it is tempting to focus on the most accessible of potential donor groups, you should consider the demographic composition of your donor base and how you might expand in the future. According to National Standards, community foundations must develop contributions from many diverse donors, representing many charitable interests in the community. In addition to organizations, consider the following individual donor groups:

- African American, Asian American, Latino and Native American individuals and families
- Women
- Gay/lesbian individuals and families
- Youth.

When your foundation broadens its donor base, it demonstrates a commitment to inclusiveness. Once you start cultivating diverse prospects, you will find that many become loyal and major donors in the future.

How can you begin your search for diverse donors? Here are some ideas:

- Invite members of selected populations to participate in the foundation's work (committee membership, use of facilities, etc.).
- Establish internal structures such as diversity policies regarding board, staff and vendors.
- Select diverse organizations as grant recipients.
- Encourage the CEO or board members to meet more community members in person by attending events or festivals, making presentations, delivering grants in person, etc.
- Offer technical assistance to new and/or grassroots organizations.

Before contacting these groups, learn what methods are appropriate to their traditions and culture. Talk to key leaders from these groups and contact the Council's inclusiveness staff for helpful information (inclusive@cof.org).

What Communication Strategies Help in Development?

Behind every specific development strategy, you have one underlying objective: to increase your community foundation's visibility and reputation. To do this, you need clear strategies for communication.

Communication strategies can range anywhere from a simple one-on-one conversation to a highly publicized campaign. Your foundation will adopt the best strategies based on its philosophy, age, size and community. For example, a new foundation might conduct a hard-hitting marketing campaign to raise operating funds, while an established foundation might work quietly behind the scenes with professional advisors. *For more information, see the "Communications, Marketing and Public Relations" chapter.*

Presentations to Donors

Presentations can make a big impression on prospective donors and the community. As resource development staff, you might present at lunches with individual prospects, speeches before civic groups and private clubs or at informal gatherings of current and potential donors. You might also be asked to help the CEO or senior staff prepare for such presentations. Work in conjunction with the communications staff, if applicable, to develop key message points. *For more information on public speaking, see the "Communications, Marketing and Public Relations" chapter.*

Before making a presentation to donors, learn about your audience. Consider:

- What are the potential donor's interests? What causes and organizations have they supported in the past?

- What are their financial assets? What form do they take and how liquid are they?

- Who influences the prospective donors' investment decisions? Do they work with an estate planner, a trust officer, an accountant or attorney?

In any presentation, you will want to articulate the community foundation's mission, its major initiatives and its ability to assist donors in meeting their charitable objectives. Be sure to focus the presentation from the audience's point of view. Instead of blandly reporting on the foundation activities, describe them as "opportunities" for donors to help the causes they care about.

You can customize your own PowerPoint presentation for donors using tools from the National Marketing Action Team. Visit www.cfmarketplace.org to learn more.

Presentations to Professional Advisors

Your community foundation should ideally maintain active relationships with the professional advisors in your region—accountants, attorneys, brokers, estate planners, insurance agents, trust officers and so forth. To find professional advisors, you might:

- Ask current donors what advisors they use/have used.

- Ask individuals you already know to introduce you to new advisors.

- Create a professional advisor council to help you do your outreach.

- Maintain a database of advisors to keep them abreast of foundation activities and giving opportunities.

Set up meetings and make presentations to advisors, stressing how they can use the community foundation to inform their clients. Educate them on the types of funds offered and the variety of gifts the foundation accepts. Tell them about the foundation's history, its credibility in the community, its grantmaking activities and its investment policies.

Here are some tips for getting your message to professional advisors:

- Give presentations before professional associations—bar associations, associations of estate planners and accountants.

- Meet with advisors one-on-one.

- Publish brochures, e-newsletters and other materials designed for professional advisors.

- Send end-of-the-year letters to those advisors who have been active with the community foundation, giving them a list of brokers through whom stock can be transferred quickly and easily.

■ FROM THE FIELD: EDUCATING PROFESSIONAL ADVISORS

A community foundation can build its unrestricted assets by educating professional advisors. A community foundation in Canada, for example, conveys to advisors how valuable unrestricted dollars are to its community. The foundation's work has led one advisor to advocate for unrestricted funds, advising his clients to keep donor-advised funds for one generation only, after which the fund becomes unrestricted. The community foundation has found that donors are more apt to listen to what their advisors say, as opposed to a foundation with a vested interest.

- Host breakfasts or lunches for professional advisors and consider offering them continuing education credits.

When working with professional advisors, it's important to consider their point of view. Each professional advisor has different specialties, different training and different values. You should customize your approach to these advisors based on your understanding of their work. Find out what's important to them as well as their clients.

Aside from presentations to potential donors and donor advisors, other communication strategies include:

- Annual campaigns
- Special events
- Mailing lists
- Publications, such as newsletters and annual reports
- Websites and e-mail.

You can customize your own PowerPoint presentation for donors using tools from the National Marketing Action Team. Visit www.cfmarketplace.org to learn more. For more information on professional advisors and other communications strategies, see the "Communications, Marketing and Public Relations" chapter.

What Ongoing Activities Make for Good Donor Relations?

Current donors are your most promising source for new gifts. For this reason, it's vital to maintain good donor relations. Donors will appreciate the administrative services your community foundations can provide. Donor relations activities range from making a simple personal visit with each donor once a year to conducting entire donor education programs. As part of your donor relations plan, your foundation should at a minimum:

- Distribute gift guidelines
- Provide fund agreements
- Acknowledge gifts
- Offer administrative support
- Report back to donors on their funds
- Keep donors informed and engaged.

Looking for Professional Advisors?

If you need help locating professional advisors in your region, start by contacting these national associations:

American Bar Association—www.abanet.org/referral/home.html

American College of Trust and Estate Councils—www.actec.org

American Institute of CPAs—www.aicpa.org

Financial Planning Association—www.fpanet.org/plannersearch/plannersearchmain.cfm

Bank Securities Association—www.bsanet.org

Independent Insurance Agents of America—www.independentagent.com

National Association of Estate Planners—www.naepc.org/estate_planners.web

National Committee on Planned Giving—www.ncpg.org

Securities Industry Association—www.sia.com

Society of Certified Public Accountants—see websites for your state.

> **NATIONAL STANDARDS**
>
> **VI**
>
> A community foundation:
>
> A. Informs and educates donors about community issues and grantmaking opportunities.
>
> B. Actively involves donors in identifying and responding to community issues and opportunities.
>
> C. Promptly and accurately acknowledges gifts.
>
> D. Provides fund statements, at least annually, to those donors who wish to receive them.
>
> E. All private information obtained with respect to donors and prospects is kept confidential to the fullest extent possible.

Distribute Gift Guidelines

Before donors make a gift, you should distribute guidelines to avoid any confusion or unrealistic expectations. Gift guidelines instruct donor advisors, for example, on how to make grant recommendations; explain procedures for processing, approving and distributing those grants; and describe the foundation's other donor services.

For sample gift guidelines, see the Standards and Effectives Practices for Community Foundations website at http://bestpractices.cof.org.

Acknowledge Gifts

The IRS has issued specific requirements for gift acknowledgments. Your foundation should have standards and procedures in place to meet those requirements. Be sure the staff clearly understands who is responsible for each step. *For more information on these requirements, see IRS publication 1771, available at www.irs.gov/pub/irs-pdf/p1771.pdf*

To show good customer service, many foundations adopt gift acknowledgement policies that exceed IRS requirements. For example, some foundations acknowledge every gift within 48 hours of receipt and personally call donors for gifts above a certain dollar value. As with all of your donor interaction, gift acknowledgments should be both professional and gracious.

To comply with National Standards, your foundation should document and describe how it acknowledges gifts and within what time period you do so. Acknowledgement letters should include: (1) the name of the community foundation, (2) the amount of cash received or description (but not value) of non-cash property received and (3) a statement that no goods or services were received. If goods or services were received, you should describe what they were and give a good-faith estimate of their value.

Gifts of property (except publicly traded stock) valued at more than $5,000 require special acknowledgements. In addition to the requirements outlined above, the community foundation must execute Part IV, Section B, of IRS Form 8283. The community foundation's signature attests that it received the property described in the form and that it will file IRS Form 8282 and provide a copy to the donor if it disposes of the property within two years of the gift. Form 8282 reports the disposition price of the property. Part IV also asks whether the community foundation will use the donated property in carrying out its charitable mission. In signing Form 8283, the community foundation does not attest to the value of the gift.

Report Back to Donors on Their Funds

Fund statements provide donors with information about the status of their charitable funds. They are also a good way for the foundation to maintain relations with donors and update them on foundation activities and community needs. Different community foundations present fund statements in many different ways. *For sample fund statements, see the Council's Standards & Effectives Practices website at http://bestpractices.cof.org.*

When designing your fund statements, consider these questions:

- How often should you send fund statements?
- How personalized should the fund statements be?
- What information do you want to give donors?
- What format should the statements take—e.g. letter, newsletter or part of the annual report?
- Should you make fund statements available to donors online?

To comply with National Standards, you should send donors at least one fund statement per year, although most community foundations provide them more frequently (some offer them on demand via the web). You should track donor preferences regarding fund statements and document how often you distribute statements.

Keep Donors Informed and Engaged

Donors are your best source for additional gifts and for larger "legacy" gifts in the future. It's important to continually involve donors with their fund to keep them interested and excited about their philanthropy.

How do you sustain donor interest over time? Here are some ideas:

- Meet with new donors, giving them a welcome packet of information about the foundation and fund.
- Gather information about the donor, their family and interests.
- Sponsor giving circles (also called collaborative donor networks), in which a group of individuals pool resources around a common interest or cause.
- Inform donors about trends, emerging issues, current needs and opportunities.
- Schedule bus tours to grantee organizations.
- Host breakfast or luncheon meetings with speakers or panels, or hold large symposiums on community issues.
- Offer donors information about philanthropy and passing charitable values to the next generation.
- Offer workshops to donors on topics such as how to conduct a site visit or how to decide whether to recommend a grant for general operating or program-specific support.
- Formally recognize donors (unless they wish to remain anonymous) to express appreciation for their generosity.

▪ FROM THE FIELD: REPORTING BACK TO DONORS

One community foundation provides an annual "Gift and Grants Report" as their fund statement. It details where donors have given money and includes graphs that illustrate it by geography and interest area. According to one development officer, "Donors love it."

Another foundation sends quarterly fund statements, including a list of five or ten "Community Grant Opportunities." These outline the organization in need, the amount requested, the date funds are needed and a short description of the program or service. A development staff member said that donors jump at these opportunities, "Publishing grant opportunities not only fills immediate needs in the community, but it keeps the foundation in closer contact with donors. We now have a better idea of our donors' programmatic interests."

How Can You Build Operating Funds?

Beyond building permanent funds and assisting donors, your development staff may be expected to generate a portion of the general operating funds. A community foundation generally must augment operational funds it receives annually from administrative fees on funds, any fees charged for services, the interest from cash awaiting distributions (a.k.a. float) and any earnings from an operating endowment, if applicable.

Developing short-term operating funds can be tricky. The quickest way may be through annual campaigns and special events. However, these events may compete with local nonprofits and can be labor intensive.

Many community foundations seek operating support through low-key efforts, focusing on selected private foundations, corporations and individuals with close ties to the community foundation. They often seek multiyear commitments so that they do not have to go back each year. Donated services and in-kind support can also be helpful.

Community foundations build operating funds through:

- Administrative fees on funds and inter-fund grants
- Campaigns/events
- Float from money transfers
- Earnings from the administrative permanent funds
- Private foundations, corporations and individuals' contributions
- Donated services and in-kind support (e.g., audit services, office space and printing).

Source: Center for Community Foundation Excellence courses. For more information on these courses, visit www.cof.org, CF CODE: **CCFE**.

Donor Bill of Rights

(1) To be informed of the organization's mission, of the way the organization intends to use donated resources, and of its capacity to use donations effectively for their intended purposes.

(2) To be informed of the identity of those serving on the organization's governing board, and to expect the board to exercise prudent judgment in its stewardship responsibilities.

(3) To have access to the organization's most recent financial statements

(4) To be assured their gifts will be used for the purposes for which they were given.

(5) To receive appropriate acknowledgement and recognition.

(6) To be assured that information about their donation is handled with respect and with confidentiality to the extent provided by law.

(7) To expect that all relationships with individuals representing organizations of interest to the donor will be professional in nature.

(8) To be informed whether those seeking donations are volunteers, employees of the organization or hired solicitors.

(9) To have the opportunity for their names to be deleted from mailing lists that an organization may intend to share

(10) To feel free to ask questions when making a donation and to receive prompt, truthful and forthright answers.

The Donor Bill of Rights was created by the American Association of Fund Raising Counsel (AAFRC), Association for Healthcare Philanthropy (AHP), the Association of Fundraising Professionals (AFP) and the Council for Advancement and Support of Education (CASE). It has been endorsed by numerous organizations, including the National Committee on Planned Giving. Printed with permission by the Association of Fundraising Professionals.

How Do You Measure Success?

Your development plan should state desired outcomes and what indicators you will use to evaluate those outcomes. As you evaluate in the short-term, think beyond what gifts you received and look to what building blocks you laid for the future. *What key relationships did staff make? What response did you receive from a donor advisor presentation? How many potential donors did you solicit as volunteers on an advisory committee?*

Some community foundations set dollar goals for each market segment and type of fund. Others find this to be impractical. Establishing dollar goals for gifts from individuals is difficult because the largest gifts tend to come as bequests, and it is impossible to predict when testamentary gifts will mature.

If you do not set specific dollar goals by market, you will want to assess the potential market and measure the extent to which you reach this market. How do you do this? Start by doing your research. Some community foundations develop methods for rating individual donors on their ability to give. For example, if a potential donor owns a corporation, you can gauge the donor's ability to give by learning the company's worth and profitability. *Learn about companies online at Dun & Bradstreet www.smallbusiness.dnb.com or by performing a general search at www.google.com.*

Community foundations measure their success in other ways as well. Sample indicators of a good development program include:

- Number and value of gifts received.
- Number and value of gifts committed but not yet received.
- Number and content of calls/in-person visits with prospects and advisors.
- Board involvement as donors.
- Board involvement in donor visits.
- Marketing materials produced and disseminated to an identified audience.
- Presentations to groups.
- Special events (fundraising, recognition, educational, celebrations).
- Objectives achieved by each event (participation, volunteer involvement, net receipts, staff resources).
- Diversity of donor base.
- Referrals from donors and advisors.
- Donor service on committees.
- Donor service quality as measured by survey results.
- Press coverage of donor stories and events.

In addition to these indicators, you can measure success from what others say. Offer donors and advisors the opportunity to give you feedback. You might consider calling them periodically or conducting a survey as to how they feel your programs are working. Create a feedback form on your website or dedicate a specific e-mail address as a place where donors and others can send their comments.

The reality of evaluating resource development is this: Because community foundations are in the forever business, it may take years to see the results of your work. By focusing on the building blocks you create for future development, you can establish benchmarks that demonstrate progress along the way.

Community Foundations of America offers a market research tool designed to help community foundations elicit knowledge to help strengthen donor relationships. For information on the Donor Survey Tool Kit, visit www.cfamerica.org.

4.
LEGAL CONSIDERATIONS FOR RESOURCE DEVELOPMENT

> **WHAT YOU WILL LEARN**
>
> You and your board must know the tax and legal rules on various gifts and funds. Learn the basics here, including information on donor restrictions and how to remove them, as well as why confidentiality policies are important.

What Are Tax and Legal Implications of Various Gifts and Funds?

By their nature, community foundations receive and manage different types of gifts and funds. Because different rules apply to each, it can be complicated from a tax and legal perspective.

Boards and CEOs should be familiar with rules and regulations regarding different kinds of gifts and funds. This will help the foundation maintain its credibility and more important, ensure its charitable status.

Community foundations must make it clear that all gifts become property of the foundation and are subject to control by the foundation's board. Donors can recommend certain restrictions or how a contribution might be used, but the decision ultimately rests with the community foundation.

Most gifts and funds will be simple and straightforward. However, when considering a new gift or fund type, you should always consult your attorney.

For a discussion on legal rules and regulations, see the "Management, Finance and Administration" chapter. For a more complete discussion, read the Legal Compendium for Community Foundations, *Council on Foundations, 1996, www.cof.org.*

What Are Donor Restrictions?

Because community foundations have public charity status and special tax privileges, rules exist for how much donors can restrict a gift they have made to the foundation.

Namely, donors may not impose a "material restriction." A material restriction is a condition that prevents a community foundation from using assets, or the income derived from assets, to further its exempt purpose.

Readers should consult the *Legal Compendium for Community Foundations* for a detailed discussion of situations in which the IRS or the courts have determined that material restrictions do and do not exist. The information below only describes the most common restrictions.

What a Donor Can Do

- A donor can dedicate funds to the use of one or more charities, at the time the gift is made, in what is called a **designated fund**.

- A donor can dedicate funds to a particular cause or area, at the time the gift is made, in what is called a **field of interest fund**.

- A donor may serve as an advisor or appoint another as an advisor to make recommendations of grants from the fund. This is often called a **donor-advised fund**.

- A donor may create an **unrestricted fund** intended to last in perpetuity or may permit the community foundation to expend principal.

- A donor may select a name for the fund, which is often called a **named fund**. These could be any type of fund including designated, field-of-interest or donor-advised funds.

Any of the above funds can be established to last in perpetuity or may permit the community foundation to expend principal.

What a Donor Can't Do

- Once a gift has been made, a donor may not direct the distribution of the fund to charities the donor names, although donors may suggest grants from their fund.

- A donor may not tell the community foundation when to make distributions.

- Normally, a donor cannot require that the community foundation hold on to particular assets that the donor contributes.

- Normally, a donor may not be given a right of first refusal with respect to transferred property. (*Note*: Some rights of first refusal are acceptable. Consult with your attorney.)

- Generally, the community foundation cannot take over the donor's liabilities. However, if the donor is a terminating private foundation, the community foundation may be able to take over its existing obligations. Consult with your attorney.

- Donors may not require the community foundation to enter into irrevocable relationships with banks, brokerage houses or investment advisors. Revocable relationships may be acceptable.

How Do You Comply With the National Standards?

The following list describes how you can comply with National Standards related to resource development functions. Your foundation should show:

- A list of the types of funds the foundation offers.
- Sample marketing materials.
- Sample fund agreements.
- Mission statement.
- Gift/fund acceptance policies.
- Sample disclosure documents or paragraphs that are used in correspondence with donors.
- Documented evidence of donor education and participation (materials, invitations, etc.).
- Gift acknowledgment procedures and sample letters.
- Documented evidence that fund statements were provided to donors, such as sample fund statements with a cover letter.
- Documentation of procedures ensuring that funds are used to meet donor's intent.
- Guidelines for donor advisors and/or sample donor-advised fund agreement.
- Investment and management of assets policies.
- Conflict of interest and confidentiality.

When determining if a donor has excessive control, the IRS applies certain tests set forth in the material restriction rules. The control test consists of favorable and unfavorable factors—the presence or absence of one or more factors will not necessarily cause the IRS to find donor control, but it is a good idea to have as many favorable factors as possible and to avoid the unfavorable ones.

Favorable Factors

A community foundation should:

- Conduct an independent investigation of the donor's recommendation.
- Have guidelines enumerating specific charitable needs.
- Educate donors about charitable needs.
- Distribute funds from non-donor-advised resources to the same or similar organizations or causes as those donors recommend.
- Clearly state, orally and in writing, that the foundation will not be bound by the donor's advice.

Unfavorable Factors

A community foundation should **not**:

- Imply that a donor's advice will be followed
- Consider only the donor's advice
- Follow the donor's advice substantially all the time.

> **NATIONAL STANDARDS VI.E**
>
> All private information obtained with respect to donors and prospects is kept confidential to the fullest extent possible.

How Can You Remove Donor Restrictions?

There are three ways to remove donor restrictions: donor consent, variance power and court action.

Using Donor Consent

The quickest and easiest way to remove donor restrictions is with the consent of the donor. The Uniform Management of Institutional Funds Act (UMIFA), enacted in most states, permits donors to consent to the removal of a restriction. Consult your attorney on whether UMIFA has been adopted in your state and whether, as adopted, the donor may release restrictions. *For more on UMIFA, read the "Management, Finance and Administration" chapter, and read the Interpretations of UMIFA (April 2002) in the Council's legal archives, www.cof.org, COF CODE:* **Legal**.

Using the Variance Power

If a donor restriction has become unnecessary, incapable of fulfillment or no longer is in the best interest of the community, the community foundation may modify it through the variance power. Examples of when a community foundation may choose to exercise the variance power are:

- A charity designated by the donor has ceased to exist.
- A fund's purpose no longer makes sense (e.g., a fund to find a vaccine for polio).
- A charity designated by the donor has become seriously dysfunctional.

In the only published court ruling on the variance power, the court held that the variance power could be applied when circumstances of the designated charity have changed so much that the donor likely would change the restriction, if he or she were alive and knew all the facts.

Court Action

UMIFA permits courts to remove donor restrictions if the restriction has become "obsolete, inappropriate, or impracticable." A court may not under UMIFA, however, change a permanent fund into one that is not permanent. Normally the variance power should make it unnecessary to seek court action.

What Are Confidentiality Policies?

As a resource development/donor relations staff, you may receive information about donors as a result of their affiliation with the foundation. Because of its confidential nature, you must avoid sharing this information within the organization and outside the community foundation.

Your foundation should have clear confidentiality policies for both board and staff. These policies should include the following:

- A written pledge to hold information gained in confidence
- A list of those to whom the policy applies (staff, board, advisors, vendors, others)
- Conflict of interest statement
- Disclosure documents
- A requirement to sign the policy.

Resource Development and Donor Relations: Questions to Consider

- What would be a good balance for types of funds?
- How do you increase your visibility and reputation within the community?
- How can you show both integrity and imagination to donors in making their charitable giving a reality?
- How do you ask donors and prospective donors what issues matter most and what role they would have you play in the community?
- How can you improve your gift acceptance policies?
- What is the best way to organize and maintain donor information?
- In what ways can you help your board understand their role in fund development?
- What is your vision for your resources in 10-20 years from now?
- It's 9:00 a.m.: Do you know where your next generation of donors is?

Resources on Resource Development and Donor Relations

Publications

Cultivating Diversity in Fundraising. John Wiley and Sons, 2002. www.wiley.co

Foote, Joseph. *Family Philanthropy and Donor Advised Funds.* The National Center for Family Philanthropy, 2000. www.ncfp.org

Guide to Donor Involvement: Basic Considerations and Best Practices. Council on Foundations, 1996. www.cof.org

The Inclusive Community: A Handbook for Managing Diversity in Community Foundations. Council on Foundations, 1992. www.cof.org

Johnson, Stephen. *Doing Well by Doing Good—Improving Client Service, Increasing Philanthropic Capital: The Legal and Financial Advisor's Role.* The Philanthropic Initiative, 2000. www.tpi.org

Livingston, Richard and Linda. *Smart & Caring: A Donor's Guide to Major Gifting.* Council on Foundations, 1999. www.cof.org

Local Marketing Tools. Available from the National Marketing Action Team. www.cfmarketplace.org

Nober, Jane. *Donor-Initiated Fundraising: Issues and Guidelines for Community Foundations.* Council on Foundations, 1997. www.cof.org

Remmer, Ellen. *What's a Donor to Do? The State of Donor Resources in America Today.* The Philanthropic Initiative, 2000. www.tpi.org

Opening Doors: Pathways to Diverse Donors. Council on Foundations, 2002. www.cof.org

Chapter 6
Communications, Marketing and Public Relations

"All I'm saying is, giving a little something to the arts might help our image."

Communications, Marketing and Public Relations

In This Chapter

Introduction 215

1) Defining Communications 217
    Communications, Marketing and Public Relations: What's the Difference? 217
    What Is Strategic Communications? 218

2) Identifying Your Audiences 220
    Who Are Your Audiences? 220
        Target Audiences: What They Need to Know 221
        Internal Audiences 221
        Current Donors 222
        Potential Donors 222
        Nonprofit Organizations 223
        Professional Advisors 223
        Other Grantmakers 224
        Community Leaders 225
    How Do You Craft a Message? 225
    How Do You Match Your Message to Your Audience? 226
    What Is the Best Way to Deliver Your Message? 227

3) Developing an Image 228
    What Is Marketing? 228
    How Do You Develop an Image? 228
        Designing a Logo 228
        Crafting a Tagline 229
        Printing Organizational Materials 229
    Why Should You Consider Regional Marketing? 230

4) Getting in the Public Eye 231
    What Is Public Relations? 231
    How Do You Work with the Media? 231
        Pitching a Story 233
        Writing News Releases 234
        Developing Press Kits 235
        Managing Press Events 235
    How Do You Communicate in Times of Crisis? 236

5) Delivering Your Message 238
    What Communications Skills Help? 238
        Writing and Editing 238
        Layout and Graphic Design 239
        Web Design 239
        Public Speaking 240
        Visual Presentations 240
    In What Ways Can You Deliver Your Message? 241
        Events 241
        Publications 242
        The Web 245
        Advertisements 247

6) Designing a Communications Plan 248
    How Do You Develop a Communications Plan? 248
    What Are the Elements of a Good Strategic Communications Plan? 248
    How Can You Include Your Colleagues in Communications? 249
    What Are the Costs in Implementing the Plan? 250
    How Can You Evaluate Success? 250

Questions to Consider 251
Sample Planning Tools 252
    Developing a Communications Plan 252
    Communications Worksheet 254
Resources on Communications, Marketing and Public Relations 255

COMMUNICATIONS, MARKETING AND PUBLIC RELATIONS: AN INTRODUCTION

"Community foundations will always mean different things to different people. This will continue to be a great challenge for communicators, as we work to help others understand what community foundations do. In an ideal world, increasing access through the Internet and increasing uniformity of our services will improve understanding— and that will really be a great story to tell."

—Emily Jones Rushing, Communications Officer, Community Foundation of Greater Birmingham

Community foundations have been called one of philanthropy's best kept secrets. Because they play so many roles in the community—fund developer, donor service provider, grantmaker and leader—it can be puzzling for people to understand the exact "niche" into which community foundations fit.

Recently, this situation has begun to change, as community foundations grow more strategic about their communications. Some have created entire departments dedicated to communications. Others have expanded the roles of current staff to include communications activities. Regardless of their size and staff, community foundations have learned that communications are essential to their work.

As foundation staff, you already do communication work every day, in every activity it takes to run the foundation. This chapter will help you become intentional about how and to whom you communicate. The more mindful you are of communications, the more awareness you spread to the community and the better your chance of attracting donors and informing grant seekers.

In this chapter, you will find tools to enhance your communications, no matter the size or stage of your foundation. Learn ways to identify your audiences, develop a message, work with the media and create—or refine—your communications plan. In the following sections, read about:

1) **Defining Communications**—Discover the difference between communications, marketing and public relations. Learn about strategic communications, why it is important and how community foundations are using it as an essential part of their work.

2) **Identifying Your Audiences**—The first step in effective communication is to know your audiences. This section describes your major audience groups—your staff and board, current and potential donors, including nonprofit organizations, professional advisors, high-net-worth individuals, other grantmakers, community leaders and more. Learn how to craft a message, match your message to individual audiences and deliver it in the best way possible.

The more intentional you are about how your foundation communicates, the more awareness you spread to the community.

> ■
> **NATIONAL STANDARDS**
> **VII.A**
> A community foundation communicates openly and welcomes public scrutiny.

3) **Developing an Image**—The techniques of developing a true brand identity are beyond the scope of this publication, but certain tools can help you create an image for your foundation. Learn how to design a logo, craft a tagline and print organizational materials. Discover the importance of branding and why you might consider regional marketing.

4) **Getting in the Public Eye**—Now that you've developed your foundation's image, how will you promote it? This section introduces public relations activities—how to work with the media, pitch stories, develop news releases and press kits, and manage media events. It also gives you the essentials on how to communicate in times of crisis.

5) **Delivering Your Message**—Discover and develop the communications skills that will help your staff deliver its message, including writing and editing, layout and graphic design, web design, public speaking and visual presentations. Find out how to plan and hold events, produce publications, use the web and advertise effectively.

6) **Your Strategic Communications Plan**—Learn how easy it is to create and evaluate a communications plan. Find out how you can use board members, donors, grantees and other grantmakers as a part of this plan.

This chapter will help you reflect on how and why you communicate. You may not be ready to add all of these suggested activities to your communications plan, but you will find ideas here for when you are.

1.

DEFINING COMMUNICATIONS

"In 1984 a board member said to me, 'The best way to market the community foundation is one-on-one.' It's a truth that still bears repeating."

—Peggy Ogden, President and CEO, Central New York Community Foundation

WHAT YOU WILL LEARN

Discover the difference between communications, marketing and public relations. Learn about strategic communications, why they are important and how community foundations are using them as an essential part of their work.

Communications, Marketing and Public Relations: What's the Difference?

Communications, marketing and public relations are inseparable from every aspect of your foundation—from meeting with potential donors, mailing fund statements, speaking publicly, going on site visits, even talking to your own board members. Every contact you make with the public is a form of communication—and everything the board and staff does and says contributes to your foundation's credibility.

If you ask different people what the terms "communications, marketing and public relations" mean, you will get a variety of answers. Even within the community foundation field, there is sometimes debate over definitions. Occasionally, people will use these three terms interchangeably. Other times, one term will be used to describe the activities of another. For the purposes of this discussion, we'll look to the literal definitions of the terms.

Communications in its simplest sense means delivering a message. To communicate, you need two things: an audience and a message. In your everyday activities, you send hundreds of messages whether you realize it or not. Every time you pick up the phone or meet someone on the street, and every time you speak on behalf of the foundation or send someone an e-mail, you are communicating. In this sense, you engage in *communications* activities all the time. You figure out what you want to say and to whom you want to say it. Communications helps your board members, donors, grantees and the community stay informed about your work, and in turn, it keeps you informed about the community.

Marketing describes the functions involved in selling a product to a consumer. In other words, marketing is about sales—or in community foundation terms, about promoting your foundation, creating a "brand," attracting donors. Marketing requires you to consider these questions: *What products do you offer? To whom do you offer them? What is the best way to "sell" the foundation and its products?*

Marketing targets certain audiences and delivers pointed messages. With activities focused on selling, marketing includes developing an image and a "brand" and communicating a consistent message.

Public relations helps your foundation establish a "favorable relationship with the public." Where marketing targets certain audiences, public relations builds your reputation across all audiences. Its purpose is to create a good impression of your foundation and improve its credibility.

Public relations keeps people thinking, talking and breathing your foundation. Examples of public relations activities include writing news releases, being interviewed by the media, distributing publications, creating a website and delivering public service announcements.

Again, there is frequent overlap in how people define marketing and public relations. For the purpose of planning your activities, however, it helps to keep them separate.

> *Community foundations have remained an enigma to much of the public—the philanthropic organization that no one seems to get.*

What Is Strategic Communications?

Like any jargon from a particular field, the phrase "strategic communications" sounds vague and somewhat confusing. The phrase evolved to help organizations plan how they communicate.

For the purposes of this discussion, *strategic communications* isn't just about conveying a message—it's about the *process* that goes into planning that message and its delivery. Strategic communications calls for you to (1) think through the information you want to convey, (2) select how you will convey it and to whom and (3) measure the results of your effort.

Why should you plan your communications? Because today, it isn't enough for people to simply know about your community foundation. They expect more of you. Your foundation must demonstrate its transparency, its accountability and its impact. If you can communicate strategically, you will gain the trust you need to do your best work.

Until recently, many foundations focused their communications purely on disseminating information. They passively issued reports and publications, expecting the public to stand up and take notice of them. As a result, community foundations have remained an enigma to much of the public—the philanthropic organization that no one seems to understand.

Strategic communications have changed that trend. Community foundations now communicate with intention. They target their outreach, addressing the questions and concerns of each key constituent. In doing so, they not only disseminate information, but also influence attitudes and generate a response.

How Do Community Foundations Use Communications?

The quick answer to this question? *In everything they do.* Community foundations use communications to:

- Share information with current and potential donors, grantees and the community.
- Build relationships and trust.
- Demonstrate accountability and transparency.
- Share new ideas and lessons learned with other grantmakers, regional associations of grantmakers and national philanthropic and nonprofit organizations.
- Heighten awareness about community foundations and philanthropy among the general public.
- Educate public policy leaders.
- Help identify and define community needs.
- Stay aware of emerging philanthropic trends.

Strategic communications isn't just about the tools of communications—for example, your newsletters or brochures. Instead, it's a holistic look at the entire process, one that focuses on results. It requires you to ask important questions: *What do you want to accomplish? Who needs to know about your work? In what ways do they need to think or act differently?*

The quicker your foundation practices strategic communications, the better it can accomplish all of its goals. The first step is to identify your audiences.

Communications and Accountability

Your communications not only inform your constituents and the public, but also demonstrate your accountability. The National Standards call for community foundations to regularly disseminate information on their programs and finances. To comply with standards, your marketing materials must show the following: (1) an intent to attract support from a variety of separate, unrelated donors, (2) an intent to address a variety of fields/issues, (3) an intent to attract a variety of fund/gift types, (4) your long-term goal of securing permanent resources to address changing community needs, (5) transparency about the foundation's investments and (6) evidence that the foundation reflects the community's diversity. Your annual report, website and other publications are excellent tools to demonstrate these requirements.

2. IDENTIFYING YOUR AUDIENCES

Who Are Your Audiences?

If you ask any professional public speaker how to communicate effectively, they will tell you the most important rule: Know your audience. If you know who you are talking to and what they care about, you can make your message appeal to them. No matter how you communicate—whether it is through public speaking, private conversations, letters or publications, the same rule holds true.

As a community foundation, you have not one but many audiences. If you learn about your audiences *before* you communicate with them, you can craft your message appropriately for each one. The more you can understand your audiences—who they are, what they think, what they want—the better you can help them understand you.

To start, ask: *Who needs to know about the community foundation?*

First, consider the people closest to you. It's easy to overlook the community foundation's own **internal audience**—the board, staff and volunteers. Be sure everyone "on the inside" speaks about the foundation with a clear, consistent message to avoid creating confusion in the outer community—where it counts.

Once you've identified your internal audience, next look to your **primary audiences**—the groups who are necessary for you to run your organization. Community foundations have three primary constituents: nonprofit organizations, current donors and prospective donors. To build your assets and distribute them effectively, these three groups must know about your community foundation.

Nonprofits need to know what your program areas are and how they can apply for a grant. Current donors need to know their giving options and how you can help them meet their charitable goals. Finally, potential donors need to know why they should consider giving through your community foundation.

Third, focus on your **intermediary audiences**—those who can help you *reach* your primary audiences. For example, professional advisors and the media are audiences that can help get your message to nonprofits and donors. Professional advisors can be your best means for reaching new donors, as they already work with donors in planning their financial futures.

Fourth, focus on the **community at large**—those people who can help you learn about community needs. You can stay informed by communicating with other local grantmakers, nonprofits, public policy makers and community leaders.

Below you will find a list of audiences and tips for communicating with them. *Please note that this list is in no particular order of importance.*

WHAT YOU WILL LEARN

The first step in effective communication is to know your audiences. This section describes your major audience groups—your staff and board, current and potential donors, including nonprofit organizations, professional advisors, high-net-worth individuals, other grantmakers, community leaders and more. Learn how to craft a message, match your message to individual audiences and deliver it in the best way possible.

THE VALUE OF COMMUNITY FOUNDATIONS
- Know the local community
- Offer flexible funding options
- Be responsive to donors
- Provide professional management
- Work with a long-term view
- Build community capacity
- Leverage community resources.

Target Audiences: What They Need To Know

- Internal (includes board, staff and volunteers).
- Current donors.
- Potential donors.
- Nonprofit organizations (includes current grantees and grant seekers).
- Professional advisors (includes attorneys, accountants, investment agents, estate planners, consultants, etc.).
- Community leaders (includes government, policy makers, civic leaders, etc.).
- Other grantmakers (includes community, private and independent foundations).
- Media (includes newspapers, radio, television outlets, online news sources, etc.).
- General public.

Internal Audiences

Communication has a ripple effect. It begins in the community foundation's inner circle—with the current staff and board. From there, it works its way out to volunteers and advisory committees, current donors and grantees, then potential donors, professional advisors, grant seekers and the public at large.

When considering how your foundation will communicate, don't forget about your most captive audience—the people already involved and working for the foundation. If you can communicate the same clear message to them, they will be more likely to communicate a clear, consistent message to everyone else.

How do you accomplish this? Orientation is your first chance to train new board, staff and volunteers on how to communicate about the foundation. Train them on the foundation's history, value and message and encourage them to spread the word to others. You should provide all new board and staff members with an orientation packet—their roadmap to your community foundation.

Where Can You Find Communications Training?

Look to these resources for regional and national training on communications:

Marketing for Community Foundations, Center for Community Foundation Excellence—www.cof.org, CF CODE: **CCFE**

Fall Conference for Community Foundations, Council on Foundations—www.cof.org, CF CODE: **Community**

CommA—A professional group of communications professionals in the community foundations field—www.cof.org or e-mail cflistadmin@cof.org

The Communications Network—www.comnetwork.org

The Forum of Regional Associations of Grantmakers—www.givingforum.org

After the initial orientation, develop an ongoing internal communications system to keep board and staff well-informed. Here are some ideas for how to do this:

- Provide board and staff with communications materials to support their work.
- Develop and promote internal organizational values.
- Develop an internal memo or newsletter (either print or e-mail) to keep colleagues informed of key decisions and activities.
- Give board, staff and volunteers a "cheat sheet"—a printed index card or mini-brochure with your foundation's vision, mission and talking points that they can carry with them.
- Provide regular communications updates at board and staff meetings.
- Provide at least one in-depth communications training each year. You can do this in-house by hiring a communications consultant to train the entire staff, or you might send select staff to outside training sessions and then ask them to give a brown-bag presentation to staff upon their return.

Current Donors

Your community foundation exists to serve donors—to help them meet their charitable needs and help their dollars make a difference. Your current donors always remain top priority in your communications plan.

Most existing donors don't know how to take full advantage of community foundation products and services. In your communications, help them understand what it is you offer—your products and services that can help them fulfill their philanthropy. Work with the resource development staff to coordinate materials to send to donors. Provide donors clear written information about their giving options, what restrictions they can and cannot place on contributions and a report on their funds. In conjunction with your foundation colleagues, you will also want to keep them updated on the activities of the foundation and grant opportunities in the community.

The National Marketing Action Team provides tools for community foundations to reach donors, such as a donor newsletter. For information, visit www.cfmarketplace.org. For more information on keeping donors engaged, see the "Resource Development and Donor Relations" chapter.

Potential Donors

To sustain the community foundation, you must constantly work to cultivate new donors. Individuals are the source of almost 90 percent of all gifts received by the community foundation. Potential donors need to know who you are and what you do. Many aren't aware that your community foundation exists, much less that you can help them fulfill their charitable goals.

For you to communicate with potential donors, you will work with the development staff. There are many ways to access potential donors. *See the "Resource Development and Donor Relations" chapter to learn how.*

E-Newsletters for Professional Advisors

Looking for new ways to reach the professional advisors in your community? Consider building relationships with advisors through an e-newsletter, with content written specifically for your professional advisor audience. If building and publishing your own professional advisor e-newsletter seems like a monumental assignment, learn more about NMATpublisher, a tool for community foundations from the National Marketing Action Team. *Visit www.cfmarketplace.org*

Once you've identified potential donors, you will want to communicate what your foundation offers. You can help the development staff by providing written materials for this purpose. These materials can explain the types of gifts they can contribute, the kinds of funds you provide and the ways those funds can benefit their families and the community.

Nonprofit Organizations

Nonprofit organizations need to know two main things from you: what your foundation supports and how they can apply for a grant. Community foundations communicate this information to grant seekers in different ways. Most have set or rolling deadlines to which they accept applications from grant seekers. Some create and maintain a mailing list of all local nonprofits and send out guidelines and grant announcements. Others announce requests for proposals (RFPs) for particular initiatives.

Some community foundations hold regular nonprofit presentations or luncheons. They openly invite nonprofits that are considering applying for a grant. In these meetings, they describe what the foundation does, how to apply for grants and the process, and when they select grantees.

At a minimum, your foundation should make its grant guidelines, proposal format and other information readily available—in printed materials and, if available, on your website. You might also post announcements in libraries, neighborhood community centers and other public places.

Site for Donors, Advisors and the Media

The Council on Foundations and Community Foundations of America offer a website to help donors, professional advisors and the media learn about community foundations. The site features resources, giving tools and a newsroom with the latest information on community foundations. Tell your colleagues and community about www.communityfoundations.net.

Professional Advisors

Working with professional advisors may be your foundation's best bet at attracting new donors—especially high-net-worth individuals. Professional advisors are often the gatekeepers of potential donors. Most high-net-worth individuals already work with a professional advisor to help them make major financial decisions. It's the advisor's business to know their clients inside and out—their assets, long-term needs and, often, what they value in life. Professional advisors include attorneys, accountants, brokers, bankers, trust officers, life insurance agents, financial planners and more.

Professional advisors need to know that your foundation can help them serve their clients better. They need your expertise on how their clients can give. They should view you as a partner in helping them do their job better—and making them look good in the eyes of their clients.

When working with professional advisors, it's important to consider their point of view. Each professional advisor has different specialties, different training and different values. You should customize your approach to these advisors based on your understanding of their work. Find out first what's important to them as well as their clients. *For more information, see the tools for advisor communications on the National Marketing Action Team website, www.cfmarketplace.org.*

Visit the Community Foundation Marketplace

CFMarketplace is your source for marketing ideas, advice and ready-to-use resources.

Developed by the National Marketing Action Team, a collaboration of the Council on Foundations and Community Foundations of America, the site features local marketing tools, advertising ideas, breaking news and more. For an overview of NMAT activities, products and services, view the online seminar *Ready, Set, Go*. Visit www.cfmarketplace.org.

As a communications staff member, how can you support the work of your resource development colleagues as they work to build relationships with professional advisors?

Here's a quick list of ideas:

- Create materials and publications geared to professional advisors.
- Craft key message points for the CEO and development staff for when they meet with professional advisors.
- Help develop PowerPoint presentations that your colleagues can use to educate professional advisors.
- Include a section on your website specifically for professional advisors.
- Use the latest marketing tools and resources for professional advisors on www.cfmarketplace.org.
- Inform your colleagues, current donors and professional advisors about www.communityfoundations.net, the website for professional advisors, donors and the media.
- Maintain a mailing list of local professional advisors.

Other Grantmakers

As a community foundation, you should get to know other funders in your community, as they are your peers working toward similar goals. Help them get to know your foundation as well, informing them of grantmaking interests and activities.

There are many ways to communicate with other grantmakers. Your CEO or program staff may already be working with them through regional associations of grantmakers or other informal networks. Consider how you can use those connections to keep in touch. Invite grantmakers to your events, such as the annual meeting or community presentations. Send them your printed materials describing your work and keep them abreast of news through your newsletter or other materials. Ask them to put you on their mailing list. This will help you stay informed about their activities and may give you ideas for new types of materials and publications.

For help in finding other grantmakers in your area, you can perform a search at www.fdncenter.org. Find other community foundations near you at www.cflocate.org.

What's Your Story?

Everyone loves a good story. Telling the "story" of your community foundation—what it does and how it makes a difference in the lives of real people—can be one of your most powerful communications tools. Telling philanthropy's story can be a real challenge for grantmakers, however. According to a recent study commissioned by the Council on Foundations and conducted by Wirthlin Worldwide, 89 percent of respondents from the general public couldn't name even one foundation. Similarly, the National Marketing Action Team conducted two national surveys of high-net-worth individuals and professional advisors and found that only 8 percent could name a community foundation—proving that the awareness level isn't high.

Are you making the most of your storytelling opportunities? For tips on how to tell your foundation's story, read *Story Telling as Best Practice* by Andy Goodman. Available online at www.agoodmanonline.com.

Community Leaders

You should regularly communicate with community leaders, including business, labor, government, policymakers and civic leaders. They need to know about your community foundation to draw on its services and resources. In turn, you can gain important information from them on community needs. These leaders not only are a source of information for you, but also are themselves potential donors, both in their personal and professional capacities.

How do you communicate with community leaders? In some cases, leaders are likely already on your board or committees, and you will communicate with them through the normal course of business.

Forming new relationships with leaders can be trickier. Include them on your mailing list to send them updates, news and grant opportunities from the foundation. Invite them to your events, although be clear what you are asking of them—for example, that they are welcome to attend, but won't be part of the agenda. Help the development staff by preparing materials and message points for when they meet community leaders in person.

How Do You Craft a Message?

Why does your community foundation exist?

If you were in an elevator and someone asked you this question, what would you say? Foundation staff members—especially those who work in the communications, resource development or donor services areas—are frequently asked to explain their job or what a community foundation does.

With sometimes only seconds to answer, your response should be a good one. You need a sound bite—what is sometimes called a "quick and dirty" explanation of 10 words or less. For example, one community foundation recites the following: "We receive, manage and disburse charitable funds." The more clear and concise your answer, the more people will remember it.

This is your starting place for crafting a message—the most important part of communications. You want to make your foundation's mission and vision compelling. You want people to care. A good message can help people understand who you are and what you do. It can help them trust the foundation and even lead them to action.

Although your foundation's message will be customized for different audiences, the basic content will always be same. The more consistent your message, the more powerful it will come across. Anytime you convey your message to any audience, you will want to speak to *their* needs, not yours. Use your message to explain:

- How the foundation can help them.
- How they can have confidence and trust that the foundation will support their values and beliefs.

Next, you can create what is called a message platform—an expanded version of your quick "10 words or less" message. This message platform will be used in your printed materials or when you have time to fully explain the foundation—for instance, during a presentation or a one-on-one meeting.

Use the following key elements to develop a message platform:

1) Your mission is…
2) The value of a community foundation is… (*See sidebar*).
3) You are known for… (Keep it to three points or less).
4) Five "fast facts"—items such as year established, asset size, number of funds, most current year's total grant amount, total grants made since established.

5) Two quick stories—a donor story and a grantee story.

6) Your "tagline"—How will audiences remember you?

Once you have your message platform ready, include it on written materials, handouts and publications. Distribute these to your constituents and the public.

Make sure the board and staff know the message platform, inside and out. Help them learn to communicate the foundation's message with clarity and consistency. You might provide them with written materials outlining the message (for example, small printed index cards or mini-brochures) that they can refer to when needed.

For more information on crafting your message, see tools from the National Marketing Action Team, including its PowerPoint presentations for donors and professional advisors, at www.cfmarketplace.org.

How Do You Match Your Message to Your Audience?

It's impossible to reach all of your audiences simultaneously. In fact, you will want to address them separately to customize your message for each one. Just as each audience has different interests, each has different knowledge, experience and vocabulary. You should always tailor your message to meet your audience's level of understanding and interest.

Here's a quick example of how you might explain a community foundation to different audiences:

WHEN TALKING TO:	TELL THEM THE COMMUNITY FOUNDATION IS:
Nonprofits	A potential source of funds for them to accomplish their goals
Donors	A flexible giving vehicle for meeting their charitable goals
The Public	A catalyst for addressing the needs of the community

To match your message to your audience, begin by doing your homework. Consider:

- Who is your target audience?

- Why should they care about your community foundation?

- Where do they get their information (publications, organizations, etc.)?

- Which spokesperson from your foundation will they find the most credible (a board member, the CEO, a volunteer, a current donor, etc.)?

With these answers in mind, you will be better able to customize your message for each audience, using the right words and ideas that will appeal to them. Language is important. Of course with any audience, you will want to speak in clear terms and avoid using jargon. But when talking to specific audiences, use the language they are accustomed to hearing. For example: *What adjectives would they use to describe community foundation work? What key phrases would most likely to catch their eye?*

When talking to professional advisors, for example, you will want to use more technical language— describing options for deferred giving. Because they work in technical arenas, professional advisors want to learn the nuts and bolts of what you can provide—and how you can help them help their clients.

When talking to potential donors—families, for instance—you will use much simpler language that steers away from the technical. You might use adjectives and ideas that appeal to their emotions— describing causes they care about, ways they can "make a difference" and ways they can "create a legacy."

What Is the Best Way to Deliver Your Message?

Not only will you adjust your message for each audience, but you will also adjust the ways by which you deliver it. For example, you might approach a potential donor with a letter from the CEO or chair of the development committee, followed by a telephone call and, you hope, a meeting. You would approach nonprofit organizations much differently.

Instead of a letter or phone call, you might design and distribute a brochure explaining your program areas and grant guidelines, or even place a public service announcement (PSA) on the radio or television advertising new grant opportunities.

Your community foundation might use many types of media, depending on its communications goals and who it intends to reach. What are your choices when it comes to different media?

The **mass media** is what people mainly think of when they hear the word media. It includes electronic media such as radio and television, as well as print media such as newspapers and magazines. Mass media reaches the maximum amount of people.

Organizational media is the material you distribute from the foundation—newsletters and brochures, handouts, annual reports, PowerPoint presentations, business cards and your website. It also includes personal communications from the foundation, such as letters, postcards, direct mail, faxes, e-mail or anything else addressed to a specific person.

Quick message media includes items such as badges, stickers, banners, billboards, posters, T-shirts, logos, symbols and mass e-mails.

Once you decide on your mode of delivery, there are certain ways to make that delivery more effective. Here are some ideas:

1) Identify yourself clearly.

2) Give the basic message three times (beginning, middle and end).

3) Back up assertions with facts.

4) Make the audience believe they have a stake in your message.

5) Always tell the audience the next steps for getting involved, along with a way to get more information.

6) Stick to your message.

This last point is the most important. Above all, make your message consistent. It's a mistake to give one message one month and change it the next. You will only confuse your audience and cause doubts about your credibility.

3.
DEVELOPING AN IMAGE

What Is Marketing?

Marketing describes the functions involved in transferring a product from producer to consumer. In other words, marketing is about sales—or in community foundation terms, about selling what it is your foundation does. To do so, you must cultivate understanding between your foundation and its audiences.

To market successfully, you first divide your audiences into segments and then cast the best message and medium to reach them. Start by learning about your separate audiences. *What do they care about? How do they receive information? Who influences them? What publications do they read? What organizations do they belong to?* Once you can learn this, you can begin to funnel information through these channels.

Before you make contact with your audiences, however, there is one crucial step: developing your foundation's image.

How Do You Develop an Image?

Your foundation makes an impression from the moment it comes into contact with someone—as soon they walk into your reception area, are greeted over the phone, receive an e-mail or see one of your printed materials.

How do people feel after having contact with your foundation? Are they greeted with attentiveness and professionalism? Do your board, staff and volunteers inspire confidence in the foundation? How will people remember who you are and what you do?

To effectively market, you must develop a clear and consistent image. Start with these simple steps.

Designing a Logo

A logo is your identity symbol—it gives donors, grant seekers and the public an icon that identifies your community foundation and embodies who you are. Your logo stands as the symbol of your organization. Keep it simple and yet powerful. And make sure it's one that your audiences will actually see. Here are some tips:

- **Your logo should reduce well.** In many cases, people will see your logo on a business card or at the bottom of a newspaper ad—locations in which it may appear quite small. If it doesn't work in those dimensions, it doesn't work.

- **Your logo should fax clearly.** Consider how much of your communication takes place via the fax machine and then take a look at your logo from the recipient's perspective. If it's a gray smudge at their end, that's a problem.

> **WHAT YOU WILL LEARN**
>
> The techniques of developing a true brand identity are beyond the scope of this publication, but certain tools can help you create an image for your foundation. Learn how to design a logo, craft a tagline and print organizational materials. Discover the importance of branding and why you might consider regional marketing.

- **Your logo should work in black and white.** If you cannot afford color in every placement, your logo will eventually be rendered in black and white, most notably in newspaper ads. Make sure the image is as clear and striking in black and white as it is in its original color.

- **Add white space around your logo.** If your logo seems to disappear when surrounded by text or images, you must factor in white space for every placement. Let your logo stand out by adding uncluttered space around it.

Some foundations hire graphic design firms to create their logo; others design their logo in-house. When considering different logos, think about what you like about other logos you see. What is it about those logos that help you remember them? Note the symbol, style and colors, or the shape and writing style. Test out a few potential logos on people who aren't directly involved with your foundation. Ask them what kind of identity or "feel" they associate with it.

Once you have your logo, print it on a placard for your building entrance, office doors and/or notice board. You will feature your logo on letterhead and other stationery as well—fax cover sheets, news releases, memos, envelopes, address labels, business cards and so forth. Print your logo on presentation materials, promotional gear, brochures, publications and your website. Some organizations include logos in their e-mail, but it might be difficult for some web servers to receive graphics by e-mail. It's best to include a written tagline in your e-mail messages and leave the pictures and icons for your printed materials.

Source: Parts of the above were adapted from www.agoodmanonline.com.

Crafting a Tagline

You logo isn't the only way to help audiences remember you. Your foundation might develop a short tagline—also called a position statement or slogan—that people can attribute to your community foundation. One example of a tagline developed by the Council of Michigan Foundations (www.cmif.org) is "For Good. For Ever."

Your tagline should capture your mission, vision and values in a clear and catchy way. It should be simple, consisting of as few words as possible. You might consider registering your tagline as a trademark. Depending on your communications plan, you might consider additional taglines at different times of the year.

Print your primary tagline in most of the same places you print your logo—letterhead and other stationary, presentation materials, publications, business cards, your website. You can also use the tagline as a signature line in staff e-mail messages.

Printing Organizational Materials

Organizational materials include letterhead, fax cover sheets, envelopes, business cards, transparencies, presentation materials, signage and so forth. They aren't only necessary for running your organization, but as stated earlier, these items are prime vehicles for communicating your image.

If you have a tagline and logo, include them on these materials. Be sure to also include the important contact information—foundation name, key contact, address, phone, fax and website address. Some foundations also print the names of board members on their letterhead. If you include board member names, plan for reordering when members change.

You can design your own materials or hire an outside design or printing firm. Unless you order a special kind of printing (embossed or raised print, for example), the costs for printing business cards, letterhead and envelopes are usually reasonable. Remember, the larger the quantities you order, the less expensive these materials are per item.

Why Should You Consider Regional Marketing?

As a way to create broader understanding of what community foundations do and the value they bring, community foundations across the country are now banding together to do marketing regionally. Regional marketing enables community foundations throughout an entire area to combine their collective talent, resources and time—and to deliver a consistent and powerful image to the same audience group (typically, professional advisors).

Regional activities can include developing a community foundation brand, producing core messages and promotional materials, conducting regional advertising, holding joint seminars and events, developing marketing capacity through joint training, sharing marketing staff and conducting regional grantmaking.

As discovered in a study conducted by the Michigan Community Foundations Ventures, community foundations must address certain key issues to market themselves regionally with success. *To find out more, download the report by author Karin E. Tice, Ph.D., at www.cmif.org, and read the "Overview of Community Foundations" chapter.*

The Business of Branding

Branding is the way you convey your identity and broadcast your image. In developing or refining your "local brand" for the community foundation, consider these questions:

- ***Do we have an effective identity?*** A clear and accurate name? A clear meaning and appeal to our logo and tagline?
- ***Is this identity consistently and appropriately applied to all communications?***
- ***Do all of our communications reinforce and build upon our core message?***
- ***Is the visual appearance of all our communications similar?***
- ***Do all of our communications reflect an appealing, professional quality and help build a quality brand image?***

Source: Marketing for Community Foundations, Center for Community Foundation Excellence, www.cof.org,
COF CODE: **CCFE**

4.

GETTING IN THE PUBLIC EYE

> **WHAT YOU WILL LEARN**
>
> Now that you've developed your foundation's image, how will you promote it? This section introduces public relations activities—how to work with the media, pitch stories, develop news releases and press kits and manage press events. It also gives you the essentials on how to communicate in times of crisis.

What Is Public Relations?

Public relations activities are a good way for your foundation to promote itself and reach a wide audience while doing so. They can raise your public profile and spread awareness about your community foundation—what it does and what it has achieved. By delivering your message through a third party such as the media, you gain credibility with your audiences.

Through public relations work, you create a strong community presence and image. You help the public understand your foundation and its value in the community. In doing so, you shape public opinion and, ideally, influence the actions of donors, grantees and community leaders.

Much of public relations work involves working with the mass media in an unpaid manner—communicating through newspapers, television, magazines and so forth. This section will give you all the basics you need to do this. Other public relations activities include networking, holding special events, advertising, printing newsletters and more.

Public relations work manages your image in good times and in bad. Occasionally, your foundation may face a public crisis. Preparing in advance for such occasions can lessen potential damage.

How Do You Work with the Media?

Mass media ("the media") is the fastest way to get your message to the most people. After all, access to the media means access to the public.

It takes persistence and planning to gain media coverage, especially in large metropolitan areas. Like fundraising, cultivating the media is an ongoing process. Your strategy for press coverage needs to go beyond trying to land one big story; instead, you want the press to know that you are THE community source to contact whenever they are doing a story that relates to your mission.

You should identify one communications staff member or experienced board member who will work with the media and respond to inquiries. In smaller community foundations with fewer staff, you might use a volunteer who has media experience to serve as the foundation's media liaison. Regardless of who serves this role—staff, board member or volunteer—be sure they are familiar with the local media outlets, knowing what they want, what kind of stories they feature, when their deadlines are and how best to approach them.

When preparing to work with the media, consider the following helpful tasks:

- **Develop a targeted media list.** Identify media and reporters who are important to your foundation and your audiences. Offer to meet with them, providing them with news releases and information.

- **Develop an information kit for the media.** *See sidebar for what a press kit should include.* Council on Foundations members can access sample press kits online at www.cof.org.

- **Pursue regular media outreach opportunities.** Pitch news stories when you have news. Invite reporters to foundation-sponsored events. Hold news conferences. Write letters to the editor and editorials.

- **Talk to members of your community.** Make speeches to local organizations. Develop, or encourage grantees to develop, an op-ed column for the local newspaper, a feature highlighting foundation goals and outcomes in relation to local "hot" issues.

- **Encourage grantees to share results and outcomes with the media.** Provide grantees with a few foundation information kits. Support your grantees' media outreach.

How do you get the media interested in your foundation? You have to think like a journalist. The media will only be interested in you if you do newsworthy things. For example, if you:

- Do something new, unusual or controversial.
- Tell an evocative human interest story.
- Host an interesting event, or one with a news angle.
- Offer a vital service.
- Show how you made a compelling, newsmaking difference in your community.
- Show that a large number of people are affected.

Answer the following questions to help you determine the newsworthiness about a topic you might pitch:

- What is the local angle?
- Is it timely or relevant to current events?
- Do you have an expert spokesperson on the topic?
- Is there human interest?
- What is new, novel or a change from the past about your topic?
- Is there a significant prediction or finding (research results, economic forecast)?
- Is there humor?
- Does it have visual potential?
- Can you say what your story is in 20 to 30 seconds? (Reporters think in quotes and sound bites.).

The more you can answer "yes" to these questions, the better your makings for a story.

Pitching a Story

There are two ways to get attention for your foundation in print or broadcast media. You can *pay* for an ad, or you can pitch a newsworthy story. "Pitching" news stories is nothing more than packaging what it is you want to communicate in a way that will spark a reporter's or editor's interest.

There are three easy steps to pitching a story:

Step One: Prepare a News Release

News releases must be about real news. If you send news releases on every move your foundation makes, you will all too quickly lose the attention and the patience of the media.

In general, reporters look for news about (1) people, (2) the environment or culture, (3) location and (4) money. Send your news releases to those reporters with whom you have a relationship or those on your media contact list. Always deliver your release in the way the media want to receive it—be it through fax, e-mail or post.

Step Two: Follow Up

After you send out your news release, always follow up with a phone call to make sure the media outlets received it and if they need additional information. This phone call is the most important part of pitching the story; it is when you "sell" the idea. Think like a reporter: Why should the readers care about the story? Explain the idea, answer questions and offer alternative angles if the reporter does not bite on your original packaging.

Step Three: Be Interviewed

Once a reporter has accepted your pitch, he or she will most likely set up an interview with a spokesperson for your community foundation and/or a relevant secondary source such as a grantee. Be prepared with three or four key talking points and a few good quotes. Whenever you are talking with a reporter, consider your statements always "on the record." Provide the reporter with an information kit and suggest photo or video opportunities.

Working with Reporters

DO:

- Write two or three points you want to make and use them early in the exchange.
- Tell the truth.
- Watch your body language and maintain eye contact.
- If you cannot answer a question, promise to get back to the reporter within an hour or two. Ask when the reporter's deadline is and meet it.
- Keep answers brief and focused.
- Speak in clear, everyday language and take time answering questions.
- Remain calm even if hostile questions are asked.

DON'T:

- Speculate; stick to the facts.
- Become defensive or argumentative or say "no comment;" it implies guilt.
- Become emotional.
- Say anything "off the record." Even if reporters tell you they are collecting background information, be aware that everything you say still could possibly be used as a direct quote.

Source: Grantmaker's Public Affairs Resource Kit, Council on Foundations, www.cof.org

Writing News Releases

A news release has one goal: to disseminate information. Typically, community foundations write news releases to announce grantmaking priorities, procedures and deadlines, major donations and grants, new funds or activities, and changes in staff or board members.

News releases aren't just for the media; they can be effective public relations tools when distributed at events, mailed to constituents, included in donor relations packets or presented at speaking engagements. You should consider sending news releases to all of your audiences.

Because news releases conform to an established format, they are easy to write. Once you learn the format, all you have to do is fill in the blanks. It's important to always follow the format, however. Otherwise, the media receiving your release won't take it seriously, let alone publish it.

There are six basic elements that every news release should have in terms of content and how it appears. All news releases:

1) Must be on foundation **letterhead** or a standard form with key **contact information**, including a name and telephone number.

2) Include **"FOR IMMEDIATE RELEASE"** written in all caps at the top.

3) Have a compelling **HEADLINE** written in BOLD/CAPS.

4) List a date/city.

5) Describe the Who, What, When, Where and Why in the BODY copy.

6) Include the following elements: basic font, page numbers, double spaced, printed on one side only and the symbol ### at the end.

You will want to keep your news release as concise as possible, ideally no more than one or two pages. With such little space to explain your news, make every word count. Be sure to write releases in every day language (no jargon) with a message that is crystal clear. Place the most important information at the beginning and use a catchy heading that will hook the reader. And of course, before you send it out, check the spelling and grammar. You don't want to let a simple typo damage your credibility.

To comply with National Standards, be sure to document your news releases and keep any press clippings that result.

Following Up on Releases

After you distribute your news release to the media, you will want to follow up with the top media outlets. This one step often separates those who get publicity from those who don't. One simple phone call or quick e-mail may prompt the media staff to read and remember your release.

■ FROM THE FIELD: GRANTEES MAKING NEWS

A small Midwest community foundation gets big returns from one of its grant requirements. The foundation asks that all of its grantees send out their own news releases about the community foundation's support of their grants and programs. The foundation provides grantees with sample press releases and contact information for the media in its region. These news releases with a "homespun" look have garnered a lot of attention for the grantees and the community foundation, with many of the grant announcements picked up by the regional media. According to the executive director, "It's an effective marketing tool. We began this practice in 1990, around the same time the foundation was started. It has gotten us very well known—and we're a small foundation."

Source: *"In Hopes They'll Be Newsworthy,"* Foundation News and Commentary, *Nov/Dec 2000,* www.foundationnews.org

One word of caution: Reporters work on tight deadlines. If you call them on their deadline day with a seemingly insignificant inquiry, it may cause resentment. Do your homework. Ask the receptionist to tell you when the deadlines are and the best times for you to call. Acknowledge that reporters may not have time to speak with you and always be courteous and gracious when they do.

Developing Press Kits

A press kit is a package you assemble for the media and others to help them understand what you do. Press kits are living, changing, collective documents that should be continuously updated with important statistics and background information, news, fact sheets, publications and any other pertinent materials you want to communicate.

Press kits usually include the following:

- Mission and vision
- Fact sheet about the foundation
- Most recent news release
- Most recent newsletter
- A brochure or handout outlining your message platform
- Brief statement of foundation's background/history
- President and/or CEO biography
- Relevant charts/graphs/figures
- Photos, if possible
- Recent press clips about your foundation
- Contact information, including website address.

Managing Press Events

If you want press coverage from many media outlets at once, you can schedule a press event. To do so, send a news release or memorandum inviting specific editors, reporters or media representatives. In the invitation, include the "who, what, when, where and why" of the event, along with a contact name and number. Consider sending this invitation out at least two to three weeks in advance of the event and follow up with a phone call closer to the date.

For your press event to be successful, it must have a newsworthy focus. A spokesperson—usually your foundation's CEO, the board chair or communications director—will give a brief presentation. It helps to have someone else from the community speak as well to give the media a human interest angle, if appropriate to the topic.

As communications staff, you can help your spokesperson prepare for the event by giving them message "sound bites" and talking points. Distribute press kits to all media who attend and be available to answer their questions. Prepare a sign-in sheet for members of the press so that you have a record of who attended. If your budget allows, consider offering simple refreshments.

After the event, follow up with all members of the press who attended. Send them a written note of thanks, either by mail or e-mail, and provide them with your contact information should they have any questions.

How Do You Communicate in Times of Crisis?

Crises can affect your reputation and put your entire organization at risk. The better you handle a crisis situation, the more likely you are to keep your foundation's image secure. The following will give you specific steps for how you can plan for when a crisis occurs.

1) Appoint a crisis team

Create a crisis communications team with a team leader. Include representatives from the board, staff and legal counsel.

Identify **one** person to serve as your organization's spokesperson, such as the board chair, CEO, the marketing/communications director or a volunteer. In times of crisis, the public may view volunteer spokespersons as more credible than staff. Provide your spokesperson with appropriate media training in advance. Make sure he or she is comfortable talking with reporters on camera.

2) Identify potential crises

Think through all possible "problem areas." Some crises you simply won't be able to foresee—a scandal involving one of your grantees, for example. However, you can always identify potential trouble and prepare in advance. Consider: *Does your foundation make grants that could be considered controversial? Could any of your programs be accused of discriminating by age, ethnicity, sexual orientation or physical challenge? Does your foundation have a disgruntled employee or ex-employee who may cause problems?*

3) Gather information about the crisis

Gather as much information about the crisis as you can. That will prepare you to answer questions and to develop your own angle. Identify potential story angles that you can pitch to the media, giving your perspective of the crisis first. Make sure that you consider both legal and public relations perceptions when doing so.

4) Develop key messages and talking points

In times of fire, you will want to arm yourselves with the foundation's finest message points. Use these messages early and often—from the very moment you smell a crisis coming on. It's sometimes better if you contact the media first before they contact you, as they might catch you off guard.

When you do talk with the media, never—under any circumstances—should you say "no comment." Whether it's true or not, "no comment" has come to imply guilt. If needed, you might say, "I don't know the answer to that at this time." If you will answer the question later, you might say, "I will gather the information and get back to you with an answer." Set a time to get back to the reporter and meet that deadline.

5) Develop your strategy

Identify all audiences that will need to be notified in the event of a crisis—the staff, board, volunteers, other grantmakers and so forth—and who will be responsible for informing them. All media inquiries should be directed to the foundation's spokesperson. Emphasize that no one else should be talking to the media.

Develop a quick approval process for all decisionmaking related to any crises that arise. For example: *Who will need to review news releases? Who will need to okay interviews?*

6) Implement your response

When a crisis occurs, brief your spokesperson on all facets of the issue. Present the spokesperson to the media as the source of information as early as possible. Make the media's job as easy as possible. The more you can do this, the more you can stay in control of the information they receive. Keep them well-informed with *facts*, not opinions or conjecture. Don't keep them waiting for information for undue periods of time; update them as often as possible.

After the crisis, continue to monitor the situation and update key audiences for several months afterward. Determine the effectiveness of your plan through the feedback you receive.

By following these steps and developing a well-thought-out plan, you can turn the danger of a crisis situation into an opportunity, one that solidifies your foundation's public image. For sample crisis plans, check with your community foundation colleagues and the Council's Media Relations Department at media@cof.org.

5.

DELIVERING YOUR MESSAGE

What Communications Skills Help?

As you work to promote your image and deliver your message, you must rely on certain skills to help you. If you work for a large foundation with a dedicated communications staff, they likely have the skills and experience needed for most marketing and public relations activities. For smaller foundations with fewer staff, it may be more difficult to find some of these skills in-house. Some solve this problem by hiring consultants to do a specific job, but there are other alternatives as well.

The skills that help deliver your foundation's message include:

- Writing and editing
- Layout and graphic design
- Web design
- Public speaking
- Visual presentations.

> **WHAT YOU WILL LEARN**
>
> Discover and develop the communications skills that will help your staff deliver its message, including writing and editing, layout and graphic design, web design, public speaking and visual presentations. Find out how to plan and hold events, produce publications, use the web and advertise effectively.

Writing and Editing

Like any organization, your foundation produces a lot of written materials. All staff members in your foundation write something throughout the normal course of their job—everything from memos, e-mails and posters to articles for the local paper. The more consistent those written materials are, the more consistent your message.

Take a sampling of your foundation's current written materials from different departments—your fact sheets, brochures and donor reports, for example. *What writing style is used in each? Do they have a consistent look and language? Would someone on the street automatically know they were from the same organization?*

Not every piece of writing will be the same, nor do you want it to be. All staff members will have their own styles, and each department may write for its own purpose. Still, there are ways to unify written materials across the foundation.

A style guide is one of those ways. As communications staff, you might develop a **style guide** for staff to use as they write and edit their work. Such a guide offers the foundation's ground rules for style, format, syntax and production.

For example, your style guide might include:

- Suggested language, style and tone for different publications.

- Grammar and syntactic rules, such as spelling, abbreviations, punctuation, capitalization, and compound and hyphenated words.
- A policy on jargon and non-discriminatory language.
- Common misused words and expressions.
- Tips for good writing style, such as identifying the audience and theme and using active voice.
- Editing tips.

Check with your colleague community foundations or other nonprofits for a sample of their style guide. Reviewing many samples, you will gain ideas for how to create your own.

Layout and Graphic Design

Layout and design make your piece of writing look interesting, appealing and easy to read. It is also what makes your message powerful, giving it pizzazz and punch.

Layout describes how you set your writing on the page, along with the headings and illustrations you use. Font, colors, symbols and photographs are just some of your many design options.

Here are some general guidelines for design and layout:

- Use a consistent typeface. A serif font (such as Times New Roman) works better for main text and a sans serif font for headings (such as Arial). Don't use more than two or three types of lettering in one publication; it will appear too busy.
- Avoid THE USE OF CAPITAL LETTERS except for proper nouns.
- Use **bold**, underlining and *italics* sparingly.
- Keep the size of the lettering comfortable to read.
- Use headings and subheadings to guide the reader.
- Use uncomplicated numbering.
- Allow for uncluttered white space. Include wide margins and let the text breathe.
- Use boxes to highlight something.
- Use photos, graphics and cartoons where appropriate to clarify your message.

Web Design

The web is a different animal than the rest of your printed materials. Because you use it differently, you must follow different rules for its design. If you are designing or writing for your website in-house, learn the rules first.

When writing for the web, remember that it can be tiring to read from a computer screen. Present everything simply and make it easy to read. Use short sentences and small paragraphs with subheadings. You can create links where visitors can click for more detailed information.

As for page layout, remember that less is more. Use a clean and uncluttered look for your website and place your most important information at the top of the screen—not where visitors have to scroll down to find it.

Screen navigation can be text, graphics or a combination of both. Keep in mind that generally people read from top to bottom, left to right. Place navigation tools in these areas for logical and easy use by the visitor.

Again, these are just a few tips for designing a site—not a comprehensive list of all you need to know. Talk to web design experts and look to other websites for examples. *For more on websites, read the "Management, Finance and Administration" chapter. Visit CF Tech at www.cftech.org.*

Public Speaking

Most everyone has to do it at one time or another. For some community foundation staff, it's their job to do it all the time. Public speaking puts a face and a voice behind your foundation's message. It creates a big impression and, if done well, can be your best communication tool.

Public speaking can be anything from a short conversation with a small group of donors, to a formal presentation in front of hundreds of community members. You will modify your style of speaking and presentation based on the context. Here are some hints to help you prepare for a presentation, or help you prepare talking points for your CEO, board and/or colleagues.

Before you make a presentation:

- Know all the facts about your presentation—the time, date, purpose, venue, topic, occasion, number of people and so forth.

- Know your objective. *What do you want people to know, think, feel or do after you speak? Are you speaking to motivate, educate, gain their support?*

- Know your audience. *What is their knowledge level on your topic? What are their needs? Why will they care about what you have to say?*

- Create an outline for what you want to say.

- Aim for one key message/point and not more than two or three. Don't try to cover too much—you will lose people.

- Keep it short, simple, clear and straightforward.

- Decide what language, style and tone will be most appropriate for your audience. Use words they will understand. Avoid jargon.

- Once you have written, edited and proofed your speech, create your speech notes on small cards. Highlight key words or phrases that will help you to remember the logical flow of your speech.

- Practice, practice, practice.

Visual Presentations

Visual presentations can bring your message to life. People like to see pictures, plain and simple. Just as people will more likely read a brochure with an attractive photograph on the front, they will pay more attention to speakers who use multimedia. As adult learning studies have shown, a "talking head" can only hold attention for so long before the audience loses interest or worse, doses off.

If you want to deliver a strong presentation—one that people will remember—use photos, graphics, films, videos or presentation slides.

Producing visual materials requires time, money and expertise. In some cases, you may be lucky enough to use outside sources. Check with grantees to see if they photograph their activities and if they will provide you with prints or, even better, digital files. Check with your local newspapers, the public library and stock photo centers for anything of interest.

If you hope to make a video of your own, ask local filmmakers in your community to consider donating some or all of their services. You might also inquire at the communications department of local colleges. They might be willing to assign students to produce your film, video or slide show as part of their coursework.

You can also create simple slide shows on PowerPoint or other presentation software. As long as you have the software in-house, most programs walk you through step by step. Pay attention to the layout of each slide and above all, keep it simple. You can also customize your own PowerPoint presentations with tools developed by the National Marketing Action Team. Visit www.cfmarketplace.org to find out more.

Before your presentation, it helps to perform a "practice run" for a colleague. Ask them for feedback on the clarity, flow and usefulness of the slides.

In What Ways Can You Deliver Your Message?

Events

Events make the community aware of your mission. For this reason, they are excellent public relations opportunities. As communications staff, even if you aren't in charge of planning the event yourself, you can help your colleagues plan for what they will say and the materials they will distribute.

Some community foundations use their **annual meeting** as a public relations tool, inviting donors, grantees, corporate and civic leaders, and the press. These events introduce donors to the grant recipients, often for the first time. They keep attendees abreast of the foundation's work, its annual accomplishments and new programs. Some community foundations invite national speakers to attract community leaders and bring more publicity.

Community foundations often hold **awards ceremonies**, where they recognize donors, grantees, leaders or other members of the community in awards programs. These programs often create good publicity for the foundation.

Most community foundation executives and development officers make themselves available for **speaking engagements** before civic groups, trade associations, nonprofit groups, professional advisors, other grantmakers and more.

Your foundation's executive director, director of development or key board members will also attend **meetings, events and social functions** throughout all local sectors. The more your foundation can make one-to-one contact, the more it can build awareness and attract support.

How to Publicize a Special Event

Here are some tips for publicizing special events. Note that not all of these activities will be appropriate or desirable for every event. You will customize your approach depending on the type of event and the audience you are trying to attract.

- Write a news release about the event.
- Make a spokesperson available for media interviews.
- Distribute the news release to your print and electronic mailing lists, at events and meetings, and to colleague organizations.
- Advertise the event in your newsletters, on your website and through e-mail lists.
- Create posters, signs and flyers for the event.

Publications

Publications can make or break your communications program. They are often your first line of contact with the public—and first impressions count.

Your publications put basic information into the hands of your constituents and the public. To work, publications must be attractive and readable without being too slick or fancy. They must use clear, consistent and concise language as well as appeal to the eye.

Community foundations often produce the following publications:

- Annual reports
- Newsletters
- Brochures
- Other publications.

Annual Reports

The National Standards call for community foundations to regularly produce a report that describes the mission, activities and financial operations. An annual report is your foundation's report to the community—a summary of the activities for the previous year and a record of grants and issues funded. Often, the annual report serves as a foundation's most important public relations tool. In smaller foundations, it may be the only publication the foundation produces.

Annual reports may be a simple, typed document listing the previous year's donors and grants, or they may be elaborately designed. They can take the form of a page, a newsletter, a brochure or a book.

An annual report may include:

- Year, name and geographic focus of the foundation.
- Address, telephone number and website address.
- Mission, vision, values, brief history and purpose of the foundation.
- Statement by the board chair and/or the executive director highlighting some aspect of the foundation or discussing the importance of philanthropy.
- Overview of the organization and governing structure, identifying members of the board, officers and staff.

Quick Tips: Creating an Annual Report

- **Start a folder** at the beginning of the year. Use it to save lists of grants, speeches by board members and staff, newspaper clips, news releases, fund reports, photos and so forth.
- **Borrow ideas** from the annual reports of similar-sized community foundations. Look for comparable annual reports at Council on Foundations conferences or through the Council's Wilmer Shields Rich Awards.
- **Write as you go** about grants and events, when the details are fresh.
- **Ask grantees for photographs** and take advantage of events that occur throughout the year by hiring a photographer or taking photos yourself.
- **Consider the tone** you want to use. Most foundations strive to be regarded as down-to-earth and accessible.
- **Visit www.cfmarketplace.org** for more tools and ideas.

> **NATIONAL STANDARDS**
> **VII.B**
>
> A community foundation has a communication strategy that includes a report, widely distributed at least annually, which describes the community foundation's mission, activities and financial operations.

- Report of gifts received during the year, perhaps accompanied by a section recognizing individual donors.

- Guide for prospective donors, explaining gifts and types of funds the foundation accepts.

- Statement of grant activity during the year, identifying the program category, recipient and amount of each grant.

- Narrative description of several key grants.

- Section outlining the grant program and policies, and detailing the application procedures.

- Description of special programs or initiatives.

- List of the financial institutions holding the foundation's funds.

- Report of the independent public accountant who audits the books, accompanied by financial statements.

Once your annual report is ready, you should distribute it widely. Take your reports to meetings with donors and professional advisors, presentations, conferences and other events. Mail your report to board members, current and potential donors, grantees, reporters, elected officials, foundation colleagues and philanthropic organizations.

Some foundations publish their annual reports online—either on their own website or through an outside service such as The Foundation Center (www.fdncenter.org).

Newsletters

Newsletters keep your community foundation's name and activities in front of your audience. Usually issued quarterly, they are a flexible means of attracting interest and support.

Newsletters appear less formal than the annual report. They are often news-related, but with a human-interest angle—a donor profile, for example, or an article on the accomplishments of volunteers. Newsletters paint a picture of how the foundation and its donors help the community. They also highlight community issues that need funding.

You can use your newsletter in different ways. Some foundations create separate editorial sections or inserts targeted to special audiences. Others include surveys or solicit contributions. Some send newsletters by mail; others deliver them electronically, via e-mail or on their website.

When developing a newsletter, consider the following:

- What do you want to achieve with this newsletter?

- How much have you budgeted for staff and production costs?

- Can you produce and design the newsletter in-house?

- Who is the target readership?

- What is the best way to reach them?
- What image do you want to promote?
- How often should the newsletter come out?
- How many copies will you print?
- Where else should you distribute the newsletter?
- How will you assess whether you are achieving your objectives?

Brochures and "Leave Behinds"

Brochures help target specific messages to your intended audiences. Some community foundations develop brochures as a set, focusing each one on a different topic, such as:

- Mission and history
- Grant purposes, program and policies
- Special fundraising programs
- Types of funds accepted by the foundation
- Tax advantages of giving
- How to use the community foundation to achieve charitable goals.

Other foundations develop brochures based on different audiences—for instance, a brochure for potential donors, for current donors, for professional advisors and so forth.

Brochures can be expensive to produce, especially if they are printed on quality stock with art and color. If you print brochures out-of-house, design them for a long shelf-life. Be careful about including information that will become outdated quickly.

Some community foundations have found it more efficient—and economical—to produce one-page "leave behinds." Rather than a full brochure, these one-pagers are tailored to one specific audience and focus on one topic. Readers find them easy and accessible, and community foundations find them effective in getting their message across. *For examples of "leave behinds" for donors and professional advisors, see the National Marketing Action Team tools at www.cfmarketplace.org.*

Many community foundations now design and print their own brochures in-house on color copiers. Doing this saves money and makes it much easier to update brochures. If you are looking for more savings, you might also print single product sheets, as opposed to full brochures, describing one aspect of the foundation per page. If you do use single product sheets, you might place them in a folder when responding to information requests.

Other Publications

In addition to newsletters and brochures, larger community foundations typically produce reports, surveys and books. Others design simple booklets for specific audiences, such as attorneys or other donor advisors, donors and grant seekers. They might send brochures to their mailing list, for example, and then follow information requests with a detailed booklet.

Some community foundations also publish special bulletins or news briefs. These bulletins usually cover a single topic and are issued occasionally. Today, it is more common—and cost effective—for these shorter publications to be distributed by blast e-mail rather than print. *Visit www.cfmarketplace.org for sample marketing tools, e-newsletters and other customizable publications.*

The Web

Websites

The web is often the first place people look when seeking information. Your website can express your foundation's mission and intent, and communicate its value for donors, nonprofits and the community. websites save valuable staff time as well, as staff can direct inquiries to the site to answer basic questions, download grant guidelines, find a copy of the annual report and so forth.

Aim for a site that enables visitors to access information in an easy and efficient way. Your site should provide background information about the foundation, its grants, its giving options, news and resources. Typical community foundation sites can include the following sections:

- About the foundation—mission, history, board and staff names
- For donors—Why to give, how to give, types of funds available
- For grant seekers—Grant guidelines, application, recent grants
- For advisors—Giving options, resources
- Community foundation news—events, press information, calendar, annual report
- Field news—news on philanthropic issues
- Contact information.

Websites can be simple or intricate, costly or cheap. Look to staff, board members, volunteers or local experts to help you design and post your site, pro bono or at a reduced rate. You might hire a web expert to develop the best content and format for your site. Check other community foundation websites for ideas and visit www.cftech.org or www.cfamerica.org for more information. You can also see the

---

How to Work with Outside Vendors on Publications

Publications require that you work with outside printers, graphic design artists, distributors and other vendors. Some community foundations distribute a request for proposals (RFPs) to various vendors, soliciting bids for their publication projects. An RFP should include specific information about your community foundation and the services you seek. It should also specify what vendors should provide you in their written proposal—for example, a description of their services or products, a price quote, work plan, timeline, references and so forth. Check with your community foundation colleagues for sample RFPs.

When working with outside vendors, these general tips will guide you:

- Get detailed quotes in writing from a range of service providers. When you are not sure what the quote covers, ask for a line item breakdown.
- Ask for samples of other work the service provider has done.
- If appropriate, ask for references so you can check quality and reliability.
- Once you have an agreement, make sure you have the final quote in writing. Where appropriate, write up a clear contract and provide each party with a signed copy.
- Be specific with your deadlines.
- Keep the lines of communication open. Make sure the service provider knows what you expect.

When working with printers, always put large projects out for bid, as price quotes can vary dramatically. Get equivalent product bids from at least three different printers, so that you can compare them effectively. This means asking for quotes on the same number of copies; type, size and qualities of paper; colors; and type of stitching/binding. Keep in mind that larger quantities usually cost less per piece.

You should proof and revise your text **before it goes to the printer**, as correcting mistakes later can be costly. Always ask the printer to provide you with a negative proof (called a "blueline") to check text, alignment, image resolution and if possible, color.

winners from a recent Wilmer Shields Rich Award, which showcases creative and strategic communications. Visit www.cof.org, COF CODE: **Council Awards**.

Some foundations use interactive features to make giving easier and grantmaking more efficient. For example, nonprofits can apply for grants online or donors can access their funds, all at the click of a button. Other foundations use their site for market research. They track the number of visitors to their site or provide online surveys and feedback forms to discern their perceptions about the foundation.

As communications staff, you not only will maintain and control the quality of your website, but also will publicize it. Some ideas include the following:

- Send out a postcard or an e-mail announcing the site.
- Announce the launch of your site, as well as any major changes, in your newsletter.
- Place your web address on all printed materials including newsletters, brochures, press releases, letterhead, fax cover sheets and business cards.
- When talking to the press, mention your web address.
- Submit your page to the top 10 web directories and search engines. There are many professional search engine submission sites that offer this service for free.
- Request links on association sites such as the Council on Foundations (Council members can e-mail webmaster@cof.org), the Foundation Center (www.fdncenter.org) and your local regional association (www.givingforum.org).
- Find complementary sites or grantee sites that offer reciprocal links.
- Place your web address as the signature line of staff e-mail messages.

Keep in mind that you must constantly maintain and update the website, which requires dedicated staff or volunteer time. Don't take a chance on your audience finding out-of-date or irrelevant material on your site. At all times, feature the most current and useful information and make sure all of the links are working properly.

For more information on creating websites, see the "Management, Finance and Administration" chapter.

E-mail

Community foundations use e-mail for both internal and external communication. E-mail speeds communication and can be an effective and efficient way to provide information, respond to requests, facilitate e-mail lists and market the foundation's activities.

Each time you and your colleagues send an e-mail, you promote a particular image of the foundation through your language, style and tone. Because e-mail is so quick and easy, you must stay wary of the image it presents. For example, e-mail messages might be too long or too abrupt, or adopt an inappropriate tone. Because senders take less time to edit e-mails, the messages might contain more spelling and grammatical errors.

Submitting Your Site to Search Engines

You should submit your site to search engines to make it as easy as possible for people to find it. Not sure how to do that? Here is where to find help: *Search Engine Watch* (http://searchenginewatch.com) is the most comprehensive website on search engines available. Visitors have access to a wealth of articles covering a multitude of search-related topics. *Web Search* (http://websearch.about.com) provides a basic primer on search engine positioning, including articles on finding search engine success.

Your foundation should develop protocol on e-mail use, reminding staff that they are at all times communicating on behalf of the foundation.

When used properly and efficiently, e-mail can be an excellent vehicle to promote your foundation and its message. Ask staff to include the mission in the "signature line" of e-mail messages, along with their individual contact information. You might also suggest that your board members add a line to their e-mail messages, such as "A proud member of the XYZ Community Foundation."

Advertisements

Advertisements allow you to control your message to a degree not possible with news stories. Advertising is media you *pay* to present and can appear in either print or electronic media. It has a simple purpose: To make audiences aware of the community foundation's products and services and to get them to act. That act may mean calling the foundation, requesting more information or making a contribution.

What makes a good advertisement? Advertisements aim to:

- **Grab** readers with a photograph or illustration
- **Appeal** to human emotion
- **Address** your readers' needs—not your needs.

The costs of mass-media advertising can be high and must be weighed against the benefits. You can advertise without incurring a major expense, however. For example, you might develop a print ad and give it to your grantees, with a request that they print it in their programs and newsletters when space is available.

Another form of free advertising is public service announcements (PSAs). PSAs get your message out, quickly. In addition to PSAs, consider underwriting announcements on public radio or television. Although these are generally brief, it is another way you can put the foundation before the public eye. Many community foundations in metropolitan areas have found that buying sponsorships on National Public Radio has been effective, especially during morning and evening "drive times" to and from work.

Many community foundations also advertise in journals for professional advisors. Some community foundations now advertise regionally in conjunction with their community foundation colleagues in nearby towns or throughout a particular state, or they advertise nationally by using products developed by the National Market Action Team.

▪ FROM THE FIELD: COMMUNICATIONS MATERIALS

When one large West Coast foundation surveyed its grantees, past and present, some of the respondents described the communication materials as "intimidating," "hard to understand" and "slick." With the help of a communications consultant, the foundation gave itself a makeover that affected all aspects of its visual identity (color, typeface, style of photography, paper stock) and every communications tool (website, newsletter, annual report, stationery, signage, etc.). The intent was to "warm up" the foundation's image and make it more accessible to worthy applicants. It worked: According to the foundation, more grant applications came in—a higher percentage of which conformed to foundation guidelines—indicating that the foundation communicated more clearly with its audience.

5.
DESIGNING A COMMUNICATIONS PLAN

How Do You Develop a Communications Plan?

Communications affects everything your community foundation does. When you dedicate time and resources toward strategic communications, you will see it is a win/win situation that helps your foundation in every aspect of its work. This section will show you just how easy communications can be and how much better it is when you're no longer the best kept secret in town.

For your communications plan to work, it must be part of the foundation's strategic plan. This way, you gain buy-in from the board and your fellow staff. Use this guide to help you educate them, if need be, on the importance of communications.

As part of the strategic plan, determine how much of the foundation's resources can be allotted to your communications efforts. As the saying goes, money talks—meaning the communications strategies you choose will likely be a result of how much you have to spend. Be sure to identify any free resources and the amount of time available from staff and volunteers.

Next, do your research. Market research helps you understand your audience. Community foundations can use research not only to inform strategic planning, but also to identify opportunities and set and measure goals.

Start by making a list of all the audiences you want to reach. *How are you currently communicating with your audiences? How do they perceive your foundation? What works, what doesn't work?* You might profile different audience groups for their feedback and ideas. This can help you understand how your message is getting across, what is working and what you need to change. Look to field research as to what your colleagues find effective for their communications. Check national and regional associations for the latest market studies.

> **WHAT YOU WILL LEARN**
>
> Learn how easy it is to create and evaluate a communications plan. Find out how you can use board members, donors, grantees and other grantmakers as a part of this plan.

What Are the Elements of a Good Strategic Communications Plan?

- **Statement of Overall Strategic Direction**
  This statement will reflect your foundation's overall strategic plan. It may be the same as your vision statement.

- **Situation Analysis**
  This information comes from your research. Consider these questions: *What's happening in your environment today, locally, regionally and nationally? What communications strategies are you currently using? What is working/what do you need to improve?*

- **Target Audiences**

    List your intended audiences. *Who do you need to talk to and why? Where do your gifts come from? Who represents the greatest opportunity—donors, prospects, advisors?*

- **Key Messages**

    Match your message to your audience. *What will motivate your audiences to act? And how are you different from their other choices?*

- **Objectives**

    Establish your objectives by audience. Be sure objectives are clear, concise, realistic and measurable.

- **Strategies**

    List your strategies for each audience. *What initiatives and methods will help you achieve your objectives?*

- **Tactics**

    What communications tools, events and activities will you engage in?

- **Action plans**

    Who is going to carry out each step? By what date?

- **Budget**

    How much is it going to cost?

- **Measurement**

    How will you measure your success?

Source: Marketing for Community Foundations, Center for Community Foundation Excellence, www.cof.org, COF CODE: **CCFE**

How Can You Include Your Colleagues in Communications?

Communications shouldn't rest solely on the communications staff. In many instances, board members, grantees, donors and other organizations make for a more successful channel.

Encourage board members who are good public speakers or interviewees to use these skills for the foundation. If you have prestigious board members, ask them to make grant and other important announcements as a way to attract publicity.

Sometimes board members, staff and volunteers may not be clear on their message about the community foundation. Here are some ideas to encourage them to "get the word out" and get it out right.

- Ask yourselves why your foundation exists. Develop a simple answer of under 10 words that members can recite when asked. Print this on your business card or other materials.

- Ask board members to generate a list of their business and personal associates to tell about the foundation.

- Give each board, staff and volunteer an index card listing the benefits of giving through a community foundation and basic facts of the foundation (vision, mission, contact information, etc.).

- Remind your colleagues to describe gifts in terms of human problems solved—either for the donor or for the community—and encourage them to share these stories with others.

- Provide them with the tools in this chapter for writing, speaking, using the web and more.

Donors can be another good way to communicate the benefits of the foundation. Many foundations organize lunches or other gatherings of prospective donors and invite a number of current donors who will explain, in their own words, why they gave to the foundation.

Grantees and other nonprofits also keep the name and activities of the community foundation in the public eye. Some community foundations put a clause in their grant contracts requiring that grantees coordinate their publicity with the foundation or give appropriate credit to the foundation any time the project receives press. Others ask grantees to include the foundation logo on their printed materials.

What Are the Costs in Implementing the Plan?

Communications should be a part of your foundation's strategic plan and administrative budget. If not, educate your board on the importance of communication and the benefits it has on your organization. Make sure they allocate money toward that function in the future.

With each communication or promotional activity strategy that you plan, you must factor in the costs. Think through what has to be done step by step so that you leave nothing out. The costs of implementing a full-scale communications plan will vary depending on the market and the number of volunteers you use.

In a recent survey, nearly all community foundation respondents reported that they allocate an annual budget for marketing communications expenditures; of those organizations that do not currently allocate a marketing budget, 21 percent indicate that they are moving toward developing one. Almost half of respondents reported annual expenditures of $25,000 or less. Slightly more than 40 percent reported receiving $5,001 to $10,000 of *gratis* communications.

Source: Community Foundations Branding and Marketing Communications Insight, *The Cleveland Foundation, 2002.*

How Can You Evaluate Success?

How do you know if your communication plan works? Remember your initial objectives and then ask lots of questions:

- Did you meet your objectives?
- What was your strategy? How did it work well?
- What can you do to build on your successful strategies?
- What can you learn from your efforts?
- What should you do differently next time?

Few community foundations have the resources or in-house expertise to conduct a formal evaluation of their communications efforts. Look for simple ways to measure the effect and response of your efforts. For example:

- Conducting surveys (by phone or in printed materials)
- Conducting interviews (one-on-one or in focus groups)
- Collecting data (number of contacts with reporters, etc.).

If you collect your own data through surveys or interviews, keep your questions basic. If your colleagues are the ones conducting the survey, work with them to develop the questions. For example,

Ask every prospect: How did you learn about us?

Ask every donor: Why did you choose to give through your community foundation?

Ask every grantee: How well do we communicate? Are our printed and web materials clear?

In a simple method, some foundations mail postcards once a year to update the mailing list and promote the website. On the postcard, they might provide a space for open-ended feedback or include a general e-mail address for people to send comments.

Other foundations work with a consultant to survey grant seekers on how they perceive the foundation—its grantmaking, its staff and its communications materials, for example. Some contract with online survey firms to conduct the surveys for them *(find the latest vendors by searching the web)*. *Community Foundations of America offers a market research tool designed to help community foundations elicit knowledge to help strengthen donor relationships. For information on the Donor Survey Tool Kit, visit www.cfamerica.org.*

If you do conduct a formal evaluation of your communications program, look beyond the basics. Instead, consider the following:

- How has your communications program added value to the work of your donors, your grantees and the community?
- What do people say to the staff and board about your presentations, publications?
- Who is the foundation reaching?
- How much do you hear from new organizations, applicants, donors?
- How well do you use the board, staff and volunteers in communicating?
- How can your foundation communicate better?

These indicators will provide you with quantitative and anecdotal data to help you measure success. One thing is sure: If your foundation is not attracting new donors and new grantees, at a minimum, you need to rethink your communications plan.

Communications, Marketing and Public Relations: Questions to Consider

- What works about our current communication strategies?
- What could we improve?
- What makes our message strong?
- How can we be sure everyone involved with the community foundation speaks the same message?
- How might donors and grantees provide feedback on our marketing materials?
- What resources can we devote to communications at this time?

Sample Planning Tools

Developing a Communications Plan

1. Who are we?
   - Who are we?
   - What is our foundation's history?
   - What do we stand for? What do we do? Why do we do it?
   - What is our identity?
   - Who do we aim to serve?
   - How effective are we in meeting our aim and objectives?
   - What has changed for the better as a result of our work?

2. How are we perceived?
   - What is our community foundation's profile at different levels?
   - Is our foundation well known?
   - Are the issues we deal with commonly known about and reported on in the media or in other forums?
   - How does the outside world respond to the issues we are involved in?
   - How does the outside world perceive our foundation and its work?
   - How is this different from how we see ourselves?
   - How do we compete with, or complement, other organizations?
   - How can we learn more about how people perceive us?

3. What are our goals and objectives?
   - What is our foundation's vision and mission?
   - What do we want to achieve and how will we achieve it?
   - What indicators have we set to measure our success?

4. What do we want to achieve through our communications plan?
   - Why do we need a communications plan?
   - What do we want to achieve through it?
   - How will this help to achieve our aims and objectives?
   - How will we measure whether we have been successful?

5. Who do we want to communicate with and why?
   - Who are our different target audiences/groups?
   - What is our reason for communicating with each one of them?
   - What do we want the people we aim to reach to know, think, feel or do as a result of our communication activity?
   - How will we measure our success?

6. What are our key messages for our different target groups?

- Develop simple, clear and compelling key messages for each different group.
- Capture your key message in a sentence, even better would be in a slogan.
- Working through the previous steps will help you to arrive at your key messages.

7. What is the best way to communicate with each target group?

- Now you are ready to come up with strategies for communicating with each group that you have identified.
- Remind yourselves what you want to achieve, and then ask yourselves how this will best be achieved.
- Develop your different strategies as part of your promotion plan, e.g. get more stories into mass media, revamp your newsletter.

8. Getting the plan into action

- What will it take to implement your communication plan?
- What will each strategy cost in time and resources?
- Develop mini-budgets for each strategy and then an overall budget.
- Do you have the money and resources to do it?
- Draw up a schedule/timelines.

9. Implementing our plan

- Decide how you will implement your plan.
- Write down who is responsible for what and by when, and who is responsible overall.

10. Monitoring and evaluation

- Check that all tasks get done.
- Monitor progress with plans.
- Evaluate afterwards in relation to measurable goals set out
- You will then be ready to develop your communications plan for the next year or two, based on your learning from this plan.

Adapted from IMPACS 1999–2000, "Promoting Your Organization," www.civicus.org.

Starting a Communication Program

COMMUNICATIONS WORKSHEET

Audience: _____

Messages: _____

_____

ACTIVITY	JAN	FEB	MAR	APR	MAY	JUN	JUL	AUG	SEPT	OCT	NOV	DEC
Publications												
Newsletter												
Annual report												
Giving tips												
Events												
Annual meeting												
Legacy luncheon												
Awards												
Reports and mailings												
President's letter												
Advertising & P.R.												

Courtesy of the Vancouver Community Foundation

Resources on Communication, Marketing and Public Relations

Publications

Communications Handbook: A Basic Publicity Guide. Council of Michigan Foundations, 1994. www.cmif.org

A Greater Voice: Nonprofit Organizations, Communications Technology and Advocacy. National Council of Nonprofit Associations, 1996. www.ncna.org

Holtz, Shel. *Public Relations on the Net: Winning Strategies to Inform and Influence the Media, the Investment Community, the Government, the Public and More!* American Management Association, 1998. www.amanet.org

Insider's Guide to Strategic Media Relations. Valerie Denney Communications, 2001. www.vdcom.com

Marketing for Community Foundations. Center for Community Foundation Excellence course. Council on Foundations. www.cof.org, CF CODE: **CCFE**

McNamara, Christopher. *Grantmakers Communications Manual.* Council on Foundations and Forum of Regional Associations of Grantmakers, 1998. www.cof.org

The Jossey-Bass Guide to Strategic Communications for Nonprofits: A Step-by-Step Guide to Working with the Media. Jossey-Bass Publishers, 1999. www.josseybass.com

Proscio, Tony. *A Plea for Plain Speaking in Foundations: In Other Words.* New York: Edna McConnell Clark Foundation, 2000.

Proscio, Tony. *How Foundations Garble Their Message and Lose Their Audience: Bad Words for Good.* New York: Edna McConnell Clark Foundation, 2001.

Web

CIVICUS—www.civicus.org

Offers several toolkits to enable organizations globally to improve their capacity.

Communications Network—www.comnetwork.org

Provides strategic communications leadership, guidance and resources for grantmakers.

Goodman, Andy. "Five Myths About Branding"—www.agoodmanonline.com

Why Marketing CD-ROM and other NMAT tools. National Marketing Action Team—www.cfmarketplace.org

SOURCES USED FOR THE COMMUNITY FOUNDATION HANDBOOK

Publications

Best Practices in Grants Management. Grants Managers Network, Council on Foundations, 2001. www.cof.org.

Bernholz, Lucy, Katherine Fulton and Gabriel Kasper. *On the Brink of a New Promise: The Future of U.S. Community Foundations.* Blue Print Research and Design, Inc., and the Monitor Institute, 2005. www.communityphilanthropy.com.

Bryson, Ellen. *What Community Foundation Boards are Saying.* Council on Foundations, 2002. www.cof.org

Bryson, Ellen, Sandra Hughes and Marla Bobwick. *The Guide for Community Foundation Board Members.* BoardSource and the Council on Foundations, 2003. www.cof.org

Center for Community Foundation Excellence courses. Council on Foundations, 2003. www.cof.org, COF CODE: **CCFE**
    Community Foundation Fundamentals
    Resource Development for Community Foundations
    Financial Administration for Community Foundations
    Community Leadership for Community Foundations

Characteristics and Roles: Community Foundation Academy Series for New Trustees and Staff. Council on Foundations, Council of Michigan Foundations, and Forum of Regional Associations of Grantmakers, 1999. www.cof.org.

Community Foundations Branding and Marketing Communications Insight. The Cleveland Foundation, September 2002. www.clevelandfoundation.org

Community Foundation Global Status Report. Worldwide Initiatives for Grantmaker Support (WINGS-CF), 2004. www.wingsweb.org

Community Foundation Portfolio: Market Readiness. National Marketing Action Team, Council on Foundations and Community Foundations of America, 2002.

Community Foundation Training Manuals, Volume I-VI. Council on Foundations, 1990. www.cof.org

Shipp-Simone, Kelly and John A. Edie, 2006. *How to Calculate the Public Support Test,* Second Edition. Council on Foundations, 1998. www.cof.org

Gast, Elaine. *The Guide to Small Foundation Management: From Groundwork to Grantmaking.* Council on Foundations, 2002. www.cof.org

Grantcraft: Practical Wisdom for Grantmakers. Ford Foundation, 2002. www.grantcraft.org

Jansen, Paul J. and Andrea R. Kilpatrick. *The Dynamic Nonprofit Board.* The McKinsey Quarterly, Number 2, 2004. www.mckinseyquarterly.com

Kibbe, Barbara D., and Fred Setterberg, *Grantmaking Basics: A Field Guide for Funders.* Council on Foundations, 1999. www.cof.org

National Standards for U.S. Community Foundations: Confirmation of Compliance Review Form. Standards Action Team of the Community Foundations Leadership Team, Council on Foundations, June 2004. www.cof.org

Principles for Community Leadership: A Guide for Community Foundations. Community Foundations of Canada, 2002. www.community-fdn.ca

Rawl, Michael J. *Exploring the Growth Cycles of Community Foundations.* Mid-Shore Community Foundation, 2003. www.mscf.org

Strengthening Community Foundations: Redefining the Opportunities. The Foundation Strategy Group, October 2003. www.foundationstrategy.com

Tice, Karin E., Ph.D. *Community Foundations: A Case for Regional Marketing.* Council of Michigan Foundations, 2002. www.cmif.org

Web

CF Tech—www.cftech.org

Central New York Community Foundation—www.cnycf.org

Center for Charity Lobbying in the Public Interest—www.clpi.org/community_foundations.html

Cleveland Foundation—www.clevelandfoundation.org

Community Foundations of America—www.cfamerica.org

Community Foundation Marketplace—www.cfmarketplace.org

Community Foundations: Local Giving Partners—www.communityfoundations.net

Community Foundations Standards & Effective Practices database—http://bestpractices.cof.org

Council on Foundations—www.cof.org

National Marketing Action Team—www.cfmarketplace.org

GrantCraft—www.grantcraft.org

Winston Salem Foundation—www.wsfoundation.org

COMMUNITY FOUNDATION RESOURCES

Organizations Serving Community Foundations

Council on Foundations (COF): www.cof.org
> The national membership organization for all grantmakers. It serves community foundations through its Community Foundation Services Department and other COF departments.

Community Foundations of Canada: www.community-fdn.ca
> The membership organization for community foundations in Canada.

Community Foundations of America: www.cfamerica.org
> An organization formed in 1999 to provide products and services for community foundations.

Regional Associations of Grantmakers: www.givingforum.org
> Regional Associations (RAs) serve all types of grantmakers in a particular region. They vary in size, structure and the extent of services offered.

Statewide Associations of Community Foundations:
> These organizations, in addition to the RAs, serve community foundations in a single state.

Community Foundation Professional Groups & Activities
> Professional groups hold their own conferences and/or have sessions at COF's Fall Conference for Community Foundations. Each of these professional groups has an e-mail list, which is maintained by the Council on Foundations' Community Foundation Services department
>
>> FAOG—Fiscal and Administrative Officers Group
>> AdNet—Advancement Network for development, donor relations officers, and senior foundation staff
>> Aff-Able—Affiliates of Council on Foundations members
>> CommA—Communications Network
>> ExecNet—CEO Network
>> ProNet—Program Officers Network
>> SuppNet—Supporting Organizations of Council on Foundations members

Affinity Groups: www.cof.org
> Affinity groups form around issues of common concern. The Council on Foundations maintains relationships with a large number of affinity groups.

Conferences, Training and Peer Networking

Center for Community Foundation Excellence—training and education programs for community foundations: www.cof.org, COF CODE: **CCFE**

Council on Foundations Fall Conference for Community Foundations—the Fall Conference is the premier event for community foundations, held in September or October each year: www.cof.org, COF CODE: **Events**

Community Foundation Professional Group Conferences—AdNet, CommA. Contact the Community Foundations Department: community@cof.org

Larger Community Foundations Meeting—for Board Chairs and CEOs, by invitation only.

Council on Foundations Annual Conference—the COF conference for all types of grantmakers, held annually in late April or May: www.cof.org, COF CODE: **Events**

BoardSource (formerly National Center for Nonprofit Boards)—annual conference and board president/CEO workshops: www.boardsource.org

The Association of Fund Raising Professionals (formerly NSFRE)—offers regional and national conferences and workshops on development and leadership: www.nsfre.org

National Committee on Planned Giving—offers a national conference as well as education, research and advocacy programs: www.ncpg.org

National Center for Family Philanthropy—focuses solely on matters of importance to families engaged in philanthropy: www.ncfp.org

Indiana University, Center on Philanthropy: www.philanthropy.iupui.edu

The Peter Drucker Foundation for Non-Profit Management: www.leadertoleader.org

The Philanthropic Initiative: www.tpi.org

Center for Creative Leadership: www.ccl.org

Women's Philanthropy Institute: www.women-philanthropy.org

Periodicals and Publications

CFSource—This monthly e-newsletter reports on the activities of the Community Foundations Leadership Team and the Council, as well as new developments in the community foundation field. Sign up by sending an e-mail: CFSource@cof.org

Breaking News—Council members can elect to receive a daily e-mail with the day's top philanthropy stories. Sign up by sending an e-mail to media@cof.org with your name, title, organization name and e-mail address.

Foundation News & Commentary—This bimonthly magazine provides you with how-to articles, case studies, opinions from the field and news about current philanthropic activities: www.foundationnews.org

FN&C Now—News can't be scheduled, so the Council offers this electronic newsletter to keep you informed about events and activities in philanthropy as they occur: www.foundationnews.org/now

Washington Update—This longtime favorite among members provides periodic updates on legislative and regulatory activities relevant to your work. All members of your board or staff are encouraged to subscribe: www.cof.org

Board Briefings—These summary papers can inform your board's discussions by presenting background information and two differing opinions on key policy issues. Previous topics have included venture philanthropy, estate taxes, funding strategies, globalization and board compensation: www.cof.org, COF CODE: **Gov Boards**

Council Columns—The Council's bimonthly, cross-constituency newsletter provides you with brief updates on important topics in the foundation world: www.cof.org

Council Publications—As a Council member you receive discounts on publications such as research reports, legal guides and how-to publications on administration, grantmaking and many other relevant topics. Publications include *What Community Foundation Board Members Are Saying, Supporting Organizations and How They Work,* and *The Guide for Community Foundation Board Members.* You may search the Council's online publications catalog by topic or for titles relevant to community foundations: www.cof.org

GLOSSARY OF COMMUNITY FOUNDATION TERMS

501(c)(3)
Section of the Internal Revenue Code that designates an organization as charitable and tax exempt. Organizations qualifying under this section include religious, educational, charitable, amateur athletic, scientific or literary groups, organizations testing for public safety or organizations involved in prevention of cruelty to children or animals. The tax code sets forth a list of sections—501(c)(4–26)—to identify other nonprofit organizations whose function is not solely charitable (e.g., professional or veterans organizations, chambers of commerce, fraternal societies).

509(a)
Section of the tax code that defines public charities (as opposed to private foundations). A 501(c)(3) organization also must have a 509(a) designation to further define it as a public charity.

Accrual Basis of Accounting
Calls for recording revenue in the period in which it is earned and recording expenses in the period in which they are incurred. The effect of events on the organization is recognized as services are rendered or consumed rather than when cash is received or paid.

Administrative Fund
See *Operating Fund.*

AdNet
Advancement Network. The association of development professionals in the community foundation field.

Affiliate Fund
A collection of assets designated to benefit a specific community, generally a geographic service area that operates under the guidance of, or in accordance with a formal agreement with, a community foundation serving a larger or a separate area. In practice, community foundations generally provide, from within their existing organizational infrastructure, the 'back office' services for these funds. Affiliate funds may be donor-advised or field of interest funds at the host community foundation or they may be separately incorporated charitable organizations that either are structured as supporting organizations to the parent community foundation or that have a written agreement with the host community foundation for the provision of services.

Affinity Group
A separate and independent coalition of grantmaking institutions or individuals associated with such institutions that shares information or provides professional development and networking opportunities to individual grantmakers with a shared interest in a particular subject or funding area.

Agency Endowment Fund
Established by a nonprofit agency for the benefit of the nonprofit agency. The community foundation regularly distributes the annual net earnings back to the agency for purposes established by the agency. Also called *Organization Endowment Fund.*

Annual Report
A report published by a foundation or corporation describing its mission, leadership, programs, services, activities and accomplishments. In the case of community foundations, it also describes its grantmaking and donor services, and includes a listing of contributors, selected policies and guidelines, and an audited financial statement.

Annualized Return
The compounded average annual return for periods greater than one year.

Appreciated Assets
Those assets that have increased in value since they were acquired. Such assets are usually subject to capital gains tax if sold.

Appreciated Securities (gift of)
Gifts of securities include publicly traded stocks, mutual funds, treasury bills, notes and closely held stock. The gift of appreciated securities held for at least one year allows the donor a charitable deduction for the market value of the gift, avoiding payment of capital gains tax.

Articles of Incorporation
A document filed with the secretary of state or other appropriate state office by persons establishing a corporation. This is the first legal step in forming a nonprofit corporation.

Asset
Cash stocks, bonds, real estate or other holdings of a foundation. Generally, assets are invested and the income is used to make grants.

Asset Allocation
The distribution of a pool of assets among various asset classes including, but not limited to, domestic and foreign bonds, cash, real estate, venture capital, etc.

Audit
An independent examination of the accounting records and other evidence relating to a business to support the expression of an impartial expert opinion about the reliability of the financial statements.

Balance Sheet (Statement of Financial Position)
A financial statement that shows the financial position of the organization at a particular date. It consists of a list of assets, liabilities and fund balances.

Bargain Sale
The sale of securities, real estate, tangible personal property or other assets to a charity for less than their current value. The donor receives a charitable deduction for the difference between the appraised value and bargain price. The charity sells the property and retains the difference between the price it paid and the price for which it sold.

Basis Point
One hundredth of a percentage point (0.01%) used frequently to measure changes in yields or fixed income securities, since they often change by very small amounts

Benchmark Portfolio
A portfolio against which the investment performance of an asset pool can be compared for the purpose of determining investment skill.

Bequest
A gift by will to a specific recipient. A charitable bequest is a transfer at death by will to a nonprofit organization for charitable purposes.

Bricks and Mortar
An informal term indicating grants for buildings or construction projects.

Building Campaign
A drive to raise funds for construction or renovation of buildings and other physical structures.

Bylaws
Rules governing the operation of a nonprofit corporation, developed according to state law requirements. Bylaws often provide the methods for selecting directors, creating committees and conducting meetings.

Capital Campaign
Also referred to as a Capital Development Campaign, a capital campaign is an organized drive to collect and accumulate substantial funds to finance major needs of an organization such as a building or major repair project.

Cash
The most common type of gift made to most organizations. Includes cash, checks and credit cards.

Cash Basis of Accounting
Revenue is recorded when received in cash and expenses are recorded in the period in which cash payment is made.

CEO Net
CEO Network. The association of CEOs in the community foundation field.

Challenge Grant
A grant that is made on the condition that other monies must be secured, either on a matching basis or via some other formula, usually within a specified period of time, with the objective of stimulating giving from additional sources.

Charitable Class [from IRS Publication 3833].
The group of individuals that may properly receive assistance from a charitable organization is called a charitable class. A charitable class must be large or indefinite enough that providing aid to members of the class benefits the community as a whole. Because of this requirement, a tax-exempt charitable organization cannot target and limit its assistance to specific individuals, such as a few persons injured in a particular fire. Similarly, donors cannot earmark contributions to a charitable organization for a particular individual or family.

Charitable Gift Annuity
A gift of cash or securities in exchange for the promise of lifetime income, immediate (CGA) or deferred (DCGA). A charitable gift annuity is a contract between the donor and charity that is part charitable gift and part purchase of an annuity. The total assets of the charity back the payments.

Charitable Intent
The philanthropic benefits or purposes assigned by the donor when making a gift. Charitable purposes include the relief of poverty, the advancement of education or religion, the promotion of health, governmental or municipal purposes, and other purposes the achievement of which is beneficial to the community. Organizations set up and operated exclusively for charitable purposes, and which serve a public rather than a private interest, are exempt from federal income tax under section 501(c)(3) of the Internal Revenue Code and are eligible recipients of tax-deductible charitable contributions.

Charitable Lead Trust
A charitable lead trust (CLT) pays the trust income to a charity first for a specified period, with the principal reverting to the donor or going to other person(s) at the end of the period. If it is established by will, it is known as a Testamentary Charitable Lead Trust (TCLT). Also called *Income Trust*.

Charitable Remainder Trust
A gift plan that provides income to one or more beneficiaries for their lifetimes, a fixed term of not more than 20 years or a combination of the two. Assets, usually cash, securities or real estate are transferred to a trust that pays income to the beneficiaries for the term of the trust. When the trust term ends, the remainder in the trust passes to the charity. Can be established as a Charitable Remainder Annuity Trust (CRAT) with a fixed payout or as a Charitable Remainder Unitrust (CRUT) with a variable payout. Can be established during the donor's lifetime (CRT) or by will (TCRT).

Chart of Accounts
Listing of the account titles and account numbers being used by an organization.

Community Foundations Leadership Team (Leadership Team)
Formerly known as the Committee on Community Foundations, this group represents the structure for advancing the community foundation field. CFLT members include representatives of the professional groups, representatives of action teams, community foundation trustees, and a core group elected by the field.

CommA
Communications Association. The professional association of community foundation communications professionals.

Community Foundation
A tax-exempt, nonprofit, autonomous, publicly supported, nonsectarian philanthropic institution with a long-term goal of building permanent, named component funds established by many separate donors for the broad-based charitable benefit of the residents of a defined geographic area, typically no larger than a state.

Community Foundation Action Teams
The Community Foundations Leadership Team conducts its work through member-driven "action teams." These groups are formed to take on short-term projects as well as long-term initiatives. The Leadership Team and/or groups of members establish them to advance the priority needs of the field. Currently, there are five action teams: Standards, Legal and Legislative, and National Marketing.

Community Foundations of America (CFA)
Organization (www.cfamerica.org) formed in 1999 to enhance the ability of foundations to build their communities and serve their donors. Membership is open to all U.S. community foundations that agree to adhere to the *National Standards for U.S. Community Foundations* and that wish to access CFA's products and services on a fee basis. Carla Dearing serves as president and CEO. www.cfamerica.org.

Component Fund
An individual fund considered by the Internal Revenue Service (IRS) to be part of the exempt assets of a foundation. The foundation's governing board must have total control over all assets of a component fund.

Consumer Price Index (CPI)
A measure of change in consumer prices, as determined by a monthly survey of the U.S. Bureau of Labor Statistics.

Corporate Form
A community foundation that is incorporated as a nonprofit corporation. Investment management of assets held is the responsibility of the board of the foundation. A community foundation may include both a corporate entity and component trusts. Also see *Trust Form*.

Corporate Foundation
Also referred to as a Company-Sponsored Foundation, this type of private foundation receives its funding from the for-profit company whose name it bears but is legally an independent entity. Corporations may establish foundations with initial endowments, make periodic contributions—generally based on a percentage of the company's profit—to the foundation or combine both methods to provide the foundation's resources.

Council on Foundations (COF)
The international membership association (www.cof.org) that serves the public good by promoting knowledge and growth and enhancing responsible and effective philanthropy. Its more than 2,000 members consist of community foundations, corporate foundations and giving programs, private and family foundations, public foundations and a new category known as emerging foundations. Suzanne Feurt is the council's director of community foundation services.

Custodian
A bank or other financial institution that has custody of stock certificates and other assets of a mutual fund, individual, corporation or institution. Custodians hold assets in safekeeping, collect income on securities in custody, settle transactions, invest cash overnight, handle corporate accounting and provide accounting reports.

Cy Pres
Also called the cy pres doctrine. Cy pres is the power vested in a court to vary the terms of a charitable trust if the charitable purpose specified by the donor becomes unlawful, impracticable or impossible to achieve. Courts applying cy pres must direct the funds to a new purpose or beneficiary that is as near as possible to the donor's original intent. The variance power possessed by community foundations is modeled on cy pres, but may be exercised without the need to seek court approval.

Deferred Gifts
Methods of giving which require the wait of a year or more before being able to use the gift assets.

Deferred Gift with No Income Benefit: A gift that the foundation will be able to use in the future, from which neither the foundation nor the donor receive any income in the interim.

Deferred Gift with Income Benefit
A gift of assets which the foundation will be able to use in the future, from which the donor or a person or entity designated by the donor receive income in the interim.

Deferred Gift with No Income Benefit
A gift that the foundation will be able to use in the future, from which neither the foundation nor the donor receive any income in the interim.

Designated Fund
A type of restricted fund held by a community foundation in which the donor specifies the fund beneficiaries.

Disqualified Person (Public Charity)
As applied to public charities, the term disqualified person includes (1) organization managers, (2) any other person who, within the past 5 years, was in a position to exercise substantial influence over the affairs of the organization, (3) family members of the above and (4) businesses they control. Paying excessive benefits to a disqualified person results in the imposition of penalty excise taxes on that person and, under some circumstances, on the charity's board of directors. Also see *Intermediate Sanctions*.

Diversification
An attempt to minimize risk by distributing assets among various asset classes or among managers within the same asset class who have different investment styles.

Dividend
A distribution of cash by a corporation to its stockholders.

Donee
See *Grantee*.

Donor
The individual or organization that makes a grant or contribution. Also called a Grantor.

Donor-Advised Fund
A fund held by a community foundation where the donor, or a person or committee appointed by the donor, may recommend eligible charitable recipients for grants from the fund. The community foundation's governing body must be free to accept or reject the recommendations.

Donor Designated Fund
A fund held by a community foundation where the donor has specified that the fund's income or assets be used for the benefit of one or more specific public charities. The community foundation's governing body must have the power to redirect resources in the fund if it determines that the donor's restriction is unnecessary, incapable of fulfillment or inconsistent with the charitable needs of the community or area served. See *Variance Power*.

Due Diligence
In grantmaking, this speaks to the practices one applies to reviewing grant requests prior to approving them. It generally includes establishing the charitable status of the grantee, the charitable purpose of the grant and the financial and organizational capacity of the organization to undertake the proposed activities

Endowment
A fund in which the principle is kept intact, and only a certain amount of earnings are available for other purposes. Donors may require that the principal remain intact in perpetuity, for a defined period of time or until sufficient assets have been accumulated to achieve a designated purpose… With a permanent endowment the principle is often invested along with some retained earnings to retain the fund's historic value.

Equities
Also called equity securities or corporate stocks. An instrument that signifies an ownership position, or equity, in a corporation and represents a claim on its proportionate share in the corporation's assets and profits. An equity holder's claim is subordinated to creditor's claims, and the equity holder will only enjoy distributions from earnings after these higher priority claims are satisfied.

Excise Tax
The annual tax of 1 or 2 percent of net investment income that must be paid to the IRS by private foundations.

Expenditure Responsibility
When a private foundation makes a grant to an organization that is not classified by the IRS as tax exempt under Section 501(c)(3) it is required by law to ensure that the funds are spent for charitable purposes and not for private gain or political activities. Special reports on the status of the grant must be filed with the IRS.

Family Foundation
"Family foundation" is not a legal term, and therefore, it has no precise definition. Yet, approximately two-thirds of the estimated 40,000 private foundations in this country are believed to be family managed. The Council on Foundations defines a family foundation as a private foundation whose funds are derived from members of a single family. At least one family member must continue to serve as an officer or board member of the foundation, and as the donor, they or their relatives play a significant role in governing and/or managing the foundation throughout its life. Members decide themselves if they wish to categorize their

private foundation as a family or independent foundation. In many cases, second- and third- generation descendants of the original donors manage the foundation. Most family foundations concentrate their giving locally, in their communities.

FAOG
Fiscal and Administrative Officers Group. This professional association includes fiscal and administrative officers, as well as human resource and technology personnel, in the community foundation field.

Fiduciary Duty (responsibility)
The legal responsibility for investing money or acting wisely on behalf of a beneficiary. More broadly, for foundation boards such responsibility must be legally exercised on behalf of the donors and the governing documents of the foundation. See *Due Diligence.*

Field of Interest Fund
A fund held by a community foundation that is used for a specific charitable purpose such as education or health research.

Financial Accounting Standards Board (FASB)
This board issues Statements of Financial Accounting Standards that represent authoritative expressions of generally accepted accounting principles.

Financial Report
An accounting statement detailing financial data, including income from all sources, expenses, assets and liabilities. A financial report may also be an itemized accounting that shows how grant funds were used by a donee organization. Most foundations require a financial report from grantees.

Financial Statements
Main source of financial information to persons outside the organization. These convey to management and to interested outsiders a concise picture of the profitability and financial position of the organization.

Fixed Income Security
A security that pays a fixed rate of interest. This usually refers to government, corporate, mortgage and municipal bonds.

Form 990/Form 990-PF
The IRS forms filed annually by public charities and private foundations respectively. The letters *PF* stand for private foundation. The IRS uses this form to assess compliance with the Internal Revenue Code. Both forms list organization assets, receipts, expenditures and compensation of officers. Form 990-PF includes a list of grants made during the year by private foundations.

Fund
An entity established for the purpose of accounting for resources used for specific activities or objectives in accordance with special regulations, restrictions or limitations. Community foundation assets are held in many named component funds established by donors or the foundation for specific or unrestricted purposes.

Fund Accounting
Economic entity is defined to be the fund. Each fund has its own chart of accounts and every transaction is accounted for at the fund level.

Fund Balance
Using the analogy to "owner's equity," the fund balance represents the resources invested by the community.

Funding Cycle
A chronological pattern of proposal review, decisionmaking and applicant notification. Some community foundations make grants at set intervals, others on an annual cycle.

Future Interest Property
The donor gives remainder interest in a personal residence, vacation home or farm, subject to the right to live in the home (or work the farm) for the lifetime of the donor and/or another person. Also known as *Retained Life Estate.*

Generally Accepted Accounting Principles (GAAP)
The accounting standards and concepts used in the measurement of financial activities and the preparation of financial statements.

Gift, Charitable
Merriam-Webster's Collegiate Dictionary, Tenth Edition, defines a gift as "something voluntarily transferred by one person to another without compensation." A charitable gift is a gift of money or other property to a qualified organization for charitable purposes for which the donor does not reasonably anticipate benefit from the donee in return. The Internal Revenue Service's Code Sec. 170, the income tax charitable contribution provision and numerous court cases further define "charitable gift."

Gift, Historical Value
The monetary value of a charitable gift at the time it is given.

Gift, Real Value
The monetary value of a charitable gift after adjustment for inflation and appreciation since the gift was completed.

Giving Pattern
The overall picture of the types of projects and programs that a donor has supported historically. The past record may include areas of interest, geographic locations, dollar amount of funding and kinds of organizations supported.

Grant
The award of funds to an organization or individual to undertake charitable activities.

Grantee
The individual or organization that receives a grant.

Grantor
See *Donor.*

Grassroots Fundraising
Efforts to raise money from individuals or groups from the local community on a broad basis. Usually an organization does grassroots fundraising within its own constituency—people who live in the neighborhood served or clients of the agency's services. Grassroots fundraising activities include membership drives, raffles, bake sales, auctions, dances and other projects. Senior staff often feel that successful grassroots fundraising indicates that an organization has substantial community support.

Growth Oriented Securities
In general two basic categories of securities are owned: 1) companies with consistent above average historical and prospective earnings growth and 2) those expected to generate above average near term earnings increases based upon company, industry or economic factors. Managers in this style are willing to pay above market multiples for the superior growth rate and profitability they anticipate. Hence P/E ratios tend to be greater than the market and dividend yields tend to be less than the S&P 500.

Guidelines
A statement of a foundation's goals, priorities, criteria and procedures for applying for a grant.

Hedging
A strategy used to offset investment risk. A perfect hedge is one eliminating the possibility of gain or loss. Selling short, put options and futures transactions may be used for hedging purposes.

Income, Earned
The interest and dividends returned from an investment. See *Return, Rate of.*

Income Statement
(Statement of Activities or Statement of Revenues, Expenses and Changes in Fund Balances) A financial statement showing the results of operating for an organization by matching revenue and related expenses for a particular accounting period.

Income Trust
See *Charitable Lead Trust.*

Independent Foundation
One individual usually establishes these private foundations, often by bequest. They are occasionally termed "non-operating" because they do not run their own programs. Sometimes individuals or groups of people, such as family members, form a foundation while the donors are still living. Many large independent foundations, such as the Ford Foundation, are no longer governed by members of the original donor's family but are run by boards made up of community, business and academic leaders. Private foundations make grants to other tax-exempt organizations to carry out their charitable purposes. Private foundations must make charitable expenditures of approximately 5 percent of the market value of their assets each year.

Although exempt from federal income tax, private foundations must pay a yearly excise tax of 1 or 2 percent of their net investment income. The Rockefeller Foundation and the John D. and Catherine T. MacArthur Foundation are two examples of well-known "independent" private foundations.

In-Kind Contribution
A donation of goods or services rather than of cash or appreciated property. See also *Technical Assistance*.

Intermediate Sanctions
Penalty taxes applied to disqualified persons of public charities that receive an excessive benefit from financial transactions with the charity. An excessive benefit may result from overcompensation for services or from other transactions such as charging excessive rent on property rented to the charity. Unlike private foundations, public charities are not barred from engaging in financial transactions with disqualified persons as long as the transaction is fair to the charity. Penalty taxes also may apply to organization managers, such as the charity's board, that knowingly approve an excess benefit transaction. Also see *Disqualified Person*.

Internal Revenue Service (IRS)
The federal agency (www.irs.gov) with responsibility for regulating foundations and their activities.

Investment Counsel
A counselor or consultant whose principal business is advising, analyzing or supervising investments managed by others. Differs from an investment manager who is responsible for the investments in a portfolio.

Investment Manager
An advisor who manages the investments of others. In general, a manager with more than $25 million must register with the Securities and Exchange Commission (SEC)

Jeopardy Investment
An investment that is found to have jeopardized a foundation's purposes. The result of a jeopardy investment may be penalty taxes imposed on a foundation and its managers. While certain types of investments are subject to careful examination, no single type is automatically a jeopardy investment. Generally, a jeopardy investment is made when a foundation's managers have "failed to exercise ordinary business care and prudence."

Letter of Inquiry
A brief outline of an organization's activities and a request for funding sent to a prospective donor to determine if there is sufficient interest to warrant submitting a full proposal. This saves the time of the prospective donor and the time and resources of the prospective applicant. Also referred to as a *Preliminary Proposal*.

Letter of Intent
A grantor's letter or brief statement indicating intention to make a specific gift.

Leverage
A method of grantmaking practiced by some foundations. Leverage occurs when a small amount of money is given with the express purpose of attracting funding from other sources or of providing the organization with the tools it needs to raise other kinds of funds. Sometimes known as the "multiplier effect."

Life Insurance (gift of)
Life insurance is easy to give and to receive. The donor must make the organization both *owner* and *beneficiary* of the insurance policy for the IRS to regard the transaction as a charitable gift.

Life Insurance (as wealth replacement)
To secure the interests of family members, the donor of a life income plan (such as a charitable remainder trust) purchases life insurance to replace the value of an asset that has been donated to charity by using the tax savings resulting from the charitable deduction. Placing the insurance policy in a separate trust permits the proceeds to pass to heirs outside the taxable estate.

Limited-Purpose Foundation
One that restricts its giving to one or very few areas of interest, such as higher education or medical care.

Liquidity
Refers to the ease and quickness of converting assets to cash. Also called marketability.

Listserv (e-mail list)
An Internet discussion group. The Council on Foundations hosts separate e-mail lists for each of the community foundation professional groups and others. www.cof.org, COF CODE: **CFLists**.

Loaned Executives
Corporate executives who work for nonprofit organizations for a limited period of time while continuing to be paid by their permanent employers.

Lobbying
Efforts to influence legislation by influencing the opinion of legislators, legislative staff and government administrators directly involved in drafting legislative proposals. The Internal Revenue Code sets limits on lobbying by organizations that are exempt from tax under Section 501(c)(3). *Public* charities may lobby as long as lobbying does not become a substantial part of their activities.

Market-oriented Equities
In this equity style, managers do not have a strong preference for either value or growth stocks. Their portfolio characteristics tend to adhere closer to market averages over a business cycle.

Matching Gifts Program
A grant or contributions program that will match employees' or directors' gifts made to qualifying educational, arts and cultural, health or other organizations. Each employer or foundation establishes specific guidelines. Some foundations also use such a program for their trustees.

Matching Grant
A grant or gift made with the specification that the amount donated must be matched one for one or according to some other prescribed formula.

Mutual Fund
A fund managed by an investment company that raises money from individuals and invests it in stocks, bonds, options, commodities or money market securities. An investment in a mutual fund is represented by shares or units. The value of the units depends on the value of assets owned by the mutual fund, less expenses incurred by the fund.

National Committee on Planned Giving (NCPG)
A professional association of gift planners.

National Standards for U.S. Community Foundations
Approved in September 2000, the National Standards are the minimum requirements for the governance, structure and activities of community foundations. Adoption of these standards throughout the field will provide a level of consistency that will help the field build capacity, distinguish itself and market nationally and regionally.

National Taxonomy of Exempt Entities (NTEE)
Classification system for nonprofit organizations recognized as tax exempt under the IRS code. It facilitates collecting and analyzing data by type of organization and by activity, especially helpful in tracking grants and grantees.

Net Asset Value
The current fair market value of each unit in a mutual fund, as determined by the total value of the fund's investments plus other assets, less liabilities. This total value is divided by the number of units outstanding, to arrive at NAV per unit.

Net of Fee
The rate of return reported on a portfolio after the removal of a money manager's fee.

Non-component Fund
An individual fund, that, because of restrictions by the donor, shared interests by the community foundation and other beneficiaries, or election of the foundation, is not included as part of its publicly supported status and is, therefore, treated as separate by both the foundation and the IRS.

Non-endowed Fund
Monies are received and distributed with little or no dollars remaining with the foundation. An example is the YWCA Capital Campaign Fund.

Operating Contribution
A contribution given to cover an organization's day-to-day, ongoing expenses, such as salaries, utilities, office supplies, etc. Also referred to as *Operating Support*.

Operating Foundation
Also called private operating foundations, operating foundations are private foundations that use the bulk of their income to provide charitable services or to run charitable programs of their own. They make few, if any, grants to outside organizations. To qualify as an operating foundation, the organization must follow specific rules in addition to the applicable rules for private foundations. The Carnegie Endowment for International Peace and the Getty Trust are examples of operating foundations.

Operating Fund
May be either nonpermanent and "spent" for the operations of the foundation or may be endowed with only the income from the fund used for operations.

Operating Support
See *Operating Contribution*.

Optimal Allocation
A predetermined asset mix that best suits the needs and requirements of an organization.

Organization Endowment Fund
See *Agency Endowment Fund*.

Outright Gift
Methods of giving that permit the immediate use of the gift assets.

Pass-through Foundation
Foundations that receive monies and make distributions to donees, with little or no principal remaining with the foundation.

Payout Requirement
The minimum amount that a private foundation is required to expend for charitable purposes (includes grants and necessary and reasonable administrative expenses). In general, a private foundation must pay out annually approximately 5 percent of the average market value of its assets.

Performance Measurement
The analysis of the returns earned on a pool of assets. Performance measurement uses accounting data as its inputs to generate rates of return.

Personal Property
Art, jewelry, furs, "collectibles" and other tangible objects owned by individuals.

Philanthropy
Philanthropy is defined in different ways. The word is of Greek origin, meaning "love for humankind." Today, philanthropy includes the concept of voluntary giving by individuals or groups to promote the common good. It also commonly refers to grants of money given by foundations to nonprofit organizations. Philanthropy addresses contributions by individuals or groups to other organizations that in turn work to alleviate the causes of poverty or social problems—improving the quality of life for all citizens. Philanthropic giving also supports a variety of activities in the areas of research, health, education, arts and culture, and environmental issues.

Planned Gift
"Any gift given for any amount and for any purpose, whether for current or deferred use, which requires the assistance of a professional staff person, a qualified volunteer or the donor's advisors to complete. In addition, it includes any gift that is carefully considered by a donor in light of estate or financial plans." (Robert F. Sharpe & Co.)

Pledge
A promise to make future contributions to an organization. For example, some donors make multiyear pledges promising to grant a specific amount of money each year.

Pooled Income Fund
Donors, each of whom contributes cash or property to a pooled fund, each (and/or other named beneficiaries) receives a pro rata share of net income earned by the fund. The donor also receives an income tax deduction for the present value of the remainder interest at the time of the gift. When each beneficiary dies, his or her share is removed from the fund and distributed to the charity.

Post-grant Evaluation
A review of the results of a grant, with the emphasis on whether the grant achieved its desired objective.

Preliminary Proposal
See *Letter of Inquiry*.

Price/Earnings Ratio
A corporation's current stock price divided by its earnings per share.

Principal Fund Balance
Corpus of the fund. Endowed funds have a principal fund balance and an income fund balance. Usually contains gifts plus realized and unrealized gains/losses. (Referred to as Non-Spendable Balance in some foundations.)

Private Foundation
A nongovernmental, nonprofit organization with funds (usually from a single source, such as an individual, family or corporation) and program managed by its own trustees or directors, established to maintain or aid social, educational, religious or other charitable activities serving the common welfare, primarily through grantmaking. Private foundation also means an organization that is tax exempt under Section 501(c)(3) of the tax code and is classified by the IRS as a private foundation as defined in the code.

Private Inurement
In general, it is the flow of money away from a nonprofit organization's public purposes to the private benefit of persons with a significant relationship with an organization, see intermediate sanctions.

Program Officer
Also referred to as a Corporate Affairs Officer, Program Associate, Public Affairs Officer or Community Affairs Officer, this staff member of a foundation or corporate giving program may do some or all of the following: recommend policy, review grant requests, manage the budget and process applications for the board of directors or contributions committee.

Program-Related Investment (PRI)
A loan or other investment made by a grantmaking organization to a profit-making or nonprofit organization for a project related to the foundation's stated purpose and interests. Often, program-related investments are made from a revolving fund; the foundation generally expects to receive its money back with limited, or below-market, interest, which then will provide additional funds for loans to other organizations. A program-related investment may involve loan guarantees, purchases of stock or other kinds of financial support.

Prohibited Transaction
One of a number of activities in which certain private foundations and/or foundation representatives may not engage. See *Disqualified Person*.

Project Fund
In looking at the needs of the community, the foundation board determines there is an unmet charitable need. By board resolution, a fund is established to meet that need. Donors contribute to the fund. Over time, the fund is expended (rather than endowed) to meet the community need.

ProNet
Program Network. The professional association of community foundation grantmaking/program staff.

Public Charity
A nonprofit organization that is exempt from federal income tax under Section 501(c)(3) of the Internal Revenue code and that receives its financial support from a broad segment of the general public. Religious, educational and medical institutions are deemed to be public charities. Other organizations exempt under Section 501(c)(3) must pass a public support test to be considered public charities, or must be formed to benefit an organization that is a public charity. Charitable organizations that are not public charities are private foundations and are subject to more stringent regulatory and reporting requirements. Also see *Private Foundation; Public Support Test; Supporting Organization*.

Public Foundation
The IRS recognizes public foundations, along with community foundations, as public charities. Although they may provide direct charitable services to the public as other nonprofits do, their primary focus is on grantmaking.

Public Support Test
There are two public support tests, both of which are designed to ensure that a charitable organization is responsive to the general public rather than a limited number of persons. One test, sometimes referred to as 509(a)(1) or 170(b)(1)(A)(vi) for the sections of the Internal Revenue Code where it is found, is for charities such as community foundations that mainly rely on gifts, grants and contributions. To be automatically classed as a public charity under this test, organizations must show that they normally receive at least one-third of their support from the general public (including government agencies and foundations). However, an organization that fails the automatic test still may qualify as a public charity if its public support equals at least 10 percent of all support and it also has a variety of other characteristics—such as a broad-based board—that make it sufficiently "public." The second test, sometimes referred to as the section 509(a)(2) test, applies to charities, such as symphony orchestras or theater groups, that get a substantial part of their income from the sale of services that further their mission, such as the sale of tickets to performances. These charities must pass a one-third/one-third test: They must demonstrate that their sales and contributions normally add up to at least one-third of their financial support, but their income from investments and unrelated business activities does not exceed one-third of support.

Real Property
Land, homes (residence or vacation) and land and the property attached to the land. Examples include farms.

Realized gains/losses
Increases/decreases in investments attributable to the sale of investments.

Regional Associations of Grantmakers (RAs)
Nonprofit membership associations of foundations and related organizations that share a common goal: to strengthen philanthropy in a distinct geographic region, e.g. a city, state or multistate area. RA members include private or independent foundations, community foundations and corporate foundations and giving programs. In addition, some RAs include in their membership related organizations, such as financial advisor firms or nonprofit grantseeking groups.

Restricted Funds
Assets or income that is restricted in its use, in the types of organizations that may receive grants from it or in the procedures used to make grants from such funds.

Retained Life Estate
The donor gives remainder interest in a personal residence, vacation home or farm, subject to the right to live in the home (or work the farm) for the lifetime of the donor and/or another person. Also known as *Future Interest Property*.

Retirement Plan Assets
Assets held in qualified retirement plans including employers' pension or profit-sharing plans or salary deferral plans such as 401(k) and 403(b).

Return, Rate of
The rate of return on an asset is a measure of investment performance and should be determined on a total-return basis, i.e., including realized and unrealized changes in market value in addition to earned income (i.e., dividend and interest income). Managers may report returns before or after management advisory fees, but returns are always reported after brokerage and trading costs.

Return, Real
A real return is the nominal or actual return adjusted for inflation as measured by the Consumer Price Index (CPI).

Return, Total
A measure of an investment's return that includes both realized and unrealized changes in market value plus earned income. See Income, Earned.

Risk
The uncertainty associated with the future value of an investment in an asset or portfolio of assets.

Scholarship Fund
Established to provide support for individuals who are pursuing some training or educational opportunity. Grants may be awarded to the individuals or they may be awarded to educational institutions.

Securities, Closely Held
Stocks and bonds not traded on public exchanges, often owned by family members or a few individuals. Also referred to as *Securities, Privately Held.*

Securities, Privately Held
See *Securities, Closely Held.*

Securities, Publicly Traded
Stocks and bonds traded on public exchanges.

Seed Money
A grant or contribution used to start a new project or organization.

Self-Dealing
An illegal financial transaction between a private foundation and any disqualified person(s). There are a few exceptions to the self-dealing rule, including the reasonable compensation of a disqualified person by a foundation for services that are necessary in fulfilling the foundation's charitable purpose. See *Disqualified Person.*

Site Visit
Visiting a donee organization at its office location or area of operation; meeting with its staff or directors or with recipients of its services.

Social Investing
Also referred to as Ethical Investing and Socially Responsible Investing, this is the practice of aligning a foundation's investment policies with its mission. This may include making program-related investments and refraining from investing in corporations with products or policies inconsistent with the foundation's values.

Spending Policy
A policy that determines what percentage of a group of assets, such as an endowment, should be spent to cover both operating costs and grants of an institution. Typical spending rules combine calculations based on previous years' spending, the current year's income and investment return rates, and the policy of the foundation covering grant commitments.

Split Interest Gifts
Gifts that have two distinct parts or "interests:" a charitable interest and a non-charitable interest, often the donor. The rights given by the donor are tax deductible as a charitable contribution.
Also see *Charitable Gift Annuity; Charitable Lead Trust; Charitable Remainder Trust; Future Interest Property; Retained Life Estate.*

Standard Deviation
In modern portfolio theory, the standard deviation is one of the primary measures of risk. It is an assessment of the volatility of a security or portfolio. Technically speaking, in statistics, standard deviation refers to the range of possible outcomes around the expected outcome of a random variable.

Supporting Organization
A charity that is not required to meet the public support test because it supports a public charity. To be a supporting organization, a charity must meet one of three complex legal tests that assure, at minimum, that the organization being supported has some influence over the actions of the supporting organization. Although a supporting organization may be formed to benefit any type of public charity, the use of this form is particularly common in connection with community foundations. Supporting organizations are distinguishable from donor-advised funds because they are distinct legal entities.

Tax-Exempt Organizations
Organizations that do not have to pay state and/or federal income taxes. Federal tax-exempt status can be obtained by applying to the IRS, and in most states, for state income tax exemptions, to the state attorney general's office.

Technical Assistance
Operational or management assistance given to a nonprofit organization. It can include fundraising assistance, budgeting and financial planning, program planning, legal advice, marketing and other aids to management. Assistance may be offered directly by a foundation or corporate staff member or in the form of a grant to pay for the services of an outside consultant. See *In-Kind Contribution.*

Tipping
A situation that occurs when a gift or grant is made that is large enough to significantly alter the grantee's funding base and cause it to fail the public support test. Such a gift or grant results in "tipping" or conversion from public charity to private foundation status.

Time-Weighted Rate of Return
The time-weighted rate of return measures the investment performance of the manager of a pool of assets, by removing the impact of cash flows external to the pool of assets.

Total Return
Measures the changes in portfolio value plus dividend or interest income plus realized capital gains or losses. Total return is expressed as a percentage of initial capital value, adjusted for net contributions or withdrawals.

Transfers
(1) The moving of dollars from one asset account to another within a fund (Pool asset account to checking account, for example).
(2) The moving of dollars from one fund to another fund (Interfund Grant from Fund A received as Interfund Gift in Fund B).

Trust
A legal device used to set aside the money or property of one person for the benefit of one or more persons or organizations.

Trust Form
For a community foundation, when the investment responsibility resides with the trust department of one or more banks or brokerage firms and such trust departments have responsibility for developing and implementing investment policy. Also see *Corporate Form*.

Trustee
The person(s) or institutions responsible for the administration of a trust.

Unrealized gains/losses
Increases/decreases in investments attributable to the fluctuations in value of the investments from one time period to another.

Unrestricted Fund
For a community foundation, an unrestricted fund is one that is not specifically designated to particular uses by the donor or for which restrictions have expired or been removed.

Value Oriented
The security's current market price is a critical variable for this equity investment style. Some measures used are low absolute or relative P/E ratios, above-market dividend yields, price/book value and price/sales ratios. Money managers who use this investment style look for the aforementioned measures as well as out of favor securities, industry sectors and potential turnaround candidates.

Variance Power
A distinguishing characteristic of community foundations, the variance power permits the community foundation's governing body to redirect resources in component funds if it determines that the donor's restriction is unnecessary, incapable of fulfillment or inconsistent with the charitable needs of the community or area served.

Will
A written instrument legally executed by which a person makes disposition of his or her estate to take effect after death.

Yield-to-Maturity
In the fixed income markets, this is the interest rate that makes the present value of a bond's future payments equal to its current market price. The yield-to-maturity, often referred to as "yield," is inversely related to the bonds price. If the price of the bond rises (falls), the yield falls (rises).

INDEX

Acceptance policies. See Gifts, acceptance policies
Accountability, 27–28, 34–35, 55, 57–58, 219
Administrative fees, 107–08, 177, 179, 203
Advertisements, 247
Aikman, Sheryl, vi, 172
Annual campaigns, 200, 203
Annual reports, 242–43, 261
Anonymous giving, 180, 184, 185, 202
Archiving, 96, 115
Articles of Incorporation, 20, 35, 81, 101, 144, 262
Assets, management of, 11, 22, 39, 85, 90–91, 93, 106, 109–10, 111, 112, 176, 183, 187, 196, 206, 272, 273
Audiences, identifying. See Communications, identifying your audiences
Audit committee, 41, 113
Audits, 112–13
Benefits. See Employee benefits
Boards
    assessment and evaluation of, 33, 53–54
    board chair, roles of, 30–31
    board officers, roles of, 30–32
    board size and structure, 45
    board, roles of, 30–32
    board/CEO relationship, 32–33
    board/staff relationship, 34
    change in leadership, 47–48
    committees of, 40–41
    diversity, 46
    duties of, 30–31
    effective meetings, 51–53
    handbook, 49–50
    job descriptions, 30–31
    legal duties, 30
    meeting book, 51
    member removal, 47
    minutes of meetings, 51–52
    orientation, 49–50
    professional development, 54–55, 83–84
    recruitment, 43–44
    retreats, 50, 52
    selection criteria, 43–44
    self-assessment, 33, 53–54
    succession planning, 47–48
    ways to connect with peers, 17, 27, 83–84
BoardSource, 259
Boston Foundation, 12
Branding, 217–19
Brochures, 227, 238, 240, 244
Budget, administrative, 107–08, 250
Budget, capital, 107–08
Budget, grants, 107, 109–10, 123, 125
Budgeting, 107–08
Bylaws, 27, 35–36
California Community Foundation, v, 12, 17
Capacity building, 141

Capital grants, 124
Carter, Rosalynn, 64
CEO
    evaluation of, 33
    orientation of, 70–71
    relationship with board, 31–33
    relationship with board chair, 31
    roles of, 31–34, 64–71
Challenge grants, 124, 143, 263
Charitable intent, 189, 263
Charitable organization, termination of, 183, 184, 196
Charles Schwab, 177
Chicago Community Trust, 7, 14
Cleveland Foundation, vi, 6, 15, 257
Clontz, Bryan, 188
Code of ethics, 38
Collaboration, 17, 159–60
Collaborative donor networks. See Giving circles
Common Grant Applications (CGA), 129
Communications
    accountability, 219
    communications plan, 248–51
    costs of, 250
    crisis, in times of, 236–37
    evaluation of, 250–51
    helping colleagues communicate, 249–50
    identifying your audiences, 215, 220
    sample documents, 237, 239, 244, 252–54
    skills, 238
    writing and editing, 238–39
Community Foundations Leadership Team, 18, 264
Community Foundation Network, 8
Community Foundations of America, 8, 16, 18, 47, 87, 204, 223, 251, 256, 258, 263
Community Foundations of Canada, 8, 258
Community Foundations Standards & Effective Practices database, 165, 257
Community foundations
    as public charities, 5–6
    definition of, 4
    field of, 7–8
    history of, 6–9
    professionalism of, 18
    roles, 5
    seeking permanent funds, 4, 6, 13, 179–80
    shift from trust to corporate structure, 13
    staff, types of, 21
    statistics, 9
    value of, 5
Community involvement, 149
Community leadership
    activities, 158–62
    convening, 158–59
    engaging the board, 136, 149, 157
    evaluation of, 162–63

roles, 157
Compensation. See Staff, compensation of
Competition, 15–16
Competitive grantmaking program, 126
Computers, backing up data, 90, 95–96
Computers, protecting, 90–91
Confidentiality policies, 38, 208
Conflict of interest, 36–38
Conflicts, management of, 68
Consultants, 78–80, 110–11
Contingency grants, 124
Contracts, 93–94, 95
Convening. See Community leadership, convening
Corporate giving, 184, 195
Council of Michigan Foundations, v, vi, 229, 255
Court action, 207, 208
Crisis. See Communications, crisis, in times of
Custodian, 110, 264
Cy pres, 264
Deadlines, 126, 128–29, 139, 223, 231, 233–37, 245
Declaration of Trust, 35, 101
Declining grant proposals, 132–33
Demonstration grants, 124
Designated funds, 123, 177, 185, 187, 264, 265
Director's and officer's liability insurance, 39, 93
Disaster grantmaking, 9, 12, 90–92, 124, 145, 146, 174, 186
Disclosure documents, 36–37, 103, 104, 208
Diversity. See Board, diversity
Donor Bill of Rights, 203
Donors
    consent, 207
    corporations, as donors, 176, 195
    education of, 198–99, 202, 207
    identifying, 173, 193–94, 195
    individuals, 173, 194–95
    intent (*see charitable intent*)
    needs, 18
    presentations to, 198–99
    private foundations, as donors, 175, 178, 196
    prospects, 173
    reasons for giving, 173–76
    relations with, 194–97
    restrictions. See Material restrictions
    services, 16, 18, 171, 201–02
Donor-advised funds, 10, 15, 123, 143, 153, 177, 185, 187, 191, 206–07, 265
    considerations of, 186
    view on, 188
Due diligence, 150, 265
Editing. See Communications, writing and editing
E-mail, use of, 229, 233, 238, 243, 246–47
Emergency grants, 124, 146
Employee benefits, 77–78
Employee manual, 81–82
Employment laws, 73–76, 80
Endowment, See Permanent funds
E–newsletters, 222, 244
Evaluations, of foundations, 151–52
Excess Benefit and Intermediate Sanctions, 103, 268
Excise tax, 265, 268

Expenditure requirements, 113, 162, 265, 266, 268
Fair Recruitment and Employment Practices, 73–74
Fax grants, 145
Financial Accounting Standards Board (FASB), 184
Federal tax withholding, 78
Feurt, Suzanne, v, 19, 264
Fidelity Investments, 10, 15, 177
Fiduciary responsibilities, 11, 29, 30, 63, 90, 93, 109
Field-of-interest funds, 123, 177, 182, 185–88, 205, 266
Filing systems, 95–96
Finance and Administration Officers Group, 105, 258, 265
Fiscal responsibility, 106
Float from money transfers, 203
Focus groups, 159
Form 990, 50, 103, 150, 268
Foundation Center, 72, 88, 89, 166, 196, 243, 246
Funds
    agreements, 191
    distributions monitoring, 154
    group memorial, 147, 185, 186
    minimum size, 189
    reporting on, 201–02
    statements, 201–02
    tax and legal implications, 205
    types of, 123, 185–87
General grants, 124
Geographic focus, 138, 143–44
Gifts of Substantiation and Disclosure, 104
Gifts
    acceptance policies, 39, 82, 180, 189–90, 206, 208
    acknowledging, 201
    attracting, 192–94
    business-related stock, 180–81
    cash, 180–81
    charitable bequests, 182
    charitable lead trust, 183
    closely-held securities, 181–82
    deferred, 182, 188
    guidelines, 201
    IRA accounts or retirement plans, 181
    life insurance, 181, 268
    lifetime income-charitable gift annuity, 183, 263
    lifetime income-fixed amount, 182
    lifetime income-pooled life income fund, 183, 194, 271
    lifetime income-variable amount, 182
    outright, 180, 188, 196, 270
    private foundation transfer, 183–84
    property, 181
    residence, farm or real estate, 181
Giving circles, 202
Goff, Frederick Harris, 6, 13, 15
Governance, 11, 27–28, 44–45, 54, 64
Governance committee, 44–45, 47
Governing documents, 81, 99, 100–01
Grants
    degree of risk, 125, 127, 132, 144, 157
    evaluation of, 135–37
    grant agreement, 133–34, 136
    grant application, 128–29
    grant award letter, 134, 136

grant guidelines, 126–28
level of community involvement, 149
monitoring, 134–35, 154
to individuals, 147–48
to non-501(c)(3) organizations, 123, 145–46, 186
types of grants, 124
types of organizations funded, 145–46
size of, 144–45
Grant proposals
approving, 133–34
declining, 132–33
recommending to the board, 131–32
review of, 130
soliciting, 128–29
summaries, 51, 131–32, 136
Grantee advisory committees, 151
Grantee relationships, 122, 151–52
Grantmaking
flow chart, 136
goals, 126
philosophy, 139
process, 125–26, 151–52
staff, 137
donor involvement, 153–54
Graphic design, 218, 228–29, 239, 245
Grassroots lobbying, 161–62
Guidelines. See Grants, grant guidelines
GuideStar, 103, 144, 150
Hiring
employment laws, 73–74
interview questions to avoid, 75
interviewing, 75
job posting, 74
offer of employment, 76
using search firms, 74
Human resources, 63, 72–84
Image, developing an, 228–30
Immigration Reform and Control Act of 1986, 12, 73
Indemnification of board members, 39, 50, 93
Indianapolis Foundation, 12
Insurance, 39, 50, 73, 77, 92–93, 181
Interactive grantmaking, 21, 139
Interim grants, 124, 148
International grantmaking, 8, 143–44, 166
International Meeting of Associations Serving Grantmakers (IMAG), 8
Internet, 18, 86–89, 91
Interviewing. See Hiring
Investment consultants, 110–11
Investment manager, 100, 106, 110–12, 268
Investment policies, 38, 109–11
Investment, basics of, 109–11
Investment, responsibility, 106
Investment, strategy, 109–11
Job descriptions, 30–32, 67, 72–74
Joint ventures, 160, 196
Jones Rushing, Emily, 215
Layout, See Graphic design
League of California Community Foundations, v, 17
Legal responsibilities, 30, 39, 50, 99

Legal rules. See Legal responsibilities
Legal structure, trusts and corporations, 63, 99–100
Length of support, 121, 142–43
Letters of inquiry, 128–29, 268
Leveraging, 148–49
Liabilities, 63, 90, 93, 206
Listening sessions, 159
Lobbying, 160–62, 165, 269
Logo, designing a, 216, 228–29
Long-term funding, 142–43
Lueders, Todd, vi, 171
Maintenance, 85, 91, 93–94
Marketing, 211–60
Marketing, regional, 16–17, 230, 247
Mass media, 227, 231–32, 247
Matau, Karri, vi, 3
Matching grants, 149, 269
Material restrictions, 63, 99, 105, 184, 186, 191, 205
Media. *See also Press events, Press kits*
pitching stories, 233
working with reporters, 233
writing news releases, 234–35
Message platform, 225–26
Message, crafting, 225–26
Michigan Community Foundations' Ventures, 17, 230
Minutes of meetings, 50–52, 56, 96
Mission statement, 22–23, 52, 126, 128, 206
Named fund, 14, 176, 180, 183–84, 194, 206
National Marketing Action Team, 16, 18, 222–24
National Standards for U.S. Community Foundations, 3, 9–11, 15, 17, 22, 28, 33, 36–38, 43–44, 46, 52, 104–10, 112, 122, 127, 150–51, 154, 157, 179, 190, 198, 201–02, 206, 234, 242, 257, 269
New York Community Trust, 12
News release. See Media, writing news releases
Newsletters, 50, 73, 88–9, 122, 124, 219, 222, 224, 242, 243–44
Office, furniture and equipment, 97–98
Office, setting up, 97–98
Ogden, Peggy, v, 32, 42, 112, 217
Operating grants, 140
Operating plan, 63, 66–67
Operating support, 124, 140, 203, 270
Organization endowment, 123, 185, 188, 191
Organizational media, 227
Orientation, 47, 49–50, 70, 81
Paid advisors. See Consultants
Paperless office, 95–96
Patriot Act, 144
Payroll, 78
Performance reviews, 70, 82–83
Permanent funds, 4, 6, 13, 16, 38, 123, 179–80
Personnel policies, 39–40, 63, 80–81
Pitching stories, See Media, pitching stories
Planning grants, 124
Pooled income fund, 183, 271
Pre-proposal meetings, 129, 136
Press events, 235
Press kits, 235
Press release. See News release
Printers. See Publications, working with outside vendors

Private foundations, 6–7, 12, 14, 99, 102, 145, 175, 178, 183–84, 196
Private foundations, termination of, 183–84
Problem solving, 69
Professional advisors, 199–200, 220–22, 223–24
Professional advisors, presentations to, 199–200
Professional and Organizational Development Action Team, v, 18
Professional development, 54–55, 83–84
Program-related investments (PRI), 114, 271
Project grants, 124, 140
Project support, 140, 142–43
Proposal summaries, 131–32, 136
Public policy, 12, 160–62, 164
Public relations, 211–57
Public speaking, 240
Public support test, 102, 272
Publications, 242–47
Publications, working with outside vendors, 245
Quick message media, 227
Rader, Donna G., vi, 121
Records management, 94–95
Regional collaborations, 17
Regional marketing. See Marketing, regional,
Request for Proposals (RFP), 80, 129, 245
Resource development, laws relating to, 205–08
Resource development, strategic plan, 192–204
Responsive grantmaking, 139, 143
Right of first refusal, 206
Risk management, 39, 90–91, 93
Rockefeller, John D., 6
Safety and security, 91–92
Salary adjustments, 78
San Francisco Foundation, 12
Scholarships, 147–49, 186, 187, 188
Search engines, 87, 89, 246
Search firms, 74
Securities, 180–81, 200
Seed grants, 124
Short-term funding, 142–3
Single-entity rules, 14–15, 99–100
Site visits, 130–31, 152
Slosser, Chuck, v, 4, 35
Special projects fund, 123, 186
Speech. See Public speaking
Spending policies, 38, 109–10, 114, 273
Staff
    compensation of, 76–78
    cross-functional teams, 18, 68–69, 72
    full-time employees, 76
    job descriptions, 32, 73–74
    part-time employees, 76
    performance reviews, 82–83
    professional development, 83–84
    size of, 72
    temporary employees, 77
    transitions of, 69–71
Standards Action Team, 18
Start up grants. See Seed grants
State Charitable Solicitation Law, 95, 104

Stewardship, 11, 30, 38, 49, 106, 112, 176, 187, 190, 203
Storytelling, 224
Strategic communications, 218–19, 249, 255
Strategic grantmaking, 121, 138–49
Strategic plan, for communications, 248–49
Strategic plan, for resource development, 192–204
Strategic plan, for technology, 85–89
Strategic planning, 41–42, 57
Succession planning, 47–48, 63, 69–71
Supporting organizations, 177–78, 186, 258, 273
Tagline, crafting a, 229
Tax deduction, 6, 104, 174, 181, 183, 185, 189, 263, 271, 273
Tax filing, 104–05
Tax Reform Act of 1969, 6–7, 10, 14
Tax Reform Act of 1986, 10, 12
Teams, managing, 67–68
Technology, 85–89
Technology Affinity Group (TAG), 115
Technology Roadmap, 89
Transfer of private foundation assets, 183–84
Transparency. See Accountability
Uniform laws, 111–12
Uniform Management of Institutional Funds Act (UMIFA), 111–12, 207
Uniform Prudent Investor Act, 112
Unrelated business income tax (UBIT), 103, 112
Unrestricted funds, 16, 20, 31, 123, 179–80, 274
Values statement, 22
Variance power, 15, 100, 208, 274
Venture philanthropy, 139
Vision statement, 22, 249
Visual presentations, 240–41
Volunteers, 21, 78–79
Web design, 88, 239–40
Websites, publicizing, 88–89
Websites, using, 86–87, 245
Whistleblower policies, 40, 81
Wilmer Shields Rich Award, 87, 242, 246
WINGs, Worldwide Initiatives for Grantmaker Support, 8–9, 24, 256
Winnipeg Foundation, 10
Writing. See Communications, writing and editing